DISCARDED

Urban Renewal and Resistance

Urban Renewal and Resistance

Race, Space, and the City in the Late Twentieth to the Early Twenty-First Century

Mary E. Triece

LEXINGTON BOOKS
Lanham • Boulder • New York • London

Published by Lexington Books
An imprint of The Rowman & Littlefield Publishing Group, Inc.
4501 Forbes Boulevard, Suite 200, Lanham, Maryland 20706
www.rowman.com

Unit A, Whitacre Mews, 26-34 Stannary Street, London SE11 4AB

Copyright © 2016 by Lexington Books

All rights reserved. No part of this book may be reproduced in any form or by any electronic or mechanical means, including information storage and retrieval systems, without written permission from the publisher, except by a reviewer who may quote passages in a review.

Library of Congress Cataloging-in-Publication Data

Names: Triece, Mary Eleanor, 1967- author.
Title: Urban Renewal and Resistance: Race, Space, and the City in the Late Twentieth to the Early Twenty-First Century / Mary E. Triece.
Description: Lanham : Lexington Books, [2016] | Includes bibliographical references and index.
Identifiers: LCCN 2016026937 (print) | LCCN 2016032856 (ebook) | ISBN 9780739193815 (cloth : alk. paper) | ISBN 9780739193822 (Electronic)
Subjects: LCSH: Urbanization--United States. | Urban renewal--United States. | Equality--United States. | Discrimination--United States. | Sociology, Urban--United States. | United States--Race relations.
Classification: LCC HT123 .T686 2016 (print) | LCC HT123 (ebook) | DDC 307.3/41606973--dc23
LC record available at https://lccn.loc.gov/2016026937

∞™ The paper used in this publication meets the minimum requirements of American National Standard for Information Sciences Permanence of Paper for Printed Library Materials, ANSI/NISO Z39.48-1992.

Printed in the United States of America

Contents

Acknowledgments	vii
Introduction	ix
1 Theoretical Considerations	1
Part I: Race and Displacement in Detroit	29
2 Narratives of Growth and Collective Resistance	31
3 Rationality vs. Demystification	63
Part II: Race and Health in Harlem	85
4 Mapping Race	87
5 Citizen Science: How we come to know what we know	117
Conclusion: Neoliberalism, Urban Spaces, and Race	139
Bibliography	149
Index	173
About the Author	177

Acknowledgments

In 2014 I read about the experiences of residents who lived at 1214 Griswold in downtown Detroit, Michigan. These folks—many of whom were elderly and/or disabled, some of whom had lived in the building for 20 plus years, and all of whom called 1214 Griswold "home"—were being evicted from their apartments to make way for renovations that would result in "luxury apartment living" ostensibly more in keeping with the newly fashioned upscale, professional nature of the neighborhood called Capitol Park. Mr. William H. Griffin Jr., one of Griswold's evicted residents worked hard to organize his neighbors and resist the evictions. My deepest thanks go to Mr. Griffin who generously gave his time for an interview in March 2014 on his experiences fighting against the displacement of the residents. I am also grateful for the time Detroit resident and housing and labor activist, Martha Grevatt, gave in an interview detailing her own efforts through Moratorium NOW! to resist evictions throughout the Detroit area. I also extend a thank you to Ogonnaya Dotson Newman, an environmental justice activist working with WE ACT For Environmental Justice in New York, New York, who taught me about the importance of citizen science in West Harlem residents' efforts to persuade authorities of the accuracy of their claims concerning health and the environment. Griffin's and Grevatt's experiences in Detroit and Dotson Newman's work in West Harlem are one with broader struggles on the part of ordinary people to hold on to the basic right to control where and under what conditions they live and work. For their efforts and inspiration I am thankful.

I would also like to extend a hearty thank you to the editors at Lexington Books, including Alison Pavan, Nicolette Amstutz, and Kasey Beduhn who guided me through the writing of this book and enabled me to see it through to publication. I am also extremely grateful to the anonymous reviewer who provided detailed and thoughtful feedback that made the manuscript stronger and more insightful.

Finally, I wish to thank my children Dashiell and Lily, my husband Mark Tidrick, and our three cats Charlotte, Nancy, and Howard for their support, hugs, and welcome interruptions. They inspire me to think more deeply, be more thoughtful, and act more courageously where it counts the most—in the broader community where ordinary people live, work, and struggle each day to live fuller, more humane lives.

Introduction

In 1830, the United States Congress passed the Indian Removal Act, which prompted the displacement of 46,000 Native Americans from their homes in southern states and opened up 25 million acres for colonial development. Throughout the 1940s–1950s, federal housing policy and deed "covenants" codified the exclusion of black homeowners from select neighborhoods (Sugrue 1996, 43–44). In a highly publicized trial in 2013, the "Stand Your Ground" law was successfully used to exonerate George Zimmerman of second degree murder for the shooting and killing of Trayvon Martin, an unarmed 17-year-old African American high school student, returning to his father's fiancée's home in a neighborhood in Sanford, Florida. Kenneth Jackson (1985) observed, "No discussion of the settlement patterns of the American people can ignore the overriding significance of race" (289). These three examples spanning over 150 years speak to the politics of space and race, including issues of displacement, exclusion, and (non) belonging. These historical instances—which are not by any means isolated—also recall for us the ways spatial practices are codified into law and reinforced through prevailing cultural discourses.

The first decades of the twenty-first century have given rise to public debates, collective efforts, and at times, violence that may be viewed through the lens of spatial politics: Palestinians struggle for statehood; Israelis erect settlements in the West Bank; Central American child-migrants travel thousands of miles to reach the United States; the Governor of Texas sends 1,000 National Guard troops to patrol the Texas-Mexico border. These examples underscore that spaces are not neutral; they are sites of contested meanings, imbued with nationalism and patriotism, they may serve as a wellspring for warfare, justification for race/ethnic/gender exclusion, or grounds for democratic resistance. This book begins with the premise that place is intimately related to well-being and inextricably linked to race and class. The examples above underscore this point.

If, as the critical geographer David Harvey (1989) points out, "those who command space can always control the politics of place" (234), a key question becomes: What are the rhetorical processes through which such control is legitimated and justified? And how is spatial control resisted? Referring back to the book's opening examples, how are land grabs that lead to the displacement of entire communities justified? How do exclusionary spatial practices gain legitimacy? And how have ordinary citizens fought back in their struggles for rights to space? Edward Said

(1993) observed that the "struggle over geography . . . is complex and interesting because it is not only about soldiers and cannons but also about ideas, about forms, about images and imaginings" (7). Said's point underscores the relevance of communication studies for scholars and ordinary citizens concerned with understanding and intervening in geographical practices tethered to economic and social processes of exploitation, exclusion, and marginalization.

Urban Renewal and Resistance brings attention to the politics of space in the U.S. city and argues that public discourses and debates over urban growth and renewal are best understood within the framework of uneven development, capitalist expansion and abandonment, economic and political exclusion, and democratic potential. Historically, urban spaces have been *spaces of struggle*, wherein a Woolworth's lunch counter, a bus seat, a factory floor, or more recently a square or park has become the physical site and trope for resistance. The following chapters study the discourses surrounding urban struggles over housing and health in Detroit and Harlem for the ways urban spaces are rhetorically structured through dominant discourses, such as those of city planners and the mainstream press, and the ways counternarratives proffered by longtime city residents challenge geographies of injustice. I argue that the assumptions of neoliberalism serve as the "common sense" of capitalist development. Specifically, I examine how neoliberal discourses concerning city growth and regeneration silence the racialized and class-based nature of housing and health, which effectively naturalizes a market logic constructed to politically and economically benefit a small elite. The following chapters also bring to life the ongoing struggles of ordinary citizens in Detroit and Harlem who are struggling for place-based justice that ensures them access to resources necessary for living a decent life.

Urban Renewal and Resistance asserts an argument concerning neoliberalism and democratic pushback in the late twentieth-early twenty-first centuries. Neoliberalism, broadly defined, refers to economic and political practices and assumptions that privilege unfettered market growth and cultural discourses that espouse individualism, opportunity, and freedom. Neoliberalism is grounded in a belief in the rationality of market processes and the basic soundness of technological and scientific progress that create the grounds for material expansion. And importantly, as David Theo Goldberg (2009) points out, "race is a key structuring technology" of neoliberalism, powered largely through invisibility (338). He explains,

> In diluting, if not erasing, race in all public affairs of the state, neoliberal proponents nevertheless seek to privatize racisms alongside most everything else. . . . Categories of race disappear as much from keeping account of discrimination as from producing the discrimination itself, thus leaving the condition it is supposed to articulate, to mark and express as well as identify and assess, as untouchable as it tends now to

be untouched. Devoid of race in the public sphere, racism—as modes of racially driven subjection and exclusion, debilitation and humiliation—is freed up to circulate as robustly as individuals or non-government . . . institutions should choose in private. (339)

Goldberg's pointed observation speaks to the urgency with which the Black Lives Matter movement has taken hold in the wake of police killings of unarmed black men in 2014–2015 as it repositions race at the fore of public dialogue and struggle over the rights of black Americans in the twenty-first century.[1]

The experiences of residents in Detroit and Harlem may be understood as a metonymy of the larger, ongoing processes—economic, political, and discursive—of urban growth, capitalist expansion, and struggles for social justice within a neoliberal context. Metonymy is a trope of reduction that enables us to understand complex issues by focusing on a representative part or aspect of the whole. The following chapters examine the neoliberal market logic embedded in dominant narratives of urban growth and explore how they contrast with urban struggles advancing counterhegemonic narratives that seek to unmask or give lie to neoliberal assumptions that have deeply affected the nature of urban growth and development. Specifically, residents used rhetorics of counter-memory (chapter 2), demystification (chapter 3), mapping (chapter 4), and street science (chapter 4) to evoke race as it is implicated in the politics of place.

Urban Renewal and Resistance draws on a wide range of public communication artifacts, including both traditional (e.g., print news, face-to-face) and online discourses, commonly referred to as cyberprotest when deployed for pro-democracy or social justice ends. To understand urban regeneration in Detroit, I looked at city planning documents, public interviews with city leaders, and accounts in the city's daily, the *Detroit News*. I conducted interviews with longtime Detroit residents active in housing justice struggles and looked at grassroots publications available online and in print, including press releases, flyers, non-corporate owned newspapers, and community created planning documents. For the chapters covering health in Harlem, I examined *New York Times* coverage of a local waste management plant, conducted an interview with a local environmental justice activist, and examined both online and print literature including city council testimony, community created newsletters, and community generated maps. The issues of housing and health in these two areas are ongoing and evolving even at the time of this writing. My goal is to draw attention to dominant narratives surrounding housing and health that obscure the racist dimensions of growth and urban regeneration; and, to highlight the ways communities come together to resist processes of gentrification and toxic dumping. The following chapters represent a call for bringing communication studies to bear on geography through a historical materialist lens that highlights the relationship between urban development and inequality and the discourses that justify and challenge such disparities. A communication studies lens offers a way for analyzing how inequality is justified and challenged, how contradictions are sewn up or split apart through public discourses.

WHY URBAN STRUGGLES?

The following study emphasizes the relevance in the lives of ordinary citizens of an economic system (capitalism) that relies on accumulation, expansion, and a constant search for profit. Within this context, urbanization represents the "field" upon which surplus value, or profit, is realized. For example, "value can be produced in a Chinese factory, and then realized by Wal-Mart in Columbus, Ohio" (Harvey 2013). Thus, Harvey (2013) points out, "there is an inner connectivity in the circulation of capital between production and realization, and struggles in the urban sphere are just as important to value production and realization as are struggles in the workplace." Zukin (1991) notes "landscape is the tabula rasa of capital accumulation" (19). She continues, "the underlying cause of repetition and singularity in the landscape is the profit motive, shifting capital between investment in industry and in property, cycling it into new construction or reconstruction, shuttling it between the downtown and the suburban periphery" (19). The book's study of urban spaces is not meant to replace or upend what I believe to be the continued importance of class-based struggles aimed at economic systems; but rather to suggest looking at the geography of capitalism and the ways social relations are expressed within, delimited by, and constituted through spatial structures. My desire is to understand the connectivity between capitalism, urban development, and race; to thread the history of city growth to the renewal of contemporary urban spaces; and importantly to shed light on the ways public discourses promote and challenge commonsense assumptions about the supposed good of growth.

Geography is not neutral or unproblematic. The development of the United States as a nation has hinged on geographical displacement, which has occurred forcefully and has been justified through ideologies of Manifest Destiny and racial superiority since European settlers pushed Native Americans off their land in the 1500s (Friedenberg 1992; Miller 2006; Slotkin 1973). Likewise, the growth and development of U.S. cities throughout the nineteenth and twentieth centuries have been accompanied by processes of displacement and exclusion resulting from capitalist processes such as de/reindustrialization, regeneration, and increased privatization of city services and spaces. City spaces create a "rhetorical situation" (Bitzer 1968) that prompts both hegemonic and resistant discourses surrounding the development of and rights to urban spaces. *Ur-*

ban Renewal and Resistance applies the insights of communication studies to the exploration of city geographies and social justice in the twenty-first century.

The historical trajectory of Detroit represents ground zero for studies of space, race, and exclusion. Once the capital of Fordist production and boasting some of the highest rates of homeownership in the United States, Detroit's economy and infrastructure collapsed over a period of fifty-plus years due to capital and white flight (Babson et al., 1986; Massey & Denton 1993; Sugrue 1996). After filing for chapter 9 bankruptcy in 2013, Detroit's city leaders—often with rhetorical buttressing from mainstream press accounts—leveraged a market logic as they celebrated the influx of young professionals and businesses to downtown Detroit. The words of billionaire Detroit developer Dan Gilbert are revealing. He said of Detroit's growth: "We're definitely all in. . . . We didn't have a sell five years ago. Now we can compete" (Dill 2015). Importantly, and often ignored by mainstream press narratives, longtime, often low-income, minority Detroit residents have often suffered as a result of city renewal projects and thus have countered the efforts of wealthy real estate moguls by activating public memory of race and exclusionary practices in Detroit's history. The following chapters interrogate the rhetorical strategies used by ordinary citizens in Detroit and Harlem as they challenge commonsense understandings of market expansion used to justify urban development and renewal that has led to unemployment, widespread displacement, and environmental toxicity for many, while holding out the promise of opportunity and wealth for a few.

Spatial rhetorics, the focus of the following chapters, are better understood through a framework of critical geography and what some scholars refer to as geographies of injustice or landscapes of power (Cross & Keith 1993; Harvey 2009; Soja 2010b; Smith 1990; Zukin 1991). Spatial organization manifested through apartheid, gerrymandering, military occupation, cartography, and urban development may all contribute to access to (or denial of) resources, employment, education, and physical security. Put differently, justice has a spatial dimension or a "consequential geography" that is "more than just a background reflection or set of physical attributes to be descriptively mapped" (Soja 2010b, 1). Geography is both physical space and social construction, understood through images, ideas, ideologies, and symbols that hold cultural significance. The following chapters explore the ways counterpublics may create more just urban geographies amidst prevailing political and cultural discourses that delineate "appropriate" uses and users of public spaces.

Critical geography scholars have also detailed the politics of place, the symbols, representations, and ideologies through which spaces become known as "polluted" (Sibley 1995), "dangerous" (Macek 2006), or "marketable." Communication scholars—particularly through the spatial turn—have drawn on geographers to explore the rhetorical dimensions of space. *Urban Renewal and Resistance* brings these bodies of work together in an effort to highlight both the rhetorical dimensions of geography and the ways control over space shape economic and political justice in the twenty-first-century American city.

CAPITALISM, COMMUNICATION, AND THE CITY: AN OVERVIEW

Over 150 years ago, Karl Marx and Friedrich Engels theorized the importance of geographic expansion to capital production and circulation processes. In *Grundrisse*, Marx (1857–8/1973) stated the "creation by capital of *absolute surplus value* . . . is conditional upon an expansion, specifically a constant expansion, of the sphere of circulation" (407). Thus, the "need of a constantly expanding market for its products chases the bourgeoisie over the whole surface of the globe. It must nestle everywhere, settle everywhere, establish connection everywhere" (Marx & Engels 1848/1965, 63). Marx (1857–1858/1973) observed "capital by its nature drives beyond every spatial barrier. Thus the creation of the physical conditions of exchange—of the means of communication and transport—the annihilation of space by time—becomes an extraordinary necessity for it" (524).

Changes in the urban landscape since the time of these writings have been indelibly marked by capitalist production, which has shown to be no less relevant in post-Fordist/postindustrial city spaces. Geographers such as David Harvey, Henri Lefebvre, Edward Soja, and Neil Smith draw, in varying degrees, on Marxist theorizing to detail the relationship between capitalism and city spaces or what Soja (2010a) calls the "fundamental spatiality of capitalist development" (55). Capital accumulation and expansion to new markets engenders crises and inequality that become routinized and normalized.

Harvey (2009) underscores the malleability of capitalism and the system's ability to overcome crises through planned obsolescence, creative destruction, and geographical expansion (196–201; see also Soja 2010b, 89). For instance, capitalist development must deal with the contradictory needs of maintaining fixed capital investments (e.g., factories and the like) and destroying them "in order to make room for accumulation" (Harvey 1975, 13). The economic system faces a "perpetual struggle in which capitalism builds a physical landscape appropriate to its own condition at a particular moment in time, only to have to destroy it" leading to a reshaping of the "geographic environment to adapt it to the needs of further accumulation" (13).

We see this issue arise in rustbelt cities in the Midwest United States, such as Cleveland, Pittsburgh, and Detroit, left in the dust after heavy industries such as iron, steel, and auto moved south or overseas in search of cheaper labor and fewer regulations. Experiences of deindustrialization present an opportunity to theorize crisis formation and the ways capital recalibrates through creative destruction (Soja 2010b, 89). The observation, "All that is solid melts into air, all that is holy is profaned..." (Marx & Engels 1848/1965, 63), resonates when we consider the experiences of Detroit—remaking both labor force and physical landscape in an effort to deal with over 100,000 properties left vacant after tens of thousands of residents have left the city over the past five decades.[2] Detroit's circumstances demonstrate how "produced geographies also work to shape capitalist development itself, at times sustaining and stimulating growth, at other times imprisoning and inhibiting the capital accumulation process" (Soja 2010b, 89). The following chapters explore how the geographical consequences of capitalist expansion and crisis lead to displacement, toxicity, and more optimistically openings for community strategizing and critique.

Bringing in Communication

Capitalist development does not occur without communicative efforts that coordinate and legitimate the course of growth. Similarly, urban spaces are more than bricks and mortar. Spaces "speak" to us, give us our identities, and delineate who belongs and who does not. Spaces are gendered (e.g., the home) and racialized (e.g., the ghetto) thus creating unjust geographies. And city spaces may provide the ground for cultivation of "subaltern counter publics" (Fraser 1990, 67). Geographical spaces are socially produced, "political and ideological" (Lefebvre 1976, 31). Soja (2010a) observes "Space hides things from us" and argues that the "demystification of spatiality and its veiled instrumentality of power is the key to making practical, political, and theoretical sense of the contemporary era" (61).

To understand the contemporary processes of U.S. imperialism abroad and urban development stateside requires attention to issues of geography, social control, race, and public discourses. Few studies have been done that offer an in-depth analysis of the communicative strategies used to justify and resist exclusionary urban geographies. *Urban Renewal and Resistance* represents a unique exploration into the *communicative processes* surrounding the "spatialities of urban regeneration" (Keith & Pile 1993, 2), which have not been fully appreciated within communication or geography studies, particularly within the context of the twenty-first century. As political pundits, city planners, and the mainstream press celebrate postindustrial urban renewal and the term "gentrification" takes on a positive spin, longtime, low-income residents in places like Detroit are displaced. And in the historically black area of Harlem, community members are struggling against toxic dumping and air pollution resulting from upscale development in high-end areas of Manhattan. These are but two examples of "unjust geographies" that have both "material manifestations" and rhetorical underpinnings.

To understand the ways capitalism, communication, and the city come together to influence people's lives in meaningful and often-detrimental ways, this book is theoretically underpinned by communication and Marxist scholarship. The communication scholar Lloyd Bitzer (1968) offered the concept, "rhetorical situation," to understand how exigencies give rise to discourses that are shaped by audiences and constraints. Bitzer explains, a "situation is rhetorical insofar as it needs and invites discourse capable of participating with situation and thereby altering its reality;" and, "discourse is rhetorical insofar as it functions, (or seeks to function) as a fitting response to a situation which needs and invites it" (6). Importantly, the "situation controls the rhetorical response" (6). Contemporary urban decline and regeneration may be viewed as a rhetorical situation in need of exploration in order to understand how racism and other exclusionary practices bear out in urban centers across the United States. Indeed, critical geographers have been spot on in their attention to the salience of urban spaces as active contexts as opposed to inert surroundings. Critical geographers have long recognized that place/location bears directly on well-being and quality of life. In this project, I suggest viewing urban spaces through the lens of the "rhetorical situation" in order to understand how dynamics of power and race create exigencies that must be addressed through public discourse and debate.

Bitzer's rhetorical situation reminds us of the relevance of a material reality that both constrains and motivates human action. A century earlier, Friedrich Engels put the matter this way: "We make our history ourselves but, in the first place, under very definite assumptions and conditions" (Engels 1890/1978, 761). More recently the critical geographer, Edward Soja (2010b), echoed Engels: "We make our geographies for good or bad, just or unjust . . . under conditions not of our own choosing but in real-world contexts already shaped by socio-spatial processes in the past and the enveloping historically and socially constituted geographies of the present" (103). Here we see an affinity between communication studies, Marxist theorizing, and critical geography that points to the influence of urban development and capitalist processes on discourses of urban growth and struggles against geographical injustice. Conducting a rhetorical analysis within a framework of historical materialism prompts us to recognize that space is marked, above all, by material systems and structures (e.g., industrial or service economies, corresponding geographical layout, and neighborhood infrastructure) that constrain and enable bodily movement and physical/mental well-being in ways that often fall along the lines of race, class, sex, ability, and so forth. This observation regarding the link between bodies and space is made clear by the fact that one's zip code is a determinant of one's health and mortality (Arrieta et al. 2008; Benson 2009).

Standpoint: Locatedness in the City

On a more optimistic note, Marx—and scholars after him, such as Georg Lukács, Antonio Gramsci, and Nancy Hartsock—also showed interest in understanding how "external forces of capitalist circulation and accumulation" shape "processes of human resistance, desire for reform, rebellion and revolution" (Harvey 1998, 405). Standpoint theory develops an understanding of how individuals gain a critical awareness of injustices and in turn struggle to change them; or as Marx put it, how a class in itself becomes a class for itself. Lukács (1968) noted that one's position, that is, standpoint, within the "economic process"—whether proletariat or capitalist—afforded different understandings and judgments of the system. Nancy Hartsock (1983a, 1983b) referred to standpoint as a "specific kind of epistemological device" derived from "'sensuous human activity'" or the "striving . . . to meet physical needs," first and foremost (Hartsock 1983b, 118–19).[3] Specifically, standpoint theory is based on the premises that "[m]aterial life . . . not only structures but sets limits on the understanding of social relations" (232). One's position in relation to the production and distribution of necessary resources influences one's access to those resources and in turn shapes one's interests in either maintaining or challenging the current socio-economic structure.

As such, standpoint theory calls forth the intimate connection between knowledge and power. Echoing Lukács, Hartsock (1983b) states, "[i]f material life is structured in fundamentally opposing ways for two different groups, one can expect that the vision of each will represent an inversion of the other, and in systems of domination the vision available to the rulers will be both partial and perverse" (232). Similarly, Sandra Harding (1993) points out, "one's social situation enables and sets limits on what one can know; some social situations—critically unexamined dominant ones—are more limiting than others . . . and what makes these situations more limiting is their inability to generate the most critical questions about received belief" (54–55). Thus, although standpoint theory sees knowledge as perspectival, it does not view all perspectives as equally valid. The perspectives derived through firsthand experience with oppression lend greater critical insight—or provide what Alcoff (2006) refers to as "epistemic advantage" (96)—regarding social relations and systems that perpetuate domination and human suffering.

Standpoint's assumptions concerning knowledge and social position have elicited debates concerning the relationship between language and reality and the possibility of asserting knowledge claims with certainty. The linguistic turn in the humanities—influenced by postmodern, poststructuralist, and relativist thinkers—has led many to conclude that all understandings of reality are discursively constructed and thus partial (Foucault 1980, Laclau & Mouffe 1985; Lyotard 1984). Additionally, feminists have introduced the notion of difference among women to complicate Hartsock's notion of *a* feminist epistemology (Hekman 1997, 349).

Certainly, reality is understood through discourse—language, framings, and hegemonic and resistant rhetorics. And the relationship between language and an extra-discursive reality is dialectical in that material conditions shape linguistic understandings and language, in turn, impacts/shapes material reality. But these acknowledgments do not then necessitate a trip down the "rabbit hole of relativism" (Cloud 2006, 329). Some knowledge claims are truer than others and the veracity of those claims may be attributed, at least in part, to their rootedness in a lived experience with matters of oppression and struggle, with experiences linked to marginalization, disenfranchisement, and lack of formal power. Standpoint, or the idea that where one stands, figuratively and literally (as in one's zip code location), offers a way to thread together communication, the spatiality and materiality of well-being, and possibilities for social change by underscoring that "our 'place' (in all its meanings) is considered fundamentally important to our perspective, our location in the world, and our right and ability to challenge dominant discourses of power" (Keith & Pile 1993, 6).

Guiding the analyses in this book is the premise that material location bears on perspective and the two in turn influence the rhetorical strategies at play in narratives that counter celebratory city development discourses. For instance, chapter 2 explores how residents in Detroit drew on firsthand experience to reactivate public memories of race and segregation with the goal of situating present day city development along the historical trajectory of racism and exclusion. Residents challenged the collective cultural amnesia and "selective forgetting" (Hasian & Frank 1999, 99) representative of dominant stories of urban regeneration by repeatedly emphasizing that Detroit's "financial crisis result[ed] from decades of revenue decline caused by redlining, housing discrimination and deindustrialization" ("D-REM Objection" 2014, 4). Residents in Harlem, the focus of chapters 4 and 5, leveraged knowledge gained from exposure to toxins, noxious fumes, and air borne particulates to exercise "street science" to back their arguments for place-based justice. The Harlem-based WE ACT For Environmental Justice relied on community based participatory research to "instruct residents on surveying and mapping" (Mock 2009), fact-finding, and analysis in order to "democratize the policy development process" (personal interview, Ogonnaya Dotson Newman, May 28, 2014). In other words, residents drew on perspectives and experiences acquired through their standpoint as primarily low-income, minority residents to create arguments for place-based justice.

DOMINANT AND COUNTERNARRATIVES OF URBAN RENEWAL IN DETROIT AND HARLEM

Urban Renewal and Resistance argues, in part, that the dynamics of economic, political, and social change in Detroit and Harlem—the rhetorical situation—set the stage for contemporary debates over race, residence, and basic rights to housing and clean air. These two cities' stories of urban development provide a lens through which to view the racialized nature of city spaces and the ways ordinary citizens struggle for spatial justice. For both locales, "centuries of racial prejudice," local and federal policies legitimating race discrimination, and "economic and social structures" "act[ed] as parameters that limit[ed] the range of individual and collective decisions" (Sugrue 1996, 11).

Discourses of neoliberalism and the "rhetorical silence" of whiteness (Crenshaw 1997. See also Nakayama & Krizek 1995; McIntosh 2011) work in tandem to naturalize the processes of urban change. Naturalization works to "render . . . beliefs natural and self-evident . . . so that nobody could imagine how they might ever be different" (Eagleton 1991, 58). Beliefs concerning urban growth and regeneration carry a "That goes without saying" quality that conveys them as "inevitable and so unalterable" (59). When it comes to urban renewal projects, the seeming obvious response is "Great! The market is back in full swing" without considering the ways market expansion excludes, displaces, and exploits as it enables a few to control city spaces, accumulate wealth, and reap millions of dollars in profit.

Accumulation and power in the hands of a few is abetted by neoliberal discourses that laud individual traits like personal responsibility and self-sufficiency and extol the benefits of privatization, free market, and welfare rollbacks (Anderson 2012; Harvey 2000, 2005). Neoliberalism has been an "often coordinated, politically directed, rarely self-propelled, often violent process of change in the global architecture of capitalist production, trade, and consumption" (Keil 2002, 580). Neoliberalism may denote a political outlook, a viewpoint characteristic of the Reagan and Thatcher years that guided policy-making (Anderson 2012, 753). Or the concept may be used in a more specifically Marxian sense to refer to the "theoretical superstructure of a more fundamental class conflict" (753). On this view, neoliberalism is "rather like a strategic discourse" that guides, but does not determine the course of the economy (753). Neoliberal discourses are instrumental insofar as they legitimate market practices, justify rollbacks in public assistance, and distort notions of "self-sufficiency" and "dependence."

Throughout the following chapters, I view neoliberal discourses as the "common sense"—that is, dominant, prevailing, and taken-for-granted assumptions—of capitalist development in the late twentieth-early twenty-first centuries. The analyses in this book focus on the ways neoliberal discourses deployed in the mainstream press and captured in the rhetorics of urban planning used by city developers and leaders naturalize urban formations rooted in racist practices. In turn, each chapter looks at how longtime residents resist the logic of neoliberalism through key rhetorical strategies.

Urban growth and development are also naturalized through what Carrie Crenshaw (1997) calls the "rhetorical silence" of whiteness. Scholars have examined the ways whiteness and white privilege have remained unexamined, invisible, the "unmarked category against which difference is constructed" (Lipsitz 2002, 61). (See also Dyer 1998; hooks 1992; McIntosh 2011; Nakayama & Krizek 1995.) Whiteness operates strategically (Nakayama & Krizek 1995) to naturalize itself, to render itself invisible and normative. Dyer (1998) notes "White power secures its dominance by seeming not to be anything in particular" (44). Whiteness's "absence of recognition is a strategy that facilitates making a group the Other" (hooks 1992, 167). In these ways whiteness participates in a "selective amnesia" about race and racism in America. "Selective amnesia" is defined as the "rhetorical processes by which public discourse routinely omits events that defy seamless narratives of national progress and unity" (Hoerl 2012, 180). Selective amnesia operates as a handmaiden to white privilege, enabling and upholding the silence/absence of whiteness, using strategic forgetfulness to enable invisibility.

Neoliberal rhetorics extolling the virtues of individualism and personal responsibility and justifying cuts to the welfare state are not race- or class-neutral. They work strategically to support white privilege and encourage a historical forgetting of the racist dimensions of welfare, housing, and employment legislation that systematically excluded African Americans from certain jobs, neighborhoods, and public aid. Absent a history of race discrimination—one that continues in the twenty-first century (Rugh & Massey, 2010)—we are encouraged to pin unemployment, substandard housing, or reliance on welfare to the shortcomings of the (black) individual who presumably did not assume personal responsibility or take advantage of the opportunities afforded through the free market. Such perceptions are part of the "possessive investment in whiteness" (Lipsitz 2002) and bear out in studies that show widespread beliefs associating welfare, unemployment, crime, and disorder with black people (Gilens 1999; Sampson & Raudenbush 2005). If we buy into neoliberal assumptions concerning opportunity, personal responsibility, and the benign nature of the free market, we are led to conclude that individual shortcomings attributable to race (rather than institutionalized processes like redlining) are the reasons folks turn to public assistance or are unable to find work.

The observation of Republican Representative and 2012 Vice-Presidential nominee, Paul Ryan, trades on this neoliberal mind-set. In 2014, Ryan claimed: "We have got this tailspin of culture, in our inner cities in particular, of men not working and just generations of men not even thinking about working or learning the value and the culture of work, and so there is a real culture problem here that has to be dealt with" (Bouie 2014). Ryan's references to "inner city men" is code for "black" and his reference to "culture" implies that "those people" don't know how to abide by standard American mores. Ryan's observation gains currency in a broader context that extols the virtues of hard work and opportunity to the neglect of systems and structures that have historically and today work to the benefit of a few. In contrast, when white folks find work or are able to make ends meet without public aid, it is attributed to their individual efforts and work ethic, rather than as a result of white privilege. The invisibility of whiteness naturalizes a market logic constructed to benefit certain groups and the racialized nature of displacement and pollution is silenced.

The following chapters offer a unique look into the *racialized and classed dimensions of neoliberal discourses* and the ways ordinary citizens employ rhetorical strategies to recenter race and class in issues of urban regeneration and growth. Chapter 1 provides an essential historical and theoretical backdrop for understanding the analyses in chapters 2–5. Specifically, I outline the history of city growth in the twentieth century and situate that trajectory in the context of changes in the economic system from the early 1900s to the present. I also introduce theoretical perspectives on space and the city.

Chapter 2 examines rhetorics surrounding the twenty-first century recovery of Detroit. The historical trajectory of Detroit, beginning with its industrial decline in the 1950s to its present day "rebirth," epitomizes the experiences of rustbelt cities that took the brunt of deindustrialization, automation, and decentralization and have found themselves rebranding perceived landscapes of decay into centers of finance, tourism, and retail (Makagon 2010; Zukin 2008, 2009). In this chapter, I look at competing narratives of Detroit's past that continue to shape how we understand that city's present day growth. Chapter 3 explores how rhetorics of market rationalization used by Detroit city leaders dehistoricize and neutralize processes of urban change so as to construct a seamless dominant narrative of progress. I then look at how ordinary residents have used websites (e.g., Detroiters Resisting Emergency Management [D-REM]) and non-corporate newspapers (e.g., *Michigan Citizen, Voice of Detroit*) to create counternarratives that demystify or unveil the raced and classed nature of urban progress.

Chapters 4 and 5 turn to issues of race and pollution in Harlem, an area that, like Detroit, has been shaped by development processes (e.g., highway construction, toxic dumping) widely understood through popular narratives as inevitable aspects of city growth and progress. These chapters focus primarily on the rhetorical efforts of New York City's first environmental justice group, WE ACT For Environmental Justice, for the ways activists and ordinary citizens used countermapping (Ewalt 2011) and citizen science that together wove a rhetoric of recognition to challenge neoliberal discourses that diverted attention from the by-products of capitalist growth disproportionately burdening the black body. The salience of racialized health disparities has gained public attention most recently when Flint, Michigan, residents called attention to the issue of lead-contaminated water in their community. In 2014, residents of Flint, a majority black town, noticed their tap water smelled, looked, and tasted strange but city officials dismissed their concerns. Despite the findings of toxic levels of lead in studies by the local Flint pediatrician Mona Hanna-Attisha and Marc Edwards, a civil engineering professor at Virginia Tech, residents were poisoned for two years before government leaders admitted action needed to be taken. Since the early 1900s, similar "lead wars" have been waged on poor, minority, and low-wage families who often lack the resources to leave older construction apartments and homes clustered in city cores that are most likely to be contaminated by lead. Documents exchanged among officials in the Lead Industries Association in the 1950s dismissed the severity of lead poisoning stating it was primarily a problem of the "slums" and due to the ignorance of "Negro and Puerto Rican families" (Markowitz & Rosner 2014, 35). Nearly a century later the urgency of the phrase "Black Lives Matter" resonates louder than ever as Hanna-Attisha notes, "If you were going to put something in a population to keep them down for generations to come, it would be lead" (Goodnough 2016).

Critical geographers have studied the taken for granted and "routine" nature of urban "exclusionary practices" (Sibley 1995, ix) and the ways "spatial discrimination" leading to the "maldistribution of vital public services and . . . resources" become "normalized" (Soja 2010b, 49). *Urban Renewal and Resistance* draws on insights afforded by critical communication studies to shed light on *how words work* in public contexts to normalize, justify, and/or naturalize geographic injustices that impact housing and health. The following chapters examine both dominant and resistant narratives, and ask: How is communication used to exercise control over urban spaces? What roles do neoliberal assumptions play in supporting dominant narratives of urban growth? How are geographies of exclusion (Sibley 1995) created rhetorically? And more optimistically, how do ordinary citizens advocate for more just use of urban spaces?

Importantly, the following chapters represent an intervention in existing studies of communication and space as they foreground the importance of a material reality that, although understood through discourse, plays a central role in shaping, delimiting, and at times motivating rhetorical choices and the exercise of agency. Presently, communication scholarship has focused to a large degree on space as metaphor, identity, location, or mobility (see chapter 1). This study of race, space, and the city urges renewed attention to the relationship between bodies—physical bodies, knowing bodies—and location and the ways spaces reinforce power disparities that impact certain groups (e.g., black Americans, low-income, women) in systematic and material ways. Consider the ways the expectations of mothering and domesticity have historically confined women to the home, the ways terms such as "alien," "illegal," and "undocumented" have precluded non-U.S. citizens from civic spaces, and the ways laws concerning the uses of public spaces have denied homeless persons a place to be. *Urban Renewal and Resistance* provides an in-depth examination of the ways geographic injustices are justified or go unnoticed and the ways ordinary citizens draw on their experiences living in marginalized areas to call out the ways race and class are tethered to location.

The twenty-first century is witnessing a revalorization of the urban. Racialized discourses lamenting the "urban nightmare" (Macek 2006) are giving way to celebrations of the "post-post-apocalyptic" city (Austen 2014), which are equally imbricated with race; this time around, the invisible centering of whiteness is tied to contemporary discourses of the city. Once considered the triumph of American industrialization, former auto capital, Detroit, Michigan, is rebranding itself to fit the contours of market financialization, tourism, and consumption. The story of struggle over urban regeneration in Detroit merits close scrutiny for the ways race and residence play out in public discourses. The Harlem neighborhood in New York City, the center of black American culture and community, finds itself in the midst of a decades-long struggle over issues of home and health that is often whitewashed by discourses of technology and growth. The residents in each city face unique, yet parallel, struggles over justice and geographic location as these issues are tied to race and class in America.

NOTES

1. In July 2014, in Staten Island, New York City, a white police officer killed unarmed Eric Garner by putting him in a chokehold. In August 2014, a white police offer shot and killed unarmed Michael Brown in Ferguson, Missouri. Also in August 2014, police in Beavercreek, Ohio, in a Walmart, shot John Crawford III. Police allegedly mistook the BB gun Crawford was holding for a real gun. In Cleveland, Ohio, in November 2014, police, who allegedly mistook an air gun for a real pistol, shot twelve-year-old Tamir Rice. In April 2015, a white police officer shot unarmed Walter Scott in the back in North Charleston, South Carolina. Also in April 2015, Freddie Gray died in police custody due to an injury sustained at the hands of the police who arrested him.

2. This statistic includes only residential lots. It does not include commercial, industrial, or institutional lots. See Gallagher 2012.

3. Hartsock is quoting from Marx's *Theses on Feuerbach*.

ONE
Theoretical Considerations

The American city is and has been fraught with contradiction and paradox. Urban sociologists like Robert Park and developers such as Daniel Burnham viewed the city as the apex of human progress, the crown jewel of modernism, a reflection of enduring optimism. For these men, urbanization and industrialization were parts of a whole that worked to the benefit of humankind. Park (1925) extolled the city as the "natural habitat of civilized man. It is for that reason a cultural area characterized by its own peculiar cultural type" (2). Not unlike Park and Burnham, Friedrich Engels and Upton Sinclair—urban sociologists in their own right—recognized the interrelated nature of urban development and industrialization but viewed the city from a very different perspective, that of the average resident who worked in the industries that made the city so profitable for a few but kept most chained to dangerous jobs and squalid living conditions. In his own observations of city life, Engels (1845/2005) remarked that "individual isolation" and "narrow self-seeking" was "nowhere so shamelessly barefaced, so self-conscious as just here in the crowding of the great city" (60).

Since the time of the writings of these urban philosophers, much about the makeup of the American city has changed even as paradox has remained a constant. The 1940s–1960s saw middle- and upper-income white families flee the city for the orderliness, open space, and racial homogeneity of the suburbs (Dreier, Mollenkopf & Swanstrom 2001; Jackson 1985; Sugrue 1996). In contrast, the early twenty-first century is witnessing a revalorization of the urban (Lambert 2012). Well-off homebuyers are settling in the city core and gentrifying areas at a rapid pace (Hackworth 2006, 87). Empty warehouses are becoming chic loft apartments (Zukin 1982). Once hollowed out rustbelt cities like Cleveland and

Detroit are now touted as good investments and the hip place to be (Austen 2014; Dill 2015; Foroohar 2014; Schneider 2011).

Even as city centers are becoming gentrified (a process elaborated upon later in the chapter), notions of the "urban" still sit uncomfortably in the public imagination. Websites and apps are now available that inform the leery (white/well-to-do) city visitor of an area's "sketch factor"[1] or the prospective home buyer of the racial makeup of a given neighborhood (Strachan 2014; Prevost 2014). In everyday conversations of where to eat out or where to rent an apartment, one may hear warnings to avoid the "bad part of town" or references to a "bad neighborhood."[2] Conversely, we hear talk of areas that have "improved" or that "aren't ratty anymore" (Finn 2014).

What does it mean to refer to a neighborhood where people live, work, and raise their families as "sketchy," "ratty," or "bad?" I argue that references like these, far from innocuous, are part of larger discourses of the "urban" steeped in a history of race and class segregation, redlining, and toxic dumping in city spaces. The "color of American politics is implicit in . . . debates about welfare, affirmative action, crime" (Crenshaw 1997, 254) and, I would add, the inner city. This chapter provides an historical and theoretical foundation for the analyses in the following chapters by tracing the growth of the capitalist city since the early 1900s and aligning this history with an examination of the rhetorical processes that variously justify or contest disparities in health and well-being tied to spaces in the city.

HISTORICAL BACKGROUND ON URBAN DEVELOPMENT AND CAPITALIST EXPANSION

Capitalism gives rise to contradiction. And as the two statements that opened this chapter underscore, no place bears this out more clearly than the city space. For the super rich[3] who live in multi-million dollar luxury apartments and mansions, the city represents the "habitat of civilized man" (Park 1925, 2). For those living in shanties from Bogotá to Mumbai, or the favelas of Rio de Janeiro city life is often a struggle to find employment, safe housing, and to provide steady education for one's children. American cities are no less marked by contradiction. In my own neighborhood on the Near West Side of Cleveland, publically subsidized housing for seniors shares the street with eateries selling $10 pancakes and $7 craft beers. Homeless men who live in the area regularly walk the neighborhood streets dotted with half-million-dollar homes that sit among foreclosed and dilapidated dwellings selling for tens of thousands of dollars. The juxtapositions generated by growth may provoke one to observe: "The city is more beautiful, but for whom? The city is richer, but for whom? Who is the city for?" (Garcia-Navarro 2014).[4]

The city—shaped by the vagaries of capitalist expansion, overaccumulation, instability, growth, and creative destruction—remains an ever-moving target chased by discourses equally malleable. The City Beautiful movement of the early twentieth century gave way to 1950s–1960s discourses of alarm over urban decay, which is currently giving way to twenty-first century valorizations of the city as antidote to suburban alienation and homogeneity. The following section overviews city development and attendant discourses in three periods: 1. early twentieth century; 2. mid-twentieth century; and, 3. late twentieth-early twenty-first century. I paint this picture with broad strokes emphasizing key trends in each period.

From Marx and Engels to the Chicago School

Although Karl Marx and Friedrich Engels did not detail geographical matters in their writings, each recognized the influence of geography in relation to capitalist development and circulation (Harvey 1983). In the *Communist Manifesto*, Marx and Engels referenced the importance of geographical expansion to capitalism's endless search for profit and in *Grundrisse*, Marx noted the "exploration of the earth in all directions, to discover new things of use as well as new useful qualities of the old . . . is . . . a condition of production founded on capital" (409). Focusing more pointedly on urban spaces, Marx's comrade, Friedrich Engels (1845/2005), provided a poignant and descriptive account of city life in mid-1800s industrial England. In some sense, we may regard Engels' writings on city life as the first "people's geography," a mapping project that "confronts ideologies and prejudice as they really are, that faithfully mirrors the complex weave of competition, struggle, and cooperation" (Harvey 1984, 7).

Engels (1845/2005) walked the streets of Manchester in order to learn firsthand the city's physical layout and living conditions. Through both description and diagram, Engels highlighted the ways workers were divided from the more well off. He noted, "the working-people's quarters are sharply separated from the sections of the city reserved for the middle class" (61). Indeed, the "town itself is built so that a person may live in it for years, and go in and out daily without coming into contact with a working-people's quarter or even with workers" (61). In other words, spatial design communicated class belonging and legitimated city growth that resulted in "brilliant shops [and] immense hotels" and physically concealed "everything which might affront the eye and the nerves of the bourgeoisie" (61).

Engels' book resonates with a theme explored in the following chapters; namely, the ways capitalism's drive for profit underwrites the cycle of development and decay of cities. Engels detailed how the search for accumulation was an economic process that directly affected the living and health conditions of the masses. "Wherever a nook or corner was free, a house has been run up; where a superfluous passage remained, it has been built up; the value of land rose with the blossoming out of manufacture, and the more it rose, the more madly was the work of building up carried on, without reference to the health or comfort of the inhabitants, with sole reference to the highest possible profit on the principle that *no hole is so bad but that some poor creature must take it who can pay for nothing better*" (65, italics in original). Engels described workers' dwellings as "cattle sheds for human beings" (63) characterized by "filth, ruin" and lack of ventilation (64). "Each house is packed close behind its neighbor and a piece of each is visible, all black, smokey, crumbling, ancient, with broken panes and window-frames" (63).

As the industrial city so vividly detailed by Engels was growing both abroad and in the United States, novelists like Upton Sinclair and Charles Dickens as well as reformers such as Jane Addams and Jacob Riis decried the deleterious effects of industry on ordinary people. At the same time, sociologists and developers remained cautiously optimistic about the potential prosperity of the city (Beauregard 2003). The Progressive Era ushered in reformers who cast urban renewal in terms of moral uplift and beautification (Schwartz 1993; Smith 2006). Charity organizations led by middle-class reformers influenced legislation such as the Tenement House Law of 1901, which stipulated minimum requirements for new tenement construction, even as these groups reinforced prevailing notions of the "deserving" vs. the "shiftless" poor (Schwartz 1993, 5–9). The City Beautiful movement also shaped urban reform in the early 1900s with its call for creating a more "beautified, unified, and efficient arrangement of" the city (Smith 2006, 14). The Chicago architect Daniel Burnham stood at the center of the City Beautiful movement with his 1909 Plan of Chicago as a blueprint for improving the layout of Chicago and addressing slums and city inefficiency (Smith 2006).

Writing during the same time period, sociologists at the University of Chicago (referred to as the Chicago School) developed a framework for understanding city growth as a "series of concentric circles" with a city core or downtown in the center and a residential zone and commuter zone as outer circles, a framework that still holds sway today (Burgess 1925; Park 1925; Harvey 2009).

From Engels to Park and Burgess, late nineteenth- to the early twentieth-century writings on the city foreshadowed present day rhetorics of the city. Like contemporary urban activists fighting for fair housing, Engels described Manchester's neighborhoods as a "landscape of exclusion" that reveals much about how "power is expressed in the monopolization of space and relegation of weaker groups to less desirable environment" (Sibley 1995, ix). Engels' observations of the ways spatial arrangements disproportionately affected the health of workers (through exposure to air pollution and contaminants) foreshadow the work of present day environmental justice advocates (Bullard 2000; Margai 2010; Shrader-Frechette 2005).

And much like present day hegemonic discourses that rely on a market logic to naturalize and thus justify disparities that arise from urban growth and renewal, Chicago School sociologist Robert Park (1925) described the "inevitable processes of human nature [that] proceed to give . . . regions and . . . buildings a character which is less easy to control" (4). Using a similar rhetorical lens, Park's colleague Ernest Burgess (1925) likened city growth to plant ecology (50) and the "anabolic and katabolic processes of metabolism in the body" (53). In stark contrast to Engels' critique of capitalism that underwrote his scathing assessment of city, Burgess (1925) attributed city segregation by race and class as the result of "natural economic and cultural groupings" (56). The Chicago School suggested a model of city growth and change that urged planners to "pay particular attention to 'undesirable' or 'least desirable' elements" that would "precipitate price declines" if they "infiltrated" a given space (Jackson 1980, 424). This understanding set up future practices of racial exclusion, such as those embraced by the Home Owners' Loan Corporation discussed in the next section.

Mid-Twentieth-Century Urban Growth

By mid-century, ambivalence was a mainstay of urban discourses, as celebrations of City Beautiful gave way to anxieties surrounding postwar urban decline (Beauregard, 2003). I argue we should understand such discourses as an outgrowth of capitalism's "uneven development," or the "concrete manifestation of the production of space under capitalism" (Smith 1990, 90). Harvey (2006b) illustrates uneven development thusly: "Vast concentrations of productive power here contrast with relatively empty regions there. Tight concentrations of activity in one place contrast with sprawling far-flung development in another" (373). Contemporary critical geographers have adeptly examined "what capitalism does to geography . . . and what geography can do for capitalism" (Smith 1990, xi; Soja 2010a, 2010b). The project of this and subsequent chapters is to add analysis of how public discourses both shape and are constrained by the materiality of economics and spatial arrangements.

From the 1930s through the 1950s, city growth and stagnation, development and decline—"uneven" to be sure—resulted in the search for what Harvey (2006b) termed a "spatial fix," which might come in the form of imported labor power, exported commodities, land expansion, regional restructuring and the like (427; see also Soja 2010b). During the Depression, the U.S. government addressed the need for a spatial fix through massive funding for roads and highways and suburban development (Hackworth 2006, 9). The creation of the Home Owners' Loan Corporation in 1933 and the Federal Housing Administration the following year supported the growth of suburban development and sanctioned redlining, which ensured racial segregation, led to white flight and further neglect of city housing where minorities had no choice but to remain (Jackson 1985; Powell 2009). Movement to the city's outer rings was abetted by postindustrialization that impacted cities such as Philadelphia, which lost the last of its pharmaceutical, manufacturing, and food processing industries to the suburbs (Bauman 1987, 83).

By 1949, cities (re)turned to urban development and revalorization spurred by the Federal Housing Act, whose stated purpose was to "provide a decent home and suitable environment for every American family" (Kleniewski, 1984, 205). The Act provided federal funds for urban renewal projects and slum clearance and proved a boon for "stimulat[ing] economic growth and making cities more profitable places for capital to invest" (Kleniewski 1984, 205; Beauregard 2003). The name most closely tied to urban development during the late 1940s–early 1950s was Robert Moses, a New York City developer who "did Title I [of the Housing Act] his way," that is, with disregard for the thousands of low income and black families displaced by his wide-sweeping developments (Schwartz 1993, xvi). The Stuyvesant Town redevelopment on New York's East Side embodied Moses' approach to city development. Garnering support from city planners and Mayor La Guardia, Moses oversaw the displacement of 11,000 working-class residents to be replaced by 8,756 middle-class families (Schwartz 1993, 84). The extensive upheaval of residents was (and still is) not unique. The sociologist Herbert Gans' classic text, *The Urban Villagers*, detailed the decimation of Boston's working class, Italian West End neighborhood in the late 1950s resulting in the displacement of nearly 7,000 residents. Similar processes occurred in Philadelphia (Kleniewski 1984) and San Francisco (Mollenkopf 1981).

The Federal Housing Act did not live up to its promise of a "home for every American family" but actually spurred projects that reduced the stock of low-cost housing and led to widespread displacement of poor, low-income, and black families (Kleniewski 1984, 216–218). Urban redevelopment projects occurred as the country caught the first glimpses of industrial divestment and the birth of the "corporate city" (Kleniewski 1984), a transition that led to further alienation and marginalization of working-class and minority families. Urban renewal projects "played midwife to the emerging corporate headquarters economy" (Mollenkopf 1981, 16). Supported by funding from Title I, developers transformed old manufacturing warehouses and lofts into "office towers . . . luxury housing, and specialized shops" (Kleniewski 1984, 209; see also Beauregard 2003), while Title II of the Housing Act provided funding for the clearance of slums to be replaced by public housing (Beauregard 2003, 113).

Above all, city projects supported by federal funding were good for the corporate bottom line. Real estate investors and city planners cleared away working-class housing and replaced it with "prestige-bearing" projects such as luxury hotels, high-rise offices, and boutiques (Zukin 2007, 43; Schwartz 1993). Boston's West End redevelopment project sought to woo public and private investors, raise rents, and attract high-end businesses (Gans 1982, 327–329).[5]

Discourses of urban renewal conveyed contradiction as economic and political policies played out on the city landscape in similarly ambivalent ways. Proclamations to ensure housing for all resulted in neighborhood upheaval and displacement. Publically expressed alarm over slum conditions were rounded out at the end of the 1950s with a cheerful outlook as expressed in a 1959 issue of *Newsweek*: "Across the nation, the cities are rebuilding, refurbishing, marching ahead" (Beauregard 2003, 120).

Ironically, the *Newsweek* headline appeared as the "rusting of the Rust Belt" (Sugrue 1996, 6) was in high gear. Urban redevelopment and the birth of the "corporate city" occurred even as federal and local policies supported industrial divestment from city centers. Throughout the 1950s, Detroit witnessed Ford, General Motors, and Chrysler shift millions of dollars and thousands of jobs to plants in the suburbs (Sugrue 1996). Between 1947–1963, Detroit workers experienced massive layoffs as plant closings resulted in a loss of over 100,000 manufacturing jobs (126). The economic ripple effect resulted in falling property values, deteriorating neighborhoods, and white flight to the suburbs where jobs were relocated.

Suburbanization throughout the 1960s further exacerbated racist spatial practices that shaped city neighborhoods under the guise of "renewal." Sugrue (1996) notes "government housing programs perpetuated racial divisions by placing public housing in already poor urban areas and bankrolling white suburbanization through discriminatory housing subsidies" (9, 10; Jackson 1985, 201). The Federal Housing Administration (FHA)—born out of the 1934 Federal Housing Act—further boosted white flight to the suburbs through explicitly racist policies that turned the "building industry against the minority and inner-city housing market" (Jackson 1985, 213). Suburbanization represented what Harvey called a "spatial fix" insofar as it expanded both space and capitalist accumulation (Hackworth 2006, 77, 78).

Detroit exemplifies the larger economic processes pressing upon the American city. Heavy industries moved south or abroad and were supported by neoliberal policies that promoted "free" trade and "free" markets for transnational corporations, and resulted in uneven development and displacement for longtime city residents.

Neoliberalism and the City: 1960s to the Early Twenty-First Century

Neoliberalism is described as a "process" (Hackworth, 2006), a political framework (Anderson 2012), and a hegemonic "mode of discourse" (Harvey 2006a, 145). Harvey's (2006a) explanation of neoliberalism as a "theory of political economic practices" illuminates the ways city growth, capitalism, and public discourses interacted from the 1960s to the early twenty-first century to produce and justify spatial practices that shape and delimit access to resources. Neoliberal theory rests on the assumption that "individual freedoms are guaranteed by freedom of the market and of trade" (Harvey 2005, 7). At least since the 1950s, neoliberal economic practices have replaced the Keynesian welfare state with laissez-faire government practices that promote entrepreneurialism, competition, and private property rights. Neoliberal political-economic policies have led to a reduction/destruction of public housing and labor unions, replacing those institutions with privatization of social goods and cuts to welfare (Hackworth 2006, 11–12; Harvey 2006a). If a profit-bearing market did not exits, neoliberal policies sought to create one, as has been the case in the privatization of education and health care in the United States (Harvey 2006a, 145) and in the institution of a neoliberal state through military intervention abroad, e.g., Chile in 1973; Iraq in 2003 (Harvey 2005, 7). Neoliberalism served as a hegemonic discourse, a commonsense logic to legitimate capitalist expansion.

In addition to rhetorical functions, neoliberalism served important material, i.e., economic, purposes; namely to restore class power. Harvey (2006a) explains that the economic effects of neoliberal policies and practices have been primarily redistributive rather than generative creating a sort of "accumulation by dispossession" marked by four elements (153–156). Through privatization, everything from prisons to genetic materials to natural resources like water has been captured for corporate profitability. Financialization entails the turnover of billions of dollars through speculative and predatory maneuvers often allowed by law. The 2007–2009 Great Recession and housing crisis that resulted in homelessness and/or displacement for thousands of middle- and low-income people was a direct result of unregulated financial markets. A third element that creates accumulation by dispossession is the management/manipulation of crises. Debt, interest rates, bailouts, and unemployment can be controlled in ways that keep individuals or entire nations (e.g., Latin American countries) under the foot of the IMF or the U.S. Treasury. Finally, through policies at the state level, redistribution of wealth occurs in ways that benefit a small elite.

Neoliberal practices and policies (Hackworth 2006; Harvey 2006a, 2006b) particularly those exercised since the 1960s have profoundly impacted middle- and low-income city residents. The reduction/eradication of low-cost housing, privatization of once-public resources, and corporate deregulation has created city spaces of contradiction: homelessness persists amidst housing construction; low-cost, often minority, occupied neighborhoods become a target for high-end real estate; the "dangerous city" is mollified by the growing presence of young, primarily white professionals, or the "hipoisie." When it comes to race and residence, the neoliberal city presents a "situation in which we can finds all kinds of contradictory statements 'true'" (Harvey 2009, 141).

At the street level, neoliberal practices such as privatization run hand in hand with gentrification and work to supplant "publicly regulated Keynesian inner city" institutions, leading to expanding zones of exclusion (Hackworth 2006, 120). The processes of city growth explored in chapters 2–5 should be understood historically as gentrification redux. Mid-twentieth-century processes of gentrification in Philadelphia (Kleniewski 1984; Smith 1996), Greenwich Village (Zukin 1982), Boston (Gans 1982) and other cities paved the way for processes of renewal, displacement, and toxicity in urban areas across the United States.

But mid- to late-twentieth-century processes of gentrification have not taken a straight road forward. Post–World War II gentrification projects were "isolated"; by the 1970s, gentrification "had become an increasingly pervasive, trenchant and systematic occurrence" that worked in tandem with broader movements of capital (Smith 1996, 140; see also Beauregard 2003, 210–235). The 1980s and 1990s gave way to both city rejuvenation (Beauregard 2007) and "degentrification" resulting from renewed "panic over the urban crisis" (Macek 2006, 130). Degentrification, a "reversal of the gentrification process," resulted in a "revanchist antiurbanism" representing a "reaction against the supposed 'theft' of the city, a desperate defense of a challenged phalanx of privileges, cloaked in the populist language of civic morality, family values and neighborhood security" (Smith 1996, 211).

Even amidst scurries to the suburbs, gentrification of city spaces from the mid-1990s to the early twenty-first century has persisted, spurred by crises both manufactured and natural. In 1995, a city deficit of $3.1 billion prompted New York City Mayor Rudy Giuliani to cut the city's budget and services in the hopes of encouraging those most dependent on the services to leave the city (Smith 1996, 230; Body-Gendrot 2000). With similar disdain for poor and low-income residents, one legislator in Louisiana stated that Hurricane Katrina's flooding of housing projects did what the city had been trying to do for the past two decades—rid the city of poor residents (Wright 2008). In a similar vein, Detroit city planners and a handful of billionaires have profited immensely from the city's 2013 bankruptcy that laid the groundwork for privatization of public services and the scooping up of millions of square feet in downtown properties that were converted from Section 8 housing to high-end condominiums. These attempts at social control over residence also track with race and policies to bleach the city core and make it "safe" once again for the white professional class.

The concept of "uneven development" touched upon earlier provides a way to understand the relationship between capitalism and gentrification, urban crises and the economic uses and disuses of space. At international, regional, and urban levels, "capital moves spatially for similar . . .

reasons, and it is this similarity of purpose and structure that engenders a similar spatial unevenness at different scales" (Smith 1982, 142). Uneven development is characterized by tendencies toward cyclical development/underdevelopment of inner cities vis-á-vis the suburbs and the related processes of valorization/devalorization of capital. Valorization of capital refers to "its investment in search of surplus value or profit" (147). Smith explains the ways valorization is twinned to devalorization:

> The physical structure [capital] must remain in use and cannot be demolished, without sustaining a loss, until the invested capital has returned its value. What this does is to tie up whole sections of land over a long period in one specific land use, and thereby to create significant barriers to new development. But new development must proceed if accumulation is to occur. As well as creating barriers to the further valorization of capital in the built environment, however, the steady devalorization of capital creates longer term possibilities for a new phase of valorization, and this is exactly what has happened in the inner city. (147)

In short, cycles of urban growth and decay are wholly shaped by capitalist processes of accumulation and profit-seeking. Gentrification, the product of capital movements in city residential spaces (Smith 1982, 151), renovates areas into "new landscape complexes that pioneer a comprehensive class-inflected urban remake" (Smith 2002, 443). The city becomes the cultural playground for the bourgeoisie replete with festivals, open market shopping, craft breweries, artisanal bakeries, and casinos. The tenets of neoliberalism come full circle in the gentrified city center: individualism, consumerism, and freedom of choice take the place of community and collective action. It becomes a sort of domestication by cappuccino (Zukin 1998).[6] Nowhere is this wholesale re-creation more apparent than Detroit in the years 2008–2014.

Corporate media frame stories of urban regeneration in ways that naturalize market processes and sanitize the consequences of urban growth. But the understandings of city growth proffered by planners and politicians (and conveyed through the mainstream media) are often challenged by ordinary citizens whose well-being is compromised by gentrification. These street level efforts have been mobilized more recently into the Right to the City movement, described as a "response to gentrification and a call to halt the displacement of low-income people, people of color, marginalized LGBTQ communities, and youths of color from their historic urban neighborhoods" ("Mission and History").

RACE AND URBAN DEVELOPMENT

"One of the core elements of colonialism is the economic gain attached to occupation of a Third space" (Dutta 2011, 45). Dutta's observation about the conquest of land can also be applied to city spaces more specifically. As the earlier section elaborated, the settling and development of space is never a neutral process but is directly tied to capitalist production and expansion. Military occupations, apartheid, redlining, gerrymandering, and gentrification represent hegemonic and often violent means for carving spaces in ways that align with the needs of capital (e.g., for the extraction of raw material such as copper or palm oil or for the use of cheap labor as in garment factories in Bangladesh). Although the geographies of injustice resulting from these processes have not gone uncontested, the focus of this section is how spatial uses track with race and class to perpetuate material inequalities.

A little over 50 years after Engels mapped the deteriorated streets and alleys of working-class Manchester, W. E. B. DuBois (1899/1996) embarked on a similar urban sociology project as he detailed the conditions of African American residents in Philadelphia's Seventh Ward. Prefiguring contemporary critical race and geography scholars who have delineated spatial practices of race exclusion, DuBois described the Seventh Ward as "a city within a city," a "large group of people . . . who do not form an integral part of the larger social group" (5). Like Engels, DuBois pointed to employment and the structure of work as key factors shaping home life and residence.[7] Fewer occupations were open to black residents and black workers labored for cheaper wages. Such employment patterns channeled black residents into neighborhoods with inferior but overpriced housing (Jones 1998, 116).

DuBois's observations regarding the tandem relationship between race and employment resonate with the trajectory of capitalist movement and urban spatial configurations throughout the first five decades of the twentieth century. Residential segregation was exacerbated through a confluence of federal and local policies, real estate practices, and not least of all deindustrialization, all of which worked to ensure tighter restrictions on black mobility, employment, and residence. Race was seamlessly woven into notions of capitalist private property so as to define "racial exclusion as an economic necessity" (Freund 2007, 129). "Economic values . . . were racially specific" (391).

From the 1930s–1950s, black residents seeking a home "faced large down payments, difficulties in financing, and high-interest land contracts, as well as the expensive maintenance costs of old houses, all of which added to their housing expenditures" (Sugrue 1996, 43). Two government agencies mentioned earlier—the Home Owners' Loan Corporation (HOLC) and the Federal Housing Administration (FHA)—used explicitly racist practices to inform housing policies. The FHA "worked assiduously to promote segregated and not integrated patterns of urban residence" (Bauman 1987, 95). The practices of the Home Owners' Loan Corporation denied financing to black home buyers by mapping and rating city neighborhoods (Massey & Denton 1993; Sugrue 1996). Neighborhoods were rated according to perceived risks associated with lending. Areas that were "homogenous" and contained new construction were rated "A" and always received financing. Neighborhoods that were home to minority residents—labeled "'a lower grade population'" (Sugrue 1996, 44)—were granted a lower rating. Black neighborhoods were always rated "D" or "'hazardous' by federal appraisers, and colored red" on residential maps, hence the term redlining (Sugrue 1996, 44; see also Massey & Denton 1993, 52; Freund 2007, 113; Jackson 1985; see figures 1.1 and 1.2).

Throughout the 1940s–1950s, restrictive covenants, neighborhood associations, highway construction, urban "renewal projects," and physical violence provided still more avenues for shaping city neighborhoods along race lines and subsidizing "white suburban growth" (Freund 2007, 128). Covenant restrictions worked both implicitly and explicitly to dictate the racial makeup of a given area (Massey & Denton 1993, 36; Sugrue 1996, 44). Some covenants restricted the construction of multi-family units in single-family areas, essentially targeting lower-income families. Others stated that homes "'shall not be used or occupied by any person or persons except those of the Caucasian race'" (Sugrue 1996, 44). In 1952, Richard Nixon, the Republican vice-presidential candidate, and his wife "coexecuted" a covenant stipulating the house they purchased never be sold or rented to a black, Jewish, Armenian, Persian, or Syrian family (Bauman 1987, 123).

Neighborhood or homeowners associations in turn reinforced race and class segregation through rules stipulating appropriate spatial configurations and behaviors and even explicit appeals to prevent black residents from moving in (Freund 2007, 392). These associations relied on ideologies of whiteness and Americanness and often vested their arguments with references to rights and citizenship. In the late 1940s–1950s, white Detroit homeowners fought against integration and open housing through an umbrella organization of homeowners' groups called the Federated Property Owners of Detroit (Sugrue 1996, 221). This group promoted a wide-reaching "network to monitor the selling of homes to blacks, to harass real estate brokers who sold homes to blacks, and to keep house prices high to deter black buyers" (221).

Federally subsidized highway construction in the mid-1950s further facilitated the movement of white professional residents to the suburbs (Mohl 1993; Powell 2009; Sugrue 1996). Highway construction had at least three consequences that further reinforced racial and class segregation. Highways served as large, concrete barriers that divided cities physically and socially along race and class lines (Falola; Powell 2009, 27). Interstate 35, which runs north-south through Austin, Texas, was "built as part of a concerted effort to create a separate (and unequal) 'negro district' east of town" (Falola). Additionally, new highways often required the decimation of existing black neighborhoods (Mohl 1993; Pow-

Figure 1.1. Home Owners' Loan Corporation map of Detroit, Michigan. NARA II RG 195 Entry 39 Folder "Greater Detroit, MI" Box 21. *Source:* Used with permission from LaDale Winling, urbanoasis.org.

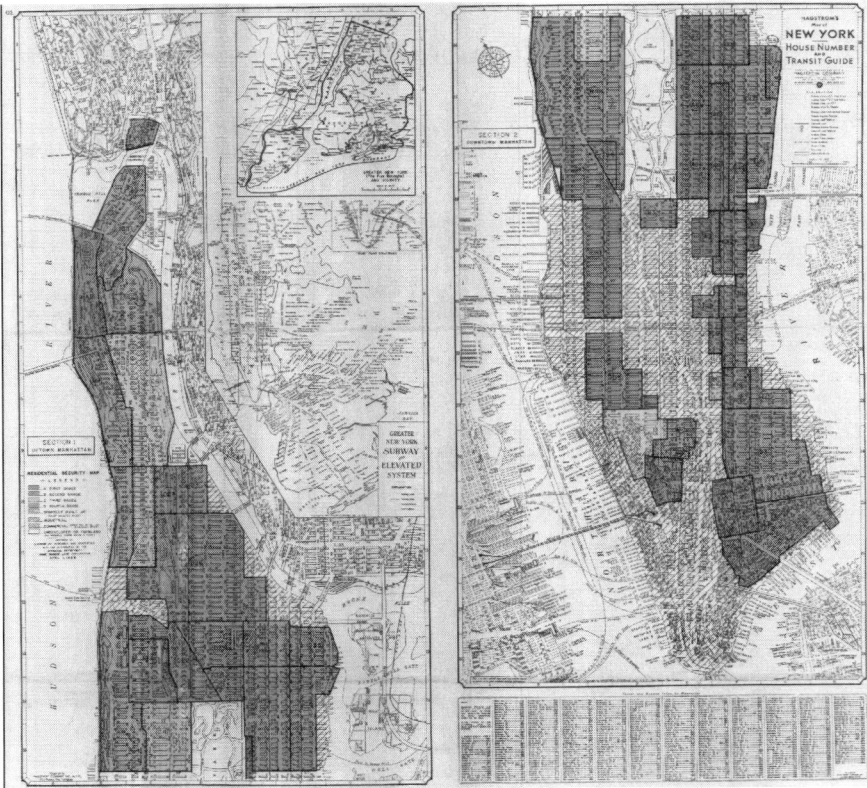

Figure 1.2. Home Owners' Loan Corporation map of Manhattan. NARA II RG 195 Entry 39 Folder "New York City Manhattan, NY Security Area Map Folder" Box 116. *Source:* Used with permission from LaDale Winling, urbanoasis.org.

ell 2009, 27; Sugrue 1996, 47). Even before the 1956 Federal Aid Highway Act promoted widespread construction, Detroit neighborhoods with primarily black residents were "devastated by highway construction" (Sugrue 1996, 47). Bustling black neighborhoods such as Paradise Valley, the Lower East Side, and the Hastings Street business district were flattened by the Oakland-Hastings Freeway.[8] Between 1957–1968, 330,000 housing units were destroyed to make room for highway construction. A majority of those displaced were black and low income (Mohl 1993, 101). City planners were unabashed when they noted that construction was "'a handy device for razing slums'" (Sugrue 1996, 47). Finally, highway construction projects siphoned federal monies away from public transit projects that would serve primarily low-income and minority residents in city centers (Powell 2009, 27).

Post–World War II urban renewal projects noted in the previous section were often motivated by race such that the "commonplace wisdom of the streets [was] that 'slum removal equals Negro removal'" (Sugrue 1996, 50). Detroit's primary redevelopment projects of the 1950s "were premised on the destruction of some of the most densely populated black neighborhoods in the city" (Sugrue 1996, 49). Those most impacted by redevelopment projects were residents least equipped to relocate. Displaced residents often ended up in homes and neighborhoods more crowded and dilapidated than the ones they left. Attempts by city officials and planners to assist displaced residents were half-hearted at best, and in many cases they "utterly failed" (Sugrue 1996, 49; Hirsch 1983).

Planning efforts in mid-century Chicago and Philadelphia provide typical examples of how expansion of "elite institutions" e.g., universities, hospitals (Massey & Denton 1993, 56), and real estate development served to eradicate slums and whitewash inner city locations (Hirsch 1983, 116; Schwartz 1993, 109). In the name of "self preservation" and "rejuvenation," the Illinois Institute of Technology and Michael Reese Hospital bought up surrounding properties and expanded facilities in order to "rid themselves of surrounding decaying areas" on Chicago's South Side (Hirsch 1983, 116). Because of existing housing segregation, replacement housing for displaced, primarily black residents was "typically built on cleared land within or adjacent to existing black neighborhoods" (Massey & Denton 1993, 56). The Chicago Urban League pointed out that the redevelopment of the South Side was simply "forcing new slums to develop in place of those it clears" (Hirsch 1983, 122).

Behind the rule of racist laws, housing policies, and redevelopment projects there always lurked the threat of physical violence, which was used repeatedly throughout the twentieth century to ensure black residents "knew their place" and their "space." Sugrue's observation about violence against black residents in Detroit is illuminating: "The violence that whites unleashed against blacks was not simply a manifestation of lawlessness and disorder. It was not random, nor was it irrational. In the arena of housing, violence in Detroit was organized and widespread, the outgrowth of one of the largest grassroots movements in the city's history" (233). The coordinated efforts of hundreds of white residents backed by racist neighborhood organizations affected thousands of black Detroiters. The experiences of black Americans in the twenty-first century point to the ways particular spaces remain racially exclusionary and thus put African Americans at risk for their lives. In 2011, Trayvon Martin, an unarmed black teen was shot to death by a white Hispanic neighborhood resident who assumed Martin was a criminal. Martin was simply walking to his father's fiancée's home in the Florida gated community after a trip to a convenience store.

Not least important, deindustrialization from the 1950s to the present has impacted housing and work patterns in profound ways for Black residents. Southern blacks that moved north as part of the Great Migration faced race discrimination on top of a tightening labor market as industries were downsizing, relocating, and closing down altogether throughout the 1950s. Detroit alone lost 134,000 manufacturing jobs between 1947–1963 (Sugrue 1996, 126). The present day economic shift from heavy manufacturing to financialization has also impacted cities and neighborhoods in racialized ways. Financialization is defined as the "long-run shift in the center of gravity of the capitalist economy from production to finance" and includes the "growth of . . . finance, insurance, and real estate as a share of national income . . . the proliferation of exotic and opaque financial instruments . . . and the expanding role of financial bubbles" (Foster 2010). In this economic context, already-existing racial segregation, predatory lending, and subprime mortgages disproportionately entangled millions of black Americans during the 2007–2009 foreclosure crisis (Rugh & Massey 2010). Rugh and Massey (2010) expose the impact of historical racist exclusion on the lives of present day black residents observing the "old inequality in home lending made the new inequality possible by creating geographic concentrations of underserved, unsophisticated consumers that unscrupulous mortgage brokers could easily target and efficiently exploit" (632).

This brief history of urban development and race suggests the ongoing significance of capitalist accumulation underwriting cycles of city growth and decline. Sociologists and urban scholars have provided important contributions explaining the processes of segregation and urban crisis throughout the twentieth century. It is equally important to understand how *discourses about* cycles of growth and decline, race and "crisis" impact prevailing views and public policies of race, community, and citizenship as we move through the new millennium.

COMMUNICATING URBAN SPACES, RACE, AND RESISTANCE

Neoliberalism is a set of processes and a network of discourses that establish a commonsense reconciliation of contradictions surrounding the "free" market of capitalism that, in fact, is replete with all manner of "control," for example through public policy and policing that delimit "appropriate" uses of space and legitimate uses of public funds (e.g., corporations receive "subsidies"; poor people get "handouts"). Indeed, widespread contradictions surrounding poverty and wealth become a seamless part of generally accepted beliefs and values surrounding neighborhood growth and development and well-being in the city. An important question to ask, then, is: How are such processes explained, justified and packaged for widespread consumption? If we accept, as numerous critical geographers have pointed out, spaces are not neutral but ideologically imbued, we would do well to study how cities and neighborhoods become spaces of exclusion. Communication studies brings a systematic study of discourses, both hegemonic and resistant, to bear on critical geography.

Communicating About Space

The ideological dimensions of space have not gone unrecognized by geographers, sociologists, and urban scholars. The French sociologist, Henri Lefebvre (2009), largely credited with bringing space to the fore of studies concerning urban growth, capitalism, and democracy, noted "space is political," meaning it is not simply a neutral object "out there" ready to be empirically observed or described (174). Space "is a product literally filled with ideologies" (1976, 31). Lefebvre (1991) recognized space as a "social product," a "means of control and hence domination" (26). He articulated three dimensions of space: 1. spatial practice or the "perceived realm of physical experience" (Saco 2002, 5); 2. representations of space or the "conceived realm of mental experience constructed as (dominant) representations of space" (Saco 2002, 5); 3. representational spaces or the "lived . . . realm of social experience in (dominated) spaces of representations" (Saco 2002, 5; see Lefebvre 1991, 33). Warf and Arias (2009) similarly explain that space is "ideological, lived, and subjective" (3). Likewise, David Harvey (2009) distinguishes "effective space" from "created space," the latter of which is "part of an intricate sign-process that give direction and meaning to daily life" (310).

Others have examined how the social construction of space and place operates to further marginalize subaltern groups while reifying privilege for elite groups. Through "spatial constraints" and "spatial control" (Goldberg 1993, 52), African Americans, poor people, and the homeless are disciplined, monitored, and regulated in the inner city. Anti-homeless and anti-panhandling laws along with bans on camping in public spaces constrain the rights of individuals to *be* in a city space (Mitchell 2003). Increasingly since the early 2000s, the well-to-do shop and dine at "life style centers" while the "spaces of the poor . . . are structured by the security-paranoid gaze which fixes bodies in carceral compounds" (Keith & Pile 1993, 26). (See figures 1.3 and 1.4.) When we consider that in the United States, there is 31 square feet of real estate per person devoted to shopping (Susser & Schneider 2003, 5), yet not enough affordable housing for working-class Americans, it becomes clear how spaces articulate identities, culture, and values even as they regulate the material well-being of millions of people.

To the insights of scholars of space, a communication perspective offers a systematic way to analyze and interpret the ways *spaces act rhetorically*, that is to say, in ways that shape attitudes, beliefs, and behaviors. Likewise, a communication perspective provides a framework for studying how dominant and resistant *representations of city spaces* operate ideo-

Figure 1.3. Riverview Towers, public housing for seniors, owned by the Cleveland Metropolitan Housing Authority, located in Cleveland, Ohio. *Source:* Photo by Mary E. Triece

logically, either justifying or pushing back against spatial constraints. Soja (2010b) notes the "political organization of space, through its material manifestations as well as representational imagery, produces oppressive and unjust geographies" (37). At the same time, these "unjust geog-

Figure 1.4. Riverview Towers, public housing for seniors, owned by the Cleveland Metropolitan Housing Authority, located in Cleveland, Ohio. *Source:* Photo by Mary E. Triece

raphies" can be "enabling, creating the foundations for resistance and potential emancipation" (37). The central question to be explored is: How—that is, through what communication strategies—do political figures, city leaders, and ordinary residents promote, legitimate, or challenge unjust geographies? And what are the discursive possibilities for creating geographies of justice?

The centrality of public space to civic life can be traced to the ancient Greek rhetorician, Aristotle, who believed humans could not reach their full potential without being actively involved in the city-state (Bambrough 1963, 379). Book 7 of Aristotle's (350 B.C.E.) treatise, *Politics*, represents some of the earliest musings on the nature and organization of the city in relation to its inhabitants. Aristotle considered numerous aspects of city life including ideal population size, the character and health of its citizens, class demarcations, and defense. Importantly, Aristotle promoted the active public involvement on the part of citizens[9] in promoting the welfare of the city. He asserted, "a city can be virtuous only when the citizens who have a share in the government are virtuous, and in our state all the citizens share in the government" (Part XIII, para. 4).

So, more than a physical space that served the general welfare of its citizens, the city represented a polis, the public space where citizens could "share in the government," that is, discuss and debate issues of public concern. Space has also been theorized by communication scholars through classical concepts such as topoi and tropes. Topoi are the places or "'regions' where one can go to find the substance for persuasive argument" (Weaver 1989, 308). Tropes, literary devices such as metaphors and similes, also carry a spatial dimension. Sutton (2012) suggests, "tropes . . . produce space" (32); they "possess this seeming ability to orient our lives, experiences, and understanding of the world"; tropes "make space imaginable" (33). Additionally, Kenneth Burke's (1969a) conceptualization of the dramatic pentad for understanding discourse and motive similarly envelops an understanding of space in the element of scene, or the background/context of the act. Burke noted that discourses/speakers may emphasize context—the location and its elements—as controlling agents and acts (Birdsell 1987; Meisenbach, Remke, Buzzanell, & Liu 2008).

Critical/cultural communication scholars have entered the study of space through the "spatial turn." These writings often draw heavily on poststructuralist thought that shifts attention from the influence of capitalist structures and relations on both oppressive and liberatory uses of space (Conley 2010; Greene 2010; Grossberg 1993; Stormer 2010; Wiley 2005). For example, Grossberg (1993) suggests that "cultural studies must move from a temporal to a spatial logic of power and it must move from a structural to a machinic theory of power" (7). On this view, "models of oppression" should give way to studies of "articulation or transformative practice" (8). Similarly, Stormer (2010) expands textual approaches to space by offering "articulation" as a concept that "allows one to study different, conflicting spatial dynamics (including textuality) by which biopower territorializes 'life'" (10).

Other scholars draw on the celebratory stance found in postmodern scholarship in order to explore modes of resistance (Conley 2010; Stormer

2010; Wiley 2005). Wiley (2005) affirms a "Deleuzean ethics" or a "theoretical stance of affirmation rather than mere negation . . . and a practical stance of 'joyful' passion and active composition rather than 'sad' reaction" (66). Conley (2010) studies Margaret Fuller's writings of her westward travels and suggests textual "clinamen" or "swerve" to explore the "raw energy of social transformation and thus the very kernel of democratic renewal" (25).

These viewpoints variously suggest "aleatory materialism" (Conley 2010), articulation, and/or "machinic power" (Grossberg 1993), to suggest the radically contingent nature of history and social change. As Wiley (2005) explains, "change and resistance to change are understood not as history but as becoming—the ongoing production of the real without evolutionary, dialectical or teleological determination" (65).

When we direct our studies to the experiences of real people and actual city spaces, I suggest it makes more sense—from a theoretical, analytical, and engaged citizen perspective—to identify and name the "territorializing machine" as capitalism and to recognize that present day democracy struggles pushing back against capitalist practices—such as transnational exploitation of land, labor, and raw materials and the policies that support those practices ("free" trade agreements, immigration restrictions, reduction of the welfare state)—cannot be reduced to text and require more than "clinamen" to confront. Here is where Marxist thought may contribute to communication studies on space.

The Rhetorical and Material Dimensions of Space

An apt starting point for spatial studies, I argue, is *The Communist Manifesto*, wherein Marx and Engels (1848/1965) derided "that single, unconscionable freedom—free trade," which deployed "political illusions" to mask "naked, shameless, direct, brutal exploitation" (62). Marx and Engels also had the prescience to recognize the never-ending movement of capital through space(s): "The need of a constantly expanding market for its products chases the bourgeoisie over the whole surface of the globe. It must nestle everywhere, settle everywhere, establish connections everywhere" (63). Present day trade agreements such as the North American Free Trade Agreement (NAFTA) and Central America Free Trade Agreement (CAFTA) as well as gentrification from Detroit to Rio de Janeiro (Garcia-Navarro 2013) illustrate their observations and reveal the ways capital's movement through/across spaces facilitates exploitation and extraction in specific locales.

Conducting rhetorical analysis within a framework of historical materialism prompts us to recognize that space is marked above all by material systems and structures—for example, geographical layout, neighborhood infrastructure, industrial or service economies—that constrain and enable bodily movement and physical/mental well-being in ways that often fall along the lines of race, class, and sex. This observation regarding the link between bodies and space is made clear by the fact that one's zip code is a determinant of one's health and mortality (Arrieta et al. 2008; Benson 2009). Having homed in on the importance of space, I do not suggest a de-emphasis on class relations in lieu of spatial relations, but rather, that we understand how spaces act to reinforce inequalities and explore how capitalism utilizes spaces to perpetuate injustices, particularly in the context of the contemporary city.

Indeed, Lefebvre's three dimensions of space—material spatial practices, representations of space, and representational spaces—cannot be fully understood absent a recognition of the uses of and control over spaces, primarily in the search for profit. Marx (1857–1858/1973) pointed out, "while capital must on one side strive to tear down every spatial barrier to intercourse, i.e. to exchange, and conquer the whole earth for its market, it strives on the other side to annihilate this space with time" (539). Capitalist imperatives shape how we use and understand spaces. And in turn, the meanings attached to money, time, and space have significance with regard to the maintenance of economic, political, and social power (Harvey 1989, 227). Historical materialism understands the relationship between language (e.g., representations of space) and the material world (e.g., capitalist practices in/on land, natural resources, city spaces) as dialectical—each influences the other—but not indeterminate. "We make our history ourselves but, in the first place, under very definite assumptions and conditions," which include, importantly, economic constraints shaping one's access to basic resources necessary for living (Engels 1890/1978, 761).

Further, global capitalist structures and processes of overaccumulation, valorization, and gentrification discussed at length earlier require conscious collective efforts to resist/transform. A historical materialist study of space overlays "geographical sensitivities" with Marxist concepts of capitalist expansion and resistance thus recognizing the ways agency is enabled and constrained by and through physical spaces of land, home, and civic engagement (Harvey 1984).[10] In this sense, space and discourses about location interact dialectically, but space cannot be reduced to text as is suggested by Stormer (2010) who makes no distinction between the space/world and meanings about such phenomena (10–11).

A historical materialist perspective focuses attention on contradictions arising from capitalism's uneven development and the ways those contradictions may be exploited for rhetorical and material gains on the part of marginalized groups. Capitalist crises, instability, recession, and land devalorization may expose contradictions that can be leveraged to launch collective action for social change. Likewise, a "reality gap"—that metaphorical space between the material struggle of daily living and hegemonic (e.g., idealized or legitimated) representations of that experience—may wedge an opening through which critique and direct action can be launched (Triece 2007, 2, 5). As Soja (2010b) states, "unjust geographies . . . can also be enabling, creating the foundations for resistance and potential emancipation" (37).

From a rhetorical perspective, I focus on the ways public discourses mediate the formation of collective identities and the mobilization of on-the-ground struggles to restore democracy in urban areas. And from a historical materialist perspective, I direct attention to the materiality of space—or the role *global capitalism* (as opposed to abstract "machine") plays in the distribution and uses of spaces that sustain individuals and communities—and I explore how ideologies/discourses of space may prompt strategic spatial occupation or may push back against dominant control of such spaces.

The analyses in the following chapters rely on public communication outlets such as corporate and grassroots news outlets, city planning documents, flyers and publicly issued statements. Additionally, I study websites, blogs, and social media sites, that is, rhetoric conveyed through information and communications technologies (ICTs), which increasingly serve as a pragmatic and often indispensible counterpart to direct actions and more traditional communicative tactics mentioned above. Since the strategic use of the Internet by the Mexican Zapatistas in 1994, ICTs have become a mainstay in the efforts of counterpublics seeking justice in the city and around the world.

CYBER-SPACE AND EFFORTS FOR SPATIAL JUSTICE

For contemporary pro-democracy movements, the Internet has proven a requisite tool for facilitating both in-group and external communication. Social media such as Facebook, Twitter, and Tumblr provide a social space through which alternative perspectives and revolutionary voices largely ignored by corporate media find a platform and can mobilize collective engagement in physical spaces of economic/political significance (Ghonim 2012; Landzelius 2006). Community activist organizations seeking urban justice have utilized websites, Facebook pages, and blogs to raise awareness and mobilize grassroots actions for spatial justice.

Online outlets often work in tandem with face to face protest efforts to shape the uses and users of space in the city. Indeed, many scholars have noted the Internet's natural affinity for social change projects (Downing 2001; Joyce 2010; Klein 2000; McCaughey & Ayers 2003; van de Donk et al. 2004). New media technologies represent a virtual sphere that may "promote citizen activity" (Papacharissi 2002, 10), provide crucial information ignored by corporate media outlets, and prompt direct actions such as rallies and marches. Kahn and Kellner (2004) optimistically assert the "internet may be deployed in a democratic and emancipatory manner by a growing planetary citizenry that is using the new media to become informed, to inform others, and to construct new social and political relations" (88).

Internet activism benefits from what has been termed "Web 2.0" (Birdsall 2007; O'Reilly 2007; Petray 2011), which "refers to technology which is multi-directional, collaborative, interactive, participatory, live and instantaneous" (Petray 2011, 924). Birdsall (2007) characterizes Web 2.0 as "democratic" and "user-orientated." Web 2.0 poses a challenge to traditional media's top-down communication by enabling "horizontal communication between citizens" (Downey & Fenton 2003, 186) such as through blogs, tweets and comments (Petray 2011, 924).

Web logs, or blogs, play a particularly important role in Internet activism (Kahn & Kellner 2004; Bennett 2004; Duffy 2010), for in-group and external communication. Blogs are dynamic and ongoing, they facilitate debate, dialogue, and commentary of "alternative information" (Kahn and Kellner 2004, 91) and they have "enhanced motivation for political movements, especially among marginal societal segments" (Rahimi 2011, 163). Further, blogs provide a vehicle for the construction of localized knowledge that empowers citizens and guards against the reification of expertise that narrowly defines what counts as "knowledge" (Galusky 2003).

The Internet has figured prominently in democratic efforts on the part of indigenous populations (Birdsall 2007; Downey & Fenton 2003; Landzelius 2006; Petray 2011); Arab Spring uprisings (Alexander & Aouragh 2014; Allagui 2014; Allam 2014; Frangonikolopoulos & Chapsos 2012; Lim, 2012); citizen push back against state and corporate powers (Downey & Fenton 2003; Pal & Dutta 2012; Rahimi 2011); efforts against globalization (Dutta & Pal 2007; Juris 2008; Kahn & Kellner 2004; Routledge, 2000); and localized, grassroots community organizations.[11] Across the globe, indigenous peoples are utilizing the Internet to advance health campaigns (Gideon 2006) and negotiate identities (Gibb 2006; Rybas & Gajjala 2007). New media technologies are being "indigenized," or "creatively integrated and indexed into practices and beliefs rooted in a local cultural logic" (Landzelius 2006, 2). The term "virtual dissidence" describes the ways Arab Spring activists used online activism to criticize their governments and organize collective actions (Allam 2014, 854). The Zapatistas in Mexico used the Internet in 1994 to transmit their demands "without mainstream media filtering," to garner international support, and to open a space/public sphere for dialogue and community transformation as they contested the Mexican government and the passage of the North American Free Trade Agreement (NAFTA) (Downey & Fenton 2003, 219, 220). And community groups have utilized the Internet as a source for everything from advancing personal and public health concerns (Ding 2013; Ginossar & Nelson 2010; Himelboim & Han 2014; Loane & D'Alessandro 2013; Persky, Sanderson, & Koehly 2013); to negotiating the politics of sexual identity (Gross 2003; Szulc & Dhoest 2013); to creating yarn and graffiti communities (Humphreys 2008; Light, Griffiths, & Lincoln 2012).

Optimistic takes on the Internet and progressive struggles contrast with dystopian views, creating a dichotomy in the literature on online media and activism (Alexander & Aouragh 2014; Fuchs 2012; Youmans & York 2012).[12] In spite of the advantages online activism affords activist and revolutionary groups, Internet communication often results in increased fragmentation (Papacharissi 2002) and polarization (Downey & Fenton 2003). Additionally, activism via the Internet may foster "slacktivism," or a false sense of democratic participation. As Downing (2008) notes, "the depth of political engagement entailed" in online civic participation is "razor-thin" and the "patient, frustrating hard work of political communication pretty well absent" (45). Real social change, that is, that which results in improved wages, clean water/air, fair elections, control over one's land, and so forth, requires time, energy, cooperation, and on-the-ground struggles, all of which may be evaded through mouse clicking and web surfing. Corporate ownership of social media directs platform construction and issues of usability in ways that maximize profit (Youmans & York 2012, 316). Galusky (2003) warns against overreliance on "expert" knowledge conveyed via websites that undermines empowerment developed through firsthand experience and articulation of needs at the community level. Additionally, authoritarian and democratic governments alike exercise power and repression through the Internet, thus making new media a "contested space" (Rahimi 2011, 160).

And, of course, accessibility remains an issue. As of 2014, just over 42 percent of the total world population uses the Internet ("Internet World Stats"). The "digital divide" remains relatively wide, particularly in Africa, the Middle East, and Asia ("Internet World Statistics"; Birdsall 2007). The "uneven nature of Internet access" underscores the importance of studying Internet activism within the broader context of other forms of political activism (Alexander & Aouragh 2014, 891). The digital divide is also measured by the quality of electronics, broadband availability, and cost of connectivity (Brodock, 2010). Each of these affects the ability to communicate effectively online. Just a decade ago, some scholars remained skeptical regarding the Internet's potential for progressive politics and democratic participation. In his 1999 book, *Rich Media, Poor Democracy*, Robert McChesney noted that the Internet will continue to be dominated by commercial interests and that the "nonprofit and civic sector has been relegated to the distant margins of cyberspace" (183). Papacharissi (2002) points out the "fact that online technologies are only accessible to, and used by, a small fraction of the population contributes to an electronic public sphere that is exclusive, elitist, and far from ideal" (14). And yet, from the 1994 Zapatista rebellion in Chiapas, Mexico, to recent events in Egypt (Ghonim 2012), Tunisia, Iran, and Ukraine (Duffy 2010), events seem to point in a more optimistic direction.

The Internet's propensity to disperse and silo suggests we would do well to examine the ways it may facilitate collective action and commonality across issues and geographic spaces. The following case studies of resistance against gentrification and toxic dumping in Detroit and Harlem address the perceived "paucity of research on collective action" (Pal & Dutta 2012, 231) in communication studies by overlaying a rhetorical perspective on new media artifacts. While it is clear the Internet can play a central role in promoting activism and facilitating political involvement (Hooghe, Vissers, Stolle, & Maheo 2010; Kruikemeier, van Noort, Vliegenthart, & de Vreese 2014), I argue traditional and new media forms of protest work in parallel fashion; one does not replace the other. New media technologies represent "one component of activism . . . an enhancement to offline activism" (Petray 2011, 925) that may augment (Ford & Gil, 2001), facilitate (Lim 2012; Salter 2003; Van de Donk, Loader, Nixon & Rucht 2004), or act as an "accelerant" (Frangonikolopoulos & Chapsos 2012) to more traditional forms of protest conducted through face to face interactions and direct action.[13] As Lim (2012) points out, "the power of networked individuals and groups who toppled [the Hosni] Mubarak presidency [in Egypt] cannot be separated from the power of social media that facilitated the formation and the expansion of the networks themselves" (232).

I am particularly interested in the ways online communication operates spatially, in essence creating a "virtual public sphere" (Papacharissi 2002; see Downing & Fenton 2003; Ford & Gil 2001; Salter 2003) or "parallel polis" that acts as an alternative space for airing grievances and encouraging civic action on the part of real bodies in physical spaces (Lagos, Coopman, and Tomhave 2014). Ford and Gil (2001) note the "Internet is potentially our first global public sphere, a medium through which politics could be made truly participatory at both regional and international levels" (202). And yet, there exist fundamental differences between the Internet—fragmented and heterogeneous—and the public sphere as conceptualized by Jürgen Habermas, which is homogenous and aligned with a "common will" (Salter 2003, 122). Still, the Internet should be viewed as more than a communicative apparatus in the activist's "toolkit" (Youmans & York 2012); rather, it may foster a space of interaction (Rahimi 2011, 160) and prompt on the ground mobilization in physical spaces marked by disparities in housing and health.

NOTES

1. The app Sketch Factor was designed by two young white professionals in New York City to enable users to assess the "relative sketchiness" of an area. The app also uses "publicly available data to help complete its sketchiness ratings" (Strachan,

"White People Create App"). The release of the app did not go without critical public reaction.

2. As a resident of a racially and economically diverse neighborhood located 2 miles from downtown Cleveland, I have been asked if my home is in a "bad" area and if the neighborhood has "improved" since I moved there in 2002.

3. CNBC aired a show, "Secret Lives of the Super Rich," which featured people who drove $4 million Lamborghinis, threw megaparties, drank $2500 cocktails, lived in megamansions with megaclosets filled with high-end clothing and jewelry, like a $40 million diamond watch.

4. This observation was made by Orlando Santos, a professor of urban planning at Rio de Janeiro Federal University who has explored the experiences of favela residents evicted to make room for the 2016 Olympics in Rio de Janeiro.

5. See Neil Smith (1996) for the way post–World War II gentrification in Philadelphia supported the inner city economy (136).

6. See Keith and Pile (1993), Susser and Schneider (2003), Zukin (2008) for similar observations. Susser and Schneider's (2003) observation of the corporate processes of privatization and reliance on government monies in New York City can easily be applied to cities across the United States, including Detroit, Cleveland, and Boston.

7. Scholars (Bay 1998; Katz & Sugrue 1998) have noted DuBois's ambivalence regarding the reasons for black struggles in the city. In *The Philadelphia Negro* DuBois pointed at once to "individual moral and behavior deficiencies" and structural "forces of racial inequality, prejudice, and discrimination" (Katz & Sugrue 1998, 25) as reasons for African American poverty in Philadelphia's Seventh Ward.

8. The destruction of black communities to make way for highway construction occurred in cities across the United States. In Miami, the construction of I-95 resulted in the decimation of the black community of Overtown. Mohl (1993) notes "one interchange alone destroyed the housing of approximately ten thousand people" (102).

9. Aristotle's definition of citizen was limited to male Athenian-born individuals. Women, children, and slaves were largely considered the property of men.

10. Harvey, 1984, 10. Harvey delineates Marx's shortcomings when it came to theorizing space. Marx relied on notions of universal class struggle but failed to incorporate geographical variations that complicate class formation and resistance.

11. The literature on Internet usage among grassroots and democratic organizations is too extensive to fully cite here. A search in the database, Communication & Mass Media Complete gives 12,313 results for a search using the terms "Internet" and "community or grassroots."

12. Alexander and Aouragh (2014) note that arguments regarding online activism should refrain from establishing a false dichotomy that sets up cyberprotest as *either* advantageous *or* harmful to pro-democracy causes (892). Similarly Allam (2014) advocates differentiating the "role of online activism from that of social media" and examining cyber activism from the standpoint of "virtual dissidence" (855).

13. Rahimi (2011) notes banned political parties and Islamist dissidents used the Internet to organize face to face street protests during the 2011 Arab uprisings (163). He explains the "diversity and complexity of online tactics and strategies cannot be seen as detached from a broader spectrum of intertwining and competing cultural, economic, political, and social forces that are changing global life in unpredictable ways" (163).

Part I: Race and Displacement in Detroit

TWO
Narratives of Growth and Collective Resistance

In 1950, Detroit Mayor Cobo supported a development plan in the Gratiot-Orleans area, a predominately African American neighborhood called Black Bottom, which was located on Detroit's Lower East Side, an area sometimes euphemistically called Paradise Valley (Sugrue 1996, 48, 49). The Gratiot Redevelopment, as the plan was called, resulted in the eviction of at least 6,000 black residents from their homes (Norris 1991; Sugrue 1996; Thomas 1997).[1] The massive displacement resulted in urban "refugees" (Norris 1991, 475) who bore the burden of finding other lodgings at a time when affordable housing was scarce. Redevelopment in the name of "renewal" upended the routines and communities of black families and often forced the separation of children from their parents (Norris 1991, 475). Residents, civil rights advocates, and at least one city planner[2] decried the project as "heartless," "inequitable," and "just plain immoral" (Norris 1991, 475).

In 2013, the real estate company 1214 Griswold, LLC, purchased an historic apartment building at 1214 Griswold, in downtown Detroit. The building housed primarily low-income residents many of whom were senior citizens, disabled, and/or minority. The purchase resulted in the eviction of over 120 residents and facilitated the transformation of once-publically subsidized units into market rate apartments. *Curbed Detroit*, an online publication that covers real estate happenings in the area, viewed the purchase as "exciting news for Capitol Park," the building's neighborhood. In contrast, a 20-year resident of 1214 Griswold, James McNeal, said of the evictions, "This is nothing but discrimination. The [residents] have been in this city and have served this city for years. But now that they [developers] want to re-do the area, they are booting the residents out" (Bukowski 2013a).

This chapter and the following one examine discourses of urban renewal in Detroit between 2009 and 2014, a five-year period that ushered the city through a foreclosure crisis, municipal bankruptcy, and wide-reaching spatial transformations. Specifically I look at dominant narratives of development proffered by urban planners and city leaders to justify city growth and concomitant displacement, and compare them to discourses of city residents who struggled against gentrification and urban white-washing of a predominately black city. Together, chapters 2 and 3 argue that Detroit's history as a (former) manufacturing giant hollowed out by deindustrialization and now experiencing an entrenchment of financialization offers a primer for understanding processes of capitalist movement, dispossession and accumulation, and the ways race has always been implicated in place-making.

In this chapter, I focus on narratives of public memory and present-day agency as they are evoked in broader discourses of (re)development in Detroit. First, discussions of *Detroit's past* were tethered to contrasting *strategies of forgetting and remembrance*. City planners relied on a "selective amnesia" (Hoerl 2012, 180) that reinforced the invisibility of whiteness and eradicated race from the history of place making in Detroit. In contrast, city residents, often finding a speaking platform in the cyber public sphere, employed counter-memories that called up the role of racial exclusion in Detroit's history of development and urban growth. Second, the issue of *agency* was conveyed through *contrasting images of individual heroism vs. people power*. As corporate news coverage of Detroit's renewal crafted city developers as urban pioneers, longtime residents deployed a rhetoric of collectivity to arouse the power of "the people" who had firsthand experience with spatial injustice.

The chapter begins with a brief history of Detroit as a geography of injustice contoured by uneven development and racist spatial practices. This background establishes the "rhetorical situation" (Bitzer 1968) to which dominant and counterhegemonic discourses respond and offers competing understandings of city growth and change, particularly in the years preceding the Great Recession of 2007–2009.

URBAN "RENEWAL": A RHETORICAL SITUATION

The interlacing of race and place in Detroit cannot be fully understood without going back to the Great Migration of the early 1900s when tens of thousands of African Americans moved north looking for work. Between 1910–1950 Detroit's black population increased from just under 6,000 to 300,000 (Sugrue 1996, 23). When black workers moved north to cities like Detroit, they faced hostility and violence at the hands of white residents. Race, space, and violence were woven together in discourses negotiating the spatial configuration of neighborhoods. At a localized level, restrictive covenants foreclosed certain areas to potential black homeowners. White homeowners' associations used intimidation tactics and direct violence to deter black families from moving into areas rhetorically and physically marked "white."

The experience of the Howard educated black doctor Ossian Sweet and his family was illustrative. When they moved in to their home in 1925 on Garland Ave., located in a fiercely guarded white neighborhood, they were surrounded by a mob of over 800 white residents who threw stones, bricks, and coal at the home and shouted obscenities as police stood idly. Gunfire from both the Sweet home and the police dispersed the crowd and the Sweets were arrested and charged with "conspiracy to murder and conspiracy to assault with the intent to kill" (Freund 2007, 2). The family was eventually acquitted but comments made by then Detroit Mayor John Smith and white witnesses reveal in no uncertain terms the ideological dimensions of space. In this case residential spaces were racialized (Smith 1993, 133) through exclusionary discourses (Sibley 1995) that spelled out who was "in place" and who was "out of place," both literally and figuratively. Mayor Smith asserted "Any colored person who endangers life and property, simply to gratify his personal pride, is an enemy of his race as well as an incitant of riot and murder" (Freund 2007, 2). Reducing the Sweets' defense of their home space as mere gratification of "personal pride" implied the Sweets had stepped "out of their place," that is, their behavior was not an appropriate response. Stripping the Sweets of the right to physical safety and agency, Mayor Smith psychologized their reaction as a matter of ego out of line with the situation. Further, as persons who "endangered life and property," the Sweets were deemed out of place/line, physically, a threat to safety, the exclusive right of white residents.

Exclusionary discourses also played out through the trope of contamination as in the statement of a white witness who testified at the Sweets' trial, "I don't believe in mixing people that way, colored and white" (Freund 2007, 2, 3). This statement indicated the Sweets' presence in the neighborhood was a transgression that created a "bad mix," a tainting of white purity associated with specific locations. The Sweets' experience settling in Detroit was typical of those faced by countless black families through the first decades of the twentieth century. Two decades after Sweet and his family were run out of their own home, black Detroiters interested in moving to the Sojourner Truth housing project in northwest Detroit were attacked by white residents and verbally assaulted with a large billboard stating "WE WANT WHITE TENANTS IN OUR WHITE COMMUNITY" (Sugrue 1996, 74; Thompson 2001, 16). The examples illustrate the extent to which residential spaces control individual bodies and family well-being and stand at the heart of white racial identities.

Racist practices exercised at the neighborhood level were buttressed by state sanctioned policies shaping urban housing, dispossession, displacement, and health. Federal housing policies authorized discriminatory practices including redlining; and, urban "renewal" projects such as the Detroit Plan mentioned above upended home and community spaces for black residents in Detroit. The result for black families was overcrowded, run-down housing that contrasted sharply with tree-shaded streets lined with the mansions of auto company executives. As southern blacks moved north in the first two decades of the 1900s, decent housing was a constant struggle. Black residents were relegated to outer area ghettos where entire families lived in one-room shacks. Most families had to take in lodgers to make ends meet, particularly in the face of exorbitant rents charged by unscrupulous landlords (Thomas 1992, 92, 94). In the black neighborhood Paradise Valley death rates from pneumonia were three times higher and the "percentage of blacks with tuberculosis was 71.5 percent higher" (Thompson 2001, 16). Black infants were much more likely than white babies to die within the first year of life (Thomas 1992, 104). Regardless of class or professional status, black residents were sequestered in the most deteriorated, densely packed neighborhoods.

As local and federal housing policies erected barriers to home ownership for black residents, for example through the Detroit Housing Commission's policy of residential segregation (Thompson 2001, 17), federal policies were created to facilitate the process for whites. The Home Owners' Loan Corporation and the Federal Housing Administration, both created in the mid-1930s, ensured low-interest, longterm, federally backed loans for homes. The HOLC and FHA's "insistence that mortgages and loans be restricted to racially homogeneous neighborhoods . . . resonated strongly with Detroit's white homeowners" (Sugrue 1996, 62). Home ownership became associated with opportunity, freedom, and citizenship—concepts tethered to white privilege and systematically denied to black Americans through Jim Crowism.

Just as the experience of Ossian Sweet stood as metonymic for the barriers faced by black families, the struggle of the Eight Mile-Wyoming neighborhood was indicative of the obstacles faced and efforts advanced by entire black neighborhoods as they fought for spatial justice. The Eight Mile neighborhood was a black enclave—three by fourteen blocks—situated amidst a sea of white, well-to-do areas to the south and east. Commercial and residential developers eyed the area as potentially profitable but blighted by the presence of black residents. At play was the racialized spaciality of urban regeneration and development wherein tracts of land became sites of struggle over identity, white privilege, and the right of black citizens to exist in the center, to resist marginalization—physical, social, and political. Racism was instituted at the federal level as the FHA refused loans to one developer of a proposed all-white subdivision due to the proximity to black residents in the Eight-Mile area. Not to be deterred, the developer erected a half-mile-long, foot-thick, six-foot-high wall to separate white from black residents in exchange for loan guarantees (Sugrue 1996, 64). The physical construction doubled as a social barrier, walling in white privilege and designating the "outside" as inferior and contaminated—in need of containment and control to prevent spreading. The wall communicated who was "in" and who was "out." In this case, space acts as "both a medium and message of domination and subordination.... It tells you where you are and it puts you there" (Keith & Pile 1993b, 37).

But Eight-Mile's black residents fought back. They wrote letters to President Roosevelt and formed the Eight Mile Road Civic Association to advocate for their right to FHA loans for home repairs and construction on land they owned. Burneice Avery, a school teacher and founder of the Eight Mile Road Civic Association, pointed out the indignities faced by black residents: "Even though we own the land, we are being told to 'Get Off' because we are not able to develop [sic] it in the way some people think it should be developed" (Sugrue 1996, 66). Avery's statement underscored the power inherent in designating (in)appropriate uses of spaces—power institutionalized in federal agencies such as the FHA.

The struggle over land in the Eight-Mile neighborhood was complicated by arguments from others, some in the black community, who wanted to see construction of public housing. In the end, Detroit's city planners worked out a compromise whereby black residents would receive FHA-backed loans for home construction and the city would construct 600 units of temporary housing, which became the Robert Brooks Homes (Sugrue 1996, 71). The success of Eight-Mile black residents underscores the potential for "marginalized groups [to] inscribe themselves into new geographies" (Keith & Pile 1993b, 36). By challenging FHA's racist policies, black residents created a space that "became a bastion of black homeownership" (Sugrue 1996, 71). By 1950, black residents, growing in numbers, bypassed the white developer's concrete wall and established roots in the formerly all-white neighborhood.

In sum, the designation of land as "blighted" and "slum," or "ripe for renewal" and "profitable" calls out the ideological dimensions and racialization of city spaces. The power in such labels points attention to the dialectical relationship between geographies as land value and discourses of geography. On one hand, economic practices—for example, the search for profitable land uses—shaped urban geographies; while on the other, racist discourses rhetorically mapped who could call what spaces home. In many ways, the struggle over the Eight-Mile neighborhood foreshadowed the efforts of Detroit residents during the city's post–Great Recession (2008–2013) renewal. In the 1940s–1960s, references to "slum removal" and "urban renewal," translated into "Negro removal" for many black residents (Sugrue 1996, 50). In 2013, long-time residents living at 1214 Griswold in downtown Detroit were forced to move out of their homes under the banner of "opportunity" and "revitalization," good terms cloaked in a cultural tradition of expansion/exploration/growth but having a similar material effect as the exclusionary rhetorics of the mid 1900s: the removal of black/minority residents to make room for profitable enterprises. The intertwining of race, place, and profit was not lost on a seventy-four-year-old resident of 1214 Griswold who had lived in the building for 19 years. James Johnson noted of the developers: "They're only doing this because we're poor. They think they can get away with anything" (McGraw 2013).

The racist politics of housing in Detroit between 1940–1970 cannot be understood outside the economic context in which the auto industry was firmly situated. Black Detroiters also experienced segregation and alienation in the automobile plants that were matched by militant worker agitation. Conditions in Detroit's auto plants were notoriously dangerous. Forced overtime, speed ups, stretch outs, and reduced times for washing up and rest periods were common in the post–World War II plants (Georgakas & Surkin 1975; Thompson 2001). Equipment was often faulty creating an environment ripe with workplace injuries and deaths. A 1973 report based on statistics compiled by the National Institute of Occupational Safety and Health revealed "65 on-the-job deaths per day among auto workers, for a total of some 16,000 annually . . . 63,000 cases of disabling diseases and about 1,700,000 cases of lost or impaired hearing" (Georgakas & Surkin 1975, 105).[3] Referring to their workplace as a "plant-ation," black auto workers faced workplace hostility, violence, and institutionalized racism. Almost all foremen and superintendents were white and white workers were given the more desirable and safer jobs. The auto workers' union, the United Auto Workers (UAW) reflected the same race bias in leadership and lack of support for black workers. Conservative rank-and-file white workers often went on strike to protest the hiring or promotion of black workers.

But there remain plenty of instances of race solidarity and resistance on the part of black workers who led their own organizations, the most well-known of which was the Dodge Revolutionary Union Movement (DRUM). DRUM formed in the midst of a 1968 wildcat strike involving 4,000 workers at the Dodge Main plant. The organization sought direct representation for black workers, elimination of racist practices, and greater worker control. DRUM inspired the formation of RUMs at other plants like Eldon Avenue (ELRUM), Jefferson Avenue (JARUM), Mack Avenue (MARUM), and at Cadillac (CADRUM) (Georgakas & Surkin 1975; Thompson 2001). In the late 1960s–early 1970s, RUMs led wildcat strikes, pickets, rallies, and boycotts with a militancy and urgency not seen in the UAW's more conciliatory approach. In 1969, RUMs organized under an umbrella organization, the League of Revolutionary Black Workers, and often connected workplace agitation to activism in the larger black community.

The anger and frustration of Detroit's black workers were the result of decades of degrading and dangerous conditions in the auto plants that were rooted in broader capitalist processes aimed at maximizing profits. Plants relied on automation, deindustrialization, and relocation to the south where labor could be more easily exploited (Sugrue 1996, 128–138).[4] Industry's efforts to reduce production costs and hire a more malleable workforce were subsidized by housing and highway expansion that furthered suburban growth and expansion. The upshot for the city of Detroit was a shrinking tax base, boarded up stores, and vacated/run-down neighborhoods. The geographical transformation impacted residents in specifically raced ways. White residents benefited from racist housing practices that supported their efforts at home ownership, while black workers' geographic and economic mobility was thwarted by housing and employment discrimination bolstered by racist ideologies. When capital left the city, black residents suffered disproportionately, as they were "in greater peril of unemployment [and] most subject to the vagaries of a troubled economy" (Sugrue 1996, 149).

In 1973, Detroit elected its first black mayor, Coleman Young, who served until 1994. As a black liberal dedicated to eradicating racism in his city, Young faced hostility throughout his tenure from conservative white residents, white officers in the Detroit police force, and the popular press who accused him of racial divisiveness and "reverse racism." Responding to the charges in 1990, Young stated, "I view racism not as a two-way street. I think racism is a system of oppression. I don't [think] Black folks are oppressive to anybody, so I don't consider that Blacks are capable of racism" (Thompson 2001, 206). Young oversaw the city government during some of the toughest economic times, including 1975 when the city lost tens of thousands of jobs and the unemployment rate for black city dwellers was 25 percent. In an attempt to save the city from white and capital flight, in the early 1980s Young took the economically conservative step of offering $200 million in tax abatements to woo General Motors and Chrysler back to the city. Looking back on the last decade of the twentieth century, now-former Mayor Coleman Young noted the "city of Detroit became abandoned to those who could not leave; it became a repository of the poor, the aged and the Blacks" (Travis 2013). Despite the gains in civil rights since the 1950s, the economy has had a similar impact on black Americans in the first decade of the twenty-first century as the Great Recession left this group in foreclosure at a far higher rate than white Americans (Rugh & Massey 2010).

As some city leaders have noted, opportunities for city renewal come in unassuming forms, including natural and manufactured disasters, such as hurricanes and bankruptcies, both of which have played out in distinctly raced ways. Speaking to a *Wall Street Journal* reporter of the aftermath of Hurricane Katrina, Republican representative Richard H. Baker of Baton Rouge quipped, "We finally cleaned up public housing in New Orleans. We couldn't do it, but God did" (Babington 2005). Five years later, facing a "clean up" of its own in 2010, Detroit hired the urban planner Toni Griffin to help rebuild the city in the wake of decades of deindustrialization. Griffin noted of the city's dire straits, "it offers such an amazing opportunity . . . to reinvent itself, reform itself, build on its strengths and position itself in a way that it hadn't been able to do before" (Bukowski 2010).

One of the "strengths" the city offered—at least from a developer's perspective—was the vast numbers of vacant acres and square feet in the city, awaiting grab and capital investment in the aftermath of a financial crisis that left the city in debt and families without homes. The story of how Detroit became a city with around 25 square miles of vacant land (Davidson, 2012) began with deindustrialization in the 1950s and was rounded out by dubious borrowing practices employed by the city in an effort to address debts resulting, in part, from a tax base reduced by manufacturing pullouts over the previous six decades. Methods of borrowing, including controversial interest rate swaps and derivatives, may have been the last nail in Detroit's financial coffin but they lined the pockets of bank executives at UBS AG, Merrill Lynch, and JP Morgan Chase who received $474 million in bank fees, an amount that "almost equals the city's 2013 budget for police and fire protection" (Bukowski 2013b). Individual investors also got in on the booty as many took advantage of Wayne County auctions where 20,000 foreclosed homes were up for grabs in 2012 (Sands 2013). Between 2009–2013, over 100,000 homes were foreclosed on in metro Detroit ("A Hurricane," 4).

The budget "crisis"[5] was used as a pretext by Michigan Governor Rick Snyder to appoint Kevyn Orr as emergency manager of Detroit in March 2013, thus handing control of much of the city's operations over to a nonelected public official. From May through July, Orr—a former partner with Jones Day, a law firm that represents corporations and financial institutions—worked with banks to restructure the city's debt obligations. In December 2013, Detroit was deemed eligible for chapter 9 protection, thus providing a way to legitimate what Dēmos pronounced as a manufactured "crisis" and gave the city a green light to strip pension funds and privatize city services in order to ensure banks and bondholders were paid first ("Detroit Bankruptcy Exit Plan" 2014; Eisenbrey 2013; "Judge Backs Snyder" 2013).[6] In his ruling, U.S. Bankruptcy Judge Steven Rhodes noted that retiree's pensions would not receive protection during the restructuring process ("Judge Backs Snyder" 2013). The Emergency Manager, Orr, expressed a desire to work "with all our creditors—pension funds, unions and lenders—to achieve a consensual agreement on a restructuring plan that balances their financial recoveries with the very real needs of the 700,000 citizens of Detroit" ("Judge backs Snyder" 2013). Part of the restructuring plan included offering 15 cents on the dollar to retirees for their pensions and privatizing Detroit's Water and Sewage Department and the city's lighting system, breathing new life into privatization proposals initially introduced by Mayor Bing in 2011 (Gaist 2013; Neavling & Helms 2011; Snavely 2014).[7]

The trajectory of (re) development in Detroit from the 1950s to the present illustrates the capitalist process of valorization/devalorization and crisis formation. Capital is invested in fixed assets—e.g., auto plants, warehouses—for the purposes of extracting surplus value; this is the process of valorization (Smith 1982, 147). Devalorization necessarily follows as over time, capital must look elsewhere to continue the process of accumulation; thus, plants move south or overseas where raw materials/labor are more easily exploited. New investment is required to enable continued accumulation but this process is often impeded by the "relative fixity of built forms" (Soja 2010b, 89).

We can turn to the Detroit of 2008–2013 to view the process of devalorization, concomitant manufactured crisis, and re-creation of valorization in the form of "renewal." Two developers, in particular, utilized the crisis to their benefit by scooping up cheap real estate devalued by decades of deindustrialization. Dan Gilbert, the founder and chair of Rock Ventures and Quicken Loans and majority owner of the Cleveland Cavaliers, owned or controlled 30 downtown buildings or nearly 8 million square feet of space as of mid-2013 (Corrigan 2013a). Gilbert's business efforts have transformed sections of downtown into a "high-tech corridor" with market rate apartments in "historical and architecturally charming buildings with a blend of renovated conveniences" ("Live It Up in the D").[8] "Opportunity Detroit"—the name attached to development and promotional efforts associated with Gilbert's Quicken Loans and Bedrock Real Estate-- has been stamped on numerous storefronts lining Woodward Avenue in downtown Detroit. (See figures 2.1 and 2.2)

Not to be outdone, Mike Ilitch, owner of the Detroit Red Wings, Detroit Tigers, and the Little Caesar's Pizza franchise, set his sights on the Midtown corridor for reinvestment. With assistance from Detroit's Downtown Development Authority, Ilitch's company Olympia Entertainment secured control of a 45-block entertainment district surrounding a new arena for the Detroit Red Wings in June 2013 to be funded with $285 million in tax dollars (Corrigan 2013b). Without an ounce of irony, the *Detroit Free Press* announced "One downtown, two empires: Mike Ilitch and Dan Gilbert reshape Detroit" (Gallagher 2014a), thus summing up the process by which restructuring within the context of the financial "crisis" enables the accumulation of wealth and control of city spaces on the part of a wealthy few. In stark contrast were the sentiments of William Williams, a city bus driver who reflected on the impact of city restructuring and crisis on ordinary folks: "I've been in this city all my life . . . it almost brings me to tears to see the city try to fix its condition on the workers' backs" (Bukowski 2011).

Figure 2.1.   Storefront on Woodward Ave., Detroit, MI. *Source:* Photo by Mary E. Triece

Rhetorics of Public Memory in Service of Creating Neoliberal Spaces

Discussions of a city's past evoke public memories, a collective understanding of how a city positions itself toward significant events, central figures, and meaningful dates. Public memory of a past is much more than historical understanding; it figures prominently in how a culture — in this case, the culture of a city — understands it's collective present and future (Blair, Dickinson, & Ott 2010; Bodnar 1992; Lipsitz 1990; Sturken 1997). In short, public memories are socially constructed, they figure into arguments "about the interpretation of reality" (Bodnar 1992, 14); they shape a public identity; and convey what behaviors and values are deemed desirable. Sturken (1997) explains "memory is crucial to understanding a culture because it indicates collective desires, needs and self definitions" (2).

Public memory is not neutral but constitutes a site of struggle, a "field of cultural negotiation" (Sturken 1997, 1; Blair, Dickinson & Ott 2010) for understanding cultural identity. Public memory is never a whole or complete picture of the past; rather, it represents a "persistent partiality" (Dickinson & Ott 2014, 19), interested and biased and thus fraught with power. The crafting of public memory — through art, memorial, literature, etc. — privileges this event over that one, one historical figure to another, and a given narrative over competing ones. Indeed, the function of public

Figure 2.2. Storefront on Woodward Ave., Detroit, MI. *Source:* Photo by Mary E. Triece

memory is to "mediate the competing restatements of reality . . . and privilege some explanations over others" (Bodnar 1992, 14).

Public memory is situated within, shaped by, and constitutive of public spaces, including cities. "Geographic spaces become *places* once meanings are ascribed upon them" (Davis 2013, 110), meanings derived, in part, from public memories of events, persons, and struggles rooted in location. And, race—whether explicitly or implicitly—cannot be divorced from considerations of space: "Racism is by nature a spatial and territorial form of power. It aims to secure and claim native/white territory but it also projects associations on to space that in turn invests racial associations and attributes in places" (Back 2005, 19).

Public memory of a city is so rich for study precisely due to its rhetorical nature, that is, to the extent that publically articulated versions of a city's past carry weight with regards to that city's future. In this way, public memory serves an inventive function (Cox 1990), as a rhetorical possibility for shaping present day debates over how to remember a war or remake a city. The past is "argument fodder" (Willard 1989, 56) as it may act "in service of the present" (Dickinson & Ott 2014, 18). Dickinson and Ott (2014) explain, we "remember the past under the pressures and opportunities of the present, [and] we often do so in ways that shape our future" (19).

Public forgetting is twinned to memory (Sturken 1997, 2). The selective nature of public memory necessitates a degree of forgetting. Of interest is what gets forgotten and why. Sturken (1997) explains there is an "organized" and "strategic" aspect to forgetting (7). Remembering involves selecting and thus deflecting various elements of the past. In this way, forgetting serves an ideological purpose that perpetuates white privilege through "selective amnesia" (Hoerl 2012, 180) that enables city planners to construct a seamless historical narrative of city growth-decay-rebirth, thus perpetuating the invisibility of whiteness woven throughout the history of city planning and threaded throughout present day city planning marked by a rhetoric of market rationality that denies the salience of race.

Collectively constituted memory is equally important for counterpublics, understood as "alternative publics" comprised of "members of subordinated social groups" and emerging "in response to exclusions within dominant publics" (Fraser 1990, 67). "Counter-memories" crafted by counterpublics stand in opposition to prevailing, generally accepted, or official memories legitimated through appeals to cultural or political authority. Counter-memories unveil the "hidden histories excluded from dominant narratives" (Lipsitz 1990, 213) and may reveal the interested/partial nature of officially accepted public memories and thus destabilize accepted cultural identities and values. Importantly, counter-memories may play a role in the formation of arguments for future action, as was the case in efforts of counterpublics to influence the remaking of Detroit.

Strategic Forgetting

Of all American cities, Detroit is one with a storied past, conveyed through a narrative whose central character is a defining American icon, the automobile. A brief outline of the auto industry from the 1950s–1980s, including deindustrialization, capital and white flight, and city decay, was relayed in chapter 1. Of interest here is how the story of Detroit's past was used rhetorically by city officials and corporate news accounts as a way to shape understandings of Detroit's present, and perhaps more importantly, how the city should look in the future. Specifically through personalization, nostalgia, and selective forgetting, Detroit's history was severed from the processes of capitalist mobility that shaped the city's geography.

Stories of Detroit's troubled past often centered on the bad doings of one person, a sort of anti-hero representing the values Detroit eschews. Dominant narratives pinned Detroit's "ruin" on the policies of past black leaders, specifically Coleman Young and Kwame Kilpatrick, who served as foils to take attention away from an ongoing history of structural racism in housing and employment. Public memory crafted this way personalized the past, psychologized issues that were structural in nature, and suggested future courses of action be grounded in the good character of city leaders. Manhattan Institute senior fellow Steve Malanga pointed a finger at the first black mayor Coleman Young who led the city from 1974–1994 as the cause of Detroit's "ruin" (Malanga, 2013). Malanga described Young as a "radical trade unionist" whose "legacy haunted Detroit long after he retired." Malanga reasoned Detroit's decline was not due to "global economic forces that displaced auto manufacturing jobs" but rather to "a virtual collapse of its municipal government during Young's 1974–1994 reign as mayor." Malanga's remarks offered a shallow and shortsighted understanding of Detroit's decline and scapegoated a black leader viewed as unruly and out of line with white normative understandings of city growth and progress. A *Detroit News* article appearing in August 2013 further supported the selective understanding of Detroit's past by casting blame on Kwame Kilpatrick, the former Detroit mayor from 2002–2008, who resigned after being convicted of various felony counts including perjury, mail and wire fraud, and racketeering ("Leadership is Key" 2013). The article asserted Kilpatrick's "cronyism and careless use of city funds" left the city in disarray thus leaving the reader to understand the history of urban growth and decline in personalized terms.

At times, the city itself was the "bad apple" in need of a character fix. The *Detroit News* warned against Detroit falling "back on old habits," like borrowing to excess ("Leadership is Key" 2013). Similarly, in a *Wall Street Journal* interview, the Emergency Manager, Kevyn Orr, described Detroit's history as "dysfunctional" stating that for a long time, the city was "dumb, lazy, happy and rich" (Finley 2013). These accounts animate the faults of a single *person* or, as the case may be, a city (personified as "dysfunctional") thus taking focus off of capitalist *processes* that shaped the contours of the city in markedly racist ways.

Recounting the story of city decay through character suggests a path for future policies similarly invested in character. In this way, the story of Detroit's past instructs present dealings with the city or acts as "rhetorical resource of the present" (Blair, Dickinson & Ott 2010, 12). According to the 2013 *Detroit News* editorial, "character is key" to rebuilding the city. But apparently, the character of "courageous leaders" is superior to that of ordinary people who are reduced to "shouting protesters" referenced in the article ("Leadership is Key" 2013). Constructing a public narrative of Detroit's past through focus on individuals effaces the roles that industry, driven by profit and accumulation, played in structuring Detroit's urban landscape and the ways housing segregation and Jim Crow necessitated the creation of black neighborhoods such as Paradise Valley that were "densely packed" with tenements and marked by extreme poverty and inadequate health care (Sugrue 1996, 37)—a far cry from the shining storefronts of places like Woodward Avenue.

Public memory of Detroit conveyed through mainstream news accounts served a conservative purpose, propagating a white nostalgia that idealized the past traditions and values linked to white privilege. The good-old-days frame—a "collective pining for America's blue collar manufacturing past"[9]—celebrated consumption and mobility without mention of the white privilege attending economies of place and movement. Articles recreated the bustling retail activity on Livernois Avenue, known as the "Avenue of Fashion" (Austen 2014, 28) and Woodward Avenue, the "show-off spot for the wealthy" in the mid-twentieth century ("Woodward Avenue" 2007). The center of another *Detroit News* article, Lakewood Street came to stand in for the happy days when "mothers stayed home, while fathers went off to jobs at Cummins Diesel, U.S. Rubber, American Motors and nearby Chrysler and Hudson plants" (Kurth, Wilkinson, & Aguilar 2013). Although this article mentioned the politics of racial exclusion (e.g., racist housing policies) that shaped the history of Detroit's landscape, the article's focus remained on the changes on Lakewood Street, in essence using the location as synecdoche for the city of Detroit.

In these articles, the street becomes a form of communication that "helps construct narratives of identity and belonging" (Davis 2013, 110) through exclusion of elements of the past. Memories of significant streets evoked a sense of group belonging and self-image linked to a time when neighborhoods were clearly demarcated by race and wealth. Race relations figured in as a thorn in an otherwise rosy picture of a city's history. For instance, one *Detroit News* article noted the move to the "sleepy suburbs" on the part of wealthy industrialists on Woodward Avenue "sped up after the July 1967 riots" ("Woodward Avenue" 2007)—a reference to the race rebellion that left 30 black residents dead at the hands of white law enforcement officials (Sugrue 1996, 259–260).

Similarly, the article that used the transformation of Lakewood Street to stand in for the story of the entire city relied on the racially charged issues of school desegregation and drug dealing to, in essence, pin the city's checkered past on the presence of black residents. The October 2013 *Detroit News* special report that recounted 60 years of Detroit's growth and decline recalled the issue of school desegregation through the eyes of a white family, the Angeleris, who decided to send their children to Catholic schools rather than see them attend a desegregated school across town. Carol Angeleri noted the family's resentment, "We were already paying taxes [for public schools] and we had to do this to keep my kids safe." Her reference to safety equated the presence of black children with danger and stood as justification for keeping her children in all-white spaces. Likewise, the crack wars of the 1980s were woven into this article's narrative of Detroit's past, similarly calling up white racist fears of black residents. According to the article, the Chambers brothers, who "migrated from the South," epitomized the worst of Detroit crime and the downfall of Lakewood, which had become a "war zone." Of interest here is how we are encouraged to remember the crack epidemic—as a problem that black residents inflicted on innocent white residents. Notably, the issue of drug usage was divorced from larger economic and political processes of the period such as Reagan era cuts in federal assistance programs and high unemployment and a lack opportunities among poor black males (Adler 1995).

Public memory is also created through strategic or organized forgetting (Sturken 1997, 7), which becomes an important tool for maintaining white privilege. Public forgetting as counterpart to memory has been described as "selective amnesia," or the "rhetorical processes by which public discourse routinely omits events that defy seamless narratives of national progress and unity" (Hoerl 2012, 180). In recounting Detroit's past, public memory singled out particular elements for amplification thus deflecting other processes that, if recalled, would require acknowledging the complex ways that industry and racism mark city landscapes. In this way, forgetting becomes an exercise of power and a way to assign blame for the present by rooting problems in a selective past. For instance, an October 2013 *Detroit News* article asserted the "many forces that propelled Detroit to such heights—autos, the might of unions, migration from the south and inexpensive housing—also contributed to its fall" (Kurth, Wilkinson, & Aguilar 2013). Another article reinforced this understanding pointing to "blight, crime and other problems" as factors contributing to the city's "decades long population decline" ("Detroit Bankruptcy Exit Plan" 2014).

The rhetorical construction of public memory of Detroit as conveyed in mainstream news accounts and by city planners aligns with Entman and Rojecki's (2000) description of "benign neglect" in news coverage of race and poverty. Entman and Rojecki assert that the corporate media rely on "*absences* of information, implicit comparisons, and visual images" (95) that elide the role of broad based structures that perpetuate racism and poverty in black communities (105). Public memory of Detroit reinforced the purity of white character and tapped in to long-standing stereotypes associating black people with poverty and crime. As Entman and Rojecki observe, there exists a "widespread sense of the prototypical Black as a poor person (and quite likely, a criminal one)" (105). The invisibility of whiteness is at work here, too, as the black resident serves as foil to highlight the good works (past and present) of the white hero (discussed later in the chapter).

In accounts of Detroit's past, public memories also engaged in forgetting by punctuating the story of Detroit's past in strategic ways. I use the term rhetorical punctuation to refer to the process by which a public memory is given a beginning and ending so as to suggest a particular interpretation of the memory (Dutta 2011, 231). Punctuation is a framing device that makes use of strategic forgetting in order to assign blame or relieve from scrutiny. For instance, news accounts of the Israeli-Palestinian conflict often punctuate or begin the crisis with events that garner greater sympathy for Israel. Framing Israeli actions (e.g., air strikes) as "retaliations" against Palestinians suggests Israel is acting defensively and that blame should be placed at the feet of Palestinians provoking "retaliation" ("CBS's Mideast" 2006; "In U.S. Media" 2002).

Punctuation functioned rhetorically during a roundtable discussion sponsored by the Manhattan Institute in March 2014. The moderator asked Michigan Governor Rick Snyder: "How did Detroit get where it is?" Snyder answered "I don't spend time on that. It's not relevant. We spend too much time on blame . . . don't figure out who did what to whom, let's figure out the solution" ("Detroit: The Next" 2014). In an effort to appear solution-oriented, Snyder denied the relevance of Detroit's past in present day discussions. Punctuation goes further than white nostalgia to completely erase the significance of past events. Figuring the past as "not relevant," denies the fluidity between past and present, obscures the extent to which past wrongs done to city residents, for example, black Detroiters, remain salient, and relieves city officials from examining the ways present day planning may rely on similar processes of exclusion.

Similarly, the nearly 200-page city planning document, *Detroit Future City* (DFC), punctuated the story of Detroit's decline by highlighting the events of 2007 when the "financial recession and foreclosure crisis . . . undermined the city's progress in diversifying its economy and bringing back residents" (*Detroit Future* 2012, 15). The long-standing role played by racist exclusion and capitalist accumulation is thus severed from memory. A different recollection of Detroit's past may begin the story as early as the 1950s when the city's "landscape was dominated by rotting hulks of factory buildings, closed and abandoned, surrounded by blocks of boarded up stores and restaurants" (Sugrue 1996, 147). Capital's chase for profit hit black residents the hardest. Middle-class whites left the city along with the jobs. Hemmed in by racist housing practices, black residents often had no choice but to remain in the city limits.

Yet to begin the story over six decades ago would require acknowledging a racist past that has borne out in the city's landscape and that needs to be addressed in present day planning. Instead, the document appeals to residents to remain focused on the present and future of Detroit thus ensuring that issues of race and capitalist processes are excluded from public memory. The document urges "everyone who cares about Detroit" to "*set aside what they think they know about the city*, and cultivate a deep, mutual understanding of what the city really is right now" (10, emphasis added). In this way, the document truncated memory to "serve contemporary and future political and economic needs" (Davis 2013, 122, 123).

Importantly, public memory that relies on personalization, nostalgia, and strategic forgetting reinscribes the invisibility of white privilege that played a central role in the shaping of Detroit as a city space throughout the twentieth century. Recalling the history of Detroit through this lens preserves the cultural myth of progress and equal opportunity while minimizing or negating the role of racism in shaping the city's landscape, past and present (see Bacon 2003, 178). The process of placemaking, establishing cultural identity and tradition through evocations of place, is racialized precisely through erasure/partiality of public memories of race. In contrast, counterpublics offered counter-memories that challenged the construction of white privilege through public memory.

Conscious Remembering

Competing constructions of memory "highlight how groups with disparate subject positions hold different ideological investments in public memory" (Hoerl 2012, 180). Memory as a site of struggle deserves attention because, as we have seen in the previous section, public memory may serve as a rhetorical resource for legitimating a course for future action. Further, race may be considered a significant factor that shapes the "social dimensions of memory" and the ways black people have developed a "shared identity by…exploring, and agreeing on memories" (Thelen 1989, 1122; see also Lewis 1996). The writer, poet, and playwright Claudia Rankine (2014) eloquently noted, "the body has memory. The physical carriage hauls more than its weight. The body is the threshold across which each objectionable call passes into consciousness—all the unintimidated, unblinking, and unflappable resilience does not erase the moments lived through" (28).

In Detroit, residents organized both loosely and formally to resist what they viewed as the city's exclusionary development practices. They regularly evoked the city's past to construct a public memory that challenged present day development efforts, using the past to serve present needs and desires of long-time residents who were marginalized from the planning process. I use the term *conscious remembering* to describe how residents recollected the role of capitalist processes and systemic racism in Detroit's history, in essence, forcing the past onto the present and rejecting "whiteness' rhetorical silence" (Crenshaw 1997) perpetuated through dominant accounts of public memory.

When covering Detroit's financial crisis between 2011–2013, the not-for-profit papers, the *Voice of Detroit* and the *Michigan Citizen*, carried numerous articles exposing a racist history and, importantly, drawing connections between the past and present day efforts at development. *Voice of Detroit*, which calls itself the "city's independent newspaper, unbossed, unbought," has been published since 2010. The *Michigan Citizen*, a Detroit weekly that ended publication on December 28, 2014, billed itself as "America's most progressive community newspaper." Both papers represented important vehicles for sharing the perspective of ordinary Detroiters, whose views were often muted against the perspectives of powerful city leaders such as the Emergency Manager, Kevyn Orr, and Mayor Mike Duggan.

The *Voice of Detroit* explored the "real cause of Detroit's fiscal crisis" by harkening back to deindustrialization and suburbanization, with race figuring prominently in the recollection (Bryant 2014; Jordan, 2013; Travis 2013). "Discriminatory federal housing policies . . . forced the city's residents to remain jobless in Detroit" (Travis 2013), while white city leaders "took out loans to build roads, water infrastructure, and all the necessities so that white workers would have the amenities they needed in their new suburban digs" (Jordan 2013). The "federal government colluded with white leaders in Michigan to steer federal funds to build roads and highways that would lead whites out of the city to their federally financed homes and INTO the city to their inner-city jobs" (Jordan, 2013). These accounts contrast sharply with the public memories offered by city leaders, which obscured the extent to which systematic exclusionary practices (e.g., deindustrialization and suburbanization) played out on city spaces in racist ways (Bryant 2014, Jordan 2013).

The grassroots organization, Detroiters Resisting Emergency Management (D-REM) provided similar recollections of Detroit's past as a way to explain the current crisis. A participant at D-REM's People's Forum in August 2013 noted the auto industry "deliberately destroyed[ed] the Black working class by shutting down city plants in the 1970s but keeping suburban plants open" ("Emergency Management Is Racism" 2013). The group's "declaration" of "grievances," released in November 2013, recounted the story of "redlining, housing discrimination and deindustrialization" to explain Detroit's current financial crisis.[10] Again, racism played a central role in the city's history: "A series of misguided and racist decisions by Wall Street bankers and regional corporate elites plunged the city into deep debt" ("Detroit State of Emergency" 2013). These grievances were reiterated in an objection filed by D-REM to U.S. Bankruptcy Court in March 2014. In the document, D-REM explained its objection to the debtor's motion to approve a settlement offered by the Emergency Manager Kevyn Orr pertaining to restructuring Detroit's debt ("D-REM Objection" 2014). D-REM member Thomas Stephens provided an assessment of the Detroit bankruptcy by comparing corporate media accounts that focused on the incompetency of a few bad leaders to what he viewed as the more deep-seated and long-running reasons for Detroit's economic demise, which he described as "the huge political economic forces of racism, neoliberalism, empire and the evisceration of social welfare by global capital" (Stephens 2014). He explained, "by the crashing fall of 2008, Detroit had already been suffering for decades in wave after wave of deindustrialization, white flight, capital flight, middle class flight, so-called 'free trade' offshoring of investment and living wage jobs, subprime mortgage predation, derivative speculation and the housing bubble" (Stephens 2014). Notably, Stephens harkened back to one of the first land grabs in North America as a comparison to the events of present day Detroit. He asked: "Are we doomed to repeat that old racist legacy of unjust enrichment, displacement and conquest? Must land speculators in cheap urban real estate be empowered to herd urban residents off to new waste lands, repeating the old patterns of conquest-followed-by-abandonment, the ones repeated already by the auto industry's relations with Detroit? Did the Wall Street crash of 2008, like the serial busts of the 19th century that accompanied the ethnic cleansing of North America, presage 'spiritual bankruptcy' as well as financial?" (Stephens 2014).

The public memory conveyed in the *Voice of Detroit*, the *Michigan Citizen*, and D-REM documents illustrates the ways past trauma may be employed by marginalized groups to shed light on present day events and, importantly, to suggest courses of future action. In contrast to Governor Rick Snyder's suggestion that the past was irrelevant to Detroit's present and future, counter-memories implicated broad based systems, entrenched in the past and at work in the present, which maintained power disparities. Public memory also served as inspiration for the present as suggested in a *Michigan Citizen* article that recalled Detroit as a "movement city," one that participated in the underground railroad, sit-down strikes, and movements for civil rights and Black Power ("Reimagine [R]evolution," 2012). The article called on readers to mark the 45th anniversary of the "Detroit Rebellion"—a reference to the 1967 race uprising—by coming together to "share ideas, learn new skills and strengthen neighborhoods" ("Reimagine [R]evolution" 2012).

George Lipsitz (1990) describes neo-conservative renderings of history as overly simplistic, uncritical accounts of the past and present, "as 'givens' independent of human agency" (27). Such accounts amount to a "mythical construct invented to impose cultural unity and obedience to the present government" (27). Public memory reinscribed in official accounts of Detroit's past aligns with Lipsitz's description. In contrast, long-time residents who stood to gain the least from city policies of redevelopment threw a wrench in the story of steady progress, instead drawing on the "hurts of history" (Lipsitz 1990, 27) to establish a connection between racist spatial policies of the past and those of the present day. The executive director of the Black Agenda Report (BAR), Glen Ford, asserted of Detroit: "We must make it possible for the people to see the city as it actually exists, so that they can rationally dream, plan and build the city as it should be" (Ford 2014). For residents, understanding the "city as it actually exists" entailed recollecting exclusionary spatial practices from the past.

AGENCY AND PLACE

Dominant understandings of the city were often tied to the ingenuity of a singular leader with vision and fortitude. In this section, I explore how the myth of heroic individualism, rooted in a neoliberal tradition prizing "opportunity" and individual success, functions in discourses of urban renewal in Detroit. I then turn to the ways personal success stories are challenged through counternarratives that emphasize the importance of people power and a "right to the city."

Stories of individual success—given structure in the myth of American individualism—are woven into the fabric of American culture and draw on strains of romantic democracy (Fisher 1982) and hegemonic masculinity (Butterworth 2007). The mythic hero is manly—a "rugged individualist" (Butterworth 2007, 228), "adventurous . . . daring and impassioned," one who "evokes the images of the American Dream" (Fisher 1982, 301). The hero often materializes as a pioneer whose self-reliance and bravery are requisite for taming the wild frontier (Carpenter 1977; Rushing 1983; Stuckey 2011). The story of the heroic individual who tames the wild frontier that is Detroit is a spatial discourse that conveys an ideology of place, a "moral landscape" or a vision of what and how to be, as embodied in the white male hero (Cooper 1999, 378).

In discourses of Detroit's redevelopment, the myth of "American individualism" was channeled through a post-racial narrative of success that masked the social structures privileging whiteness and thus foreclosed a discussion of a long-standing history of systemic racism. Examination of dominant narratives support Gray's (1989) observation that the media present "an open class structure, racial tolerance, economic mobility, and sanctity of individualism, and the availability of the American dream for black Americans" (376). Narratives of Detroit often emphasized the ingenuity and daring of one man, at times the white business tycoon, others the black Governor-appointed Emergency Manager, Kevyn Orr, suggesting a multi-cultural recovery of Detroit. Portrayals of city leadership that emphasized the heroics of one man operated rhetorically to elide the history of U.S. struggles to dismantle structures of oppression; instead constructing a narrative of a nation whose past and present "depends on personal acts and identities" (Berlant 1997, 4) as opposed to systemically rooted oppression or collectively supported resistance. In this way, the heroic individual figures prominently in dominant constructions of public memory that, as explained earlier, exile race to the margins of geographical histories and resident well-being. These narratives work in tandem with public memories of white nostalgia to decenter the geographically exclusionary past and reposition a neoliberal understanding of individual success and urban growth.

The Hero Tames Detroit

George Lipsitz's (2002) observation could not be more apt when trying to explain mainstream media accounts of Detroit's recovery: "Whiteness is everywhere . . . but it is very hard to see" (61). The story of the white hero was one commonly used avenue for conveying the story of Detroit's rebirth. In these narratives, race was coded through references to the dangers of the city (e.g., crime, drugs) associated with the racialized "Other," highlighting the qualities of success embodied in white masculinity.[11] The pioneer/hero story of Detroit's renewal gained twenty-first-century appeal through post-racial portrayals of Kevyn Orr. Portrayals of Orr worked in conjunction with racial memory of civil unrest, black leadership, and black life in Detroit. News portrayals set up Orr as the good black who contrasts with the incivility associated with the "riots" of the late 1960s, crime, and drugs, issues racially coded black. The multicultural cast of the hero reinforced the American myth that "anyone can succeed" so long as s/he works hard and plays by the rules.

Billionaire developers Dan Gilbert (who owns over 8 million square feet of downtown Detroit real estate) and Mike Ilitch (who controls a 45-block entertainment district and five neighborhoods in Detroit) were constructed as the (white) pioneer against a backdrop of the wild frontier, populated by racialized "Others." This narrative structure worked to reinforce qualities of white masculinity such as leadership and daring, and it sustained white privilege by providing a foil—the racialized, untamed cityscape—against which the two men's actions could be compared.

News accounts variously described Gilbert as "the hottest name in town" (Whyte 2014), the "city savior" (Berman 2014), the "city's biggest booster" (Gallagher 2014b), and the "Motor City missionary" (Segal 2013). These descriptions cast Gilbert in the mold of the mythic hero—he was a bold pioneer, brimming with ingenuity and good intentions for his community. Local and national newspaper articles related how Gilbert has (re)tamed Detroit, "physically transforming downtown" and turning "once-abandoned buildings" into a "series of hip offices" (Whyte 2014). His efforts—along with those of Mike Ilitch, billionaire owner of the Little Caesars Pizza franchise and the Detroit Red Wings—are "helping to transform what had been a long-dormant downtown into a 24-hour live, work, and play district" (Gallagher & Walsh 2014). Gilbert's projects under the umbrella, "Opportunity Detroit," represent a "rescue mission" for the city (Segal 2013). Gilbert and his ilk are shaping "policy decisions, public safety and future planning investment" (Aguilar 2014c). Like a true American hero, he is bold, having moved the headquarters of his company, Quicken Loans, and 12,500 employees to downtown. He is "undaunted" and "full of restless energy" (Segal 2013). He is worthy of emulation. A highway billboard in the downtown area depicts a boy and states: "The next Dan Gilbert. The Detroit of tomorrow starts with a donation today" (Whyte, 2014).

The *Detroit News* covered the Ilitch family's plans for a new Red Wings stadium and entertainment district explaining the project as a boon for the city. "If things go as planned . . . the Ilitches' vision will have created something bigger than the current downtown Detroit. Bigger than New York City's Greenwich Village or Washington's Georgetown" (Aguilar 2014c). The Ilitch's plans were cast in terms of a moral uplift for the urban landscape. The *Detroit News* noted the "family knows what it wants, as well as what it doesn't want: bail bond services, topless clubs and tarot card readers" (Aguilar 2014c). A website promoting the new district explained the geographical transformation of the area noting the new Red Wings arena "will be surrounded by a soaring glass-covered concourse pulsating with nightclub electricity, where food vendors, restaurants and shops will cater to a high energy crowd that comes together to celebrate" (Aguilar 2014a). The before and after spatial descriptions gain significance for ways race and class remain unspoken yet are present through cultural associations with urban spatial markers and marginalized groups deemed "unworthy," "morally degenerate" or "unproductive" simply because they do not patronize high-end eateries and retail establishments. The narrative of the heroic individual resonates through a language of geography that relies on commonly held presumptions and stereotypes of race and class in the city.

The *Detroit News* and *Wall Street Journal* upheld Kevyn Orr as a face of Detroit's renewal efforts. The *Detroit News* covered Orr's "upbeat assessment" ("Snyder, Orr strike" 2014) of Detroit's recovery and explained that Orr's plan proposes "spending $1.5 billion over the next decade on improving city services to combat blight, crime and other problems that contributed to a decades long population decline" in the city ("Detroit Bankruptcy Exit Plan" 2014). The *Detroit News* noted how Orr "touts successes and maps out . . . improvements" (Ferretti 2014b). The *Wall Street Journal* looked favorably upon Kevyn Orr describing him as a "youthful attorney" who "cut his chops" in Miami "after graduating from the University of Michigan Law School in 1983" (Finley 2013).

Above all, the hero embodied in Gilbert, Ilitch, and Orr has good intentions for the people he serves/saves. The *Detroit News* reassured that "Orr continues to meet opposition from retirees and other city creditors but says his main focus is getting Detroit on track for its 700,000 residents" (Ferretti 2014b). Orr himself praised both Gilbert and Mike Ilitch noting "All great cities have patrons who come to their assistance in times of need" (Corrigan, 2013a). The *Detroit News* pointed out Gilbert is a "signatory of the Giving Pledge" and has "poured his money into downtown parks, housing aid, small business development and transportation improvements" (Whyte 2014). He "preaches a vision of Detroit that is almost idyllic—and is working relentlessly to make it happen"

(Gallagher 2014b). In response to critics who charge Gilbert with ignoring "systemic problems," the *Detroit News* article cites a CEO of one of Gilbert's companies who reassures that he and Gilbert are "contributing where they think they can give the most help" (Whyte 2014).

Notably, Ilitch and Gilbert attained the status of hero against the backdrop of the city landscape. Rhetorically speaking, the city is a contested space, politically charged, an arena through which white privilege remains centered and racialized "Others" are coded through references to the city's dark side, for example, crime, drugs, low-performing schools. In mainstream accounts of Detroit, the once forlorn, dangerous, abandoned city was "rescued" by Gilbert, who attained status as hero through juxtaposition to what he—and by extension, other white professionals—was not. Here whiteness functioned as a "strategic rhetoric" to "resecure the center, the place, for whites" (Nakayama & Krizek 1995, 295) while drawing on racist associations of blackness with the dangers of the inner city. De/re-generation became the metaphor that bound race and space (Goldberg 1993, 54). Gilbert's revitalization efforts were portrayed as antidote to "crime, low-performing public schools" (Whyte 2014). Conversely, "workers without needed skills" can "stall or hold back the renaissance" spearheaded by Gilbert (Gallagher 2014b).

This racially coded story of upward mobility in the city was reinforced in a *Detroit News* photo gallery, "Detroit: A Tale of Two Cities." Photos relayed the downtrodden Detroit through pictures of abandoned homes and burned out buildings. The photo of a "long-time Detroit artist," an African American named Olayami Dobls, connoted a Detroit of the past as he was shown standing in front his African Language Wall mural. In contrast, a photo depicted a formidable, muscular white construction worker, the President of Beal Properties, standing on the balcony of the 33rd floor of the Broderick Building, a building that, readers learn, "will soon feature three $5,000-per-month penthouse apartments that are already reserved." This photo and the three following suggest the new and improved Detroit, a space made habitable through penthouse apartments available only to the financially well off. The now tamed Detroit was raced through other photos showing a young and notably white crowd enjoying Tofurky sandwiches and "raw juice" drinks prepared by a "mix master" at new vegetarian restaurant. In these pictures, food serves as the signifier of white upward mobility.

Just as the American pioneer was celebrated as bringing the Native American Indians "to the solid and safe ground of civilization" (Morse 1999 [1822], 232), the contemporary "urban pioneer" (Zukin 1982) embodied in heroes such as Dan Gilbert, Mike Ilitch, and Kevyn Orr was portrayed as bringing safety and civilization to the formerly devastated city landscape. But this public narrative was not without challenge. The *Detroit News* reporter who exclaimed, "everyone sings his [Gilbert's] praises," may have wanted to check with a few other sources, such as long-time residents who took a different tack when it came to identifying who or what could save Detroit (Whyte 2014).

A "People's Plan" to Save Detroit

It would be difficult to get a sense of what ordinary Detroiters think of the changes in the city landscape without turning to the Internet for grassroots efforts that sprang into existence between 2008 and 2014. As the Facebook page of Detroiters Resisting Emergency Management notes, "There is a resistance!" But Detroiters may need to bypass mainstream media and instead look to the streets or online to find evidence of this grassroots activism. Three of the most active organizations (in terms of both online presence and face to face interactions) include, Detroiters Resisting Emergency Management, Moratorium NOW! Coalition to Stop Foreclosures, Evictions, and Utility Shutoffs, and Detroit Eviction Defense. The three groups work in conjunction with one another. Moratorium NOW! (MNOW) and Detroit Eviction Defense (DED) are member organizations of D-REM; DED and D-REM are "allies" with MNOW.

In Detroit, particularly during the 2013–2014 time period, D-REM, MNOW, and DED centered on empowering ordinary Detroit residents to ensure basic rights to housing, jobs, and education. D-REM organized to "protect and advance democracy" in Detroit after Governor Snyder instituted emergency management in the city in March 2013. DED, formed in 2011, is a "coalition of homeowners, union members, faith-based activists, community activists, and allied groups united in the struggle against foreclosure and eviction" ("Detroit Eviction Defense: Who We Are"). DED amasses power in numbers to block evictions of families. Like D-REM and DED, MNOW (organized in 2008) focuses on issues surrounding emergency management and foreclosure, but often ties issues of racism and capitalist exploitation explicitly into discussions of Detroit's recovery. As of mid-2015, each group has a Facebook page. DED and MNOW meet weekly and can be followed on Twitter.

In contrast to the myth of heroic individualism found in mainstream news accounts of Detroit, D-REM, DED, and MNOW as well as the noncorporate weekly, *Voice of Detroit*, emphasized a people's right to the city through a narrative of collective struggle over place-making. In place of the individual white male at the center of the myth of heroic individualism, the narrative of collective struggle articulated a "we the people" that was not only an "ideological effect of constitutive rhetoric" (Charland 1987, 139), but an identity rooted in material experience.

Scholars (Althusser 1984; Black 1970; Campbell 1973; Charland 1987; McGee 1975; Perelman & Olbrechts-Tyteca 1969; Triece 2003) have theorized the relationship between audience and rhetor, with most seeming to privilege the role of language in *creating* "the people." Borrowing from Althusser, Charland (1987) suggests the audience is "interpellated" through ideology, or constituted through discourse (138). McGee (1975) understands "the people" as both fiction/socially created and real/objective (240), but gives weight to the rhetorical sway of rhetors that "create" a "people" disposed to the message of the speaker (241). Others suggest concepts such as the "second persona" (Black, 1970) and the "universal audience" (Perelman & Olbrechts-Tyteca, 1969) as a way of understanding the transformative potential of rhetoric, a rhetorical tool for establishing a "model of what the rhetor would have his real auditor become" (Black 1970, 113; Hammerback 1994; Jensen & Hammerback 1998).

Standpoint theory, grounded in Marxist thought and extended by feminists throughout the twentieth century, provides a useful intervention in discussions of language and audience identity, whether understood as rhetorically constituted, objectively grounded, or operating as a medium for becoming. Standpoint (also discussed in the Introduction) suggests an "epistemological device" (Hartsock 1983a, 118) that derives from our position within and relationship to material structures (namely, the economic system), which shapes how we experience and in turn interpret the world (Lukács 1968). Consciousness of one's surroundings—and thus the way one judges or values those surroundings—differs depending upon whether one experiences life as a worker on the factory floor or the owner of the factory; whether one is black or white in a culture that privileges whiteness; whether one is male or female in a patriarchal society; whether one has been evicted from their downtown apartment of 20 years or owns over 8 million square feet of real estate in that city. Standpoint theory is based on the premise that "material life . . . not only structures but sets limits on the understanding of social relations" (Hartsock 1983b, 232). The perspectives derived from firsthand experience with oppression lend greater critical insight—what Alcoff (2006) refers to as "epistemic advantage" (96)—regarding social relations and structures that perpetuate economic and political disparities.

Importantly, standpoint theory (re)directs our attention to epistemological issues calling forth the at times neglected relationship between language, knowledge (including how we understand ourselves), and a material reality that interacts dialectically with discourse. Individual/collective identities and knowledges of the world are created not only through discourse but through what Marx (1844/1978) called "sensuous activity," that is, "labor and creation" (171) and the adjoining experience of exploitation and struggle to meet basic needs. Our identities are created, developed, altered not only by persuasive messages but in and through our experiences as humans who are "conditioned and limited" by needs (115). I make this argument elsewhere in a study of working-class women whose experiences of workplace exploitation "spoke volumes" and "made listeners more receptive" to the appeals of labor leaders who attempted to shape their identities as agents capable of transforming their living circumstances for the better (Triece 2003, 8).

Here we may circle back to examining a narrative of collectivity that appeals to "the people" bound by common struggle for a right to city spaces and resources. This narrative draws on understandings of right to the city as the "need for those most negatively affected by the urban condition to take greater control over the social production of urbanized space" (Soja 2010b, 6). In contrast to the myth of heroic individualism figuring pioneer and frontier, the narratives provided by D-REM, DED, and MNOW, offer a new way of understanding the city and how it can be transformed, reflecting the notion of a right to the city. A "right to the city," grounded in Henri Lefebvre's 1968 writing on the subject, has been variously conceived as the right to access basic resources, the right to reconfigure urban spaces, and the right to exercise urban spaces—streets, squares, parks—as political platforms. Right to the city efforts seek "spatial reappropriation" (Soja 2010b, 96) and center on "who has access to public space and who is excluded" (Mitchell 2003, 6). A primary assumption threading these views is that the "production of urban spaces reproduces social injustice" (Plyushteva 2009).

In this study of urban spaces, race, and housing, I look at right to the city efforts specifically as they are situated in a context shaped by capitalist processes of growth and competing with widely accepted discourses of market logic. Detroiters' struggles for city rights challenged privatized control over domestic, public, and workplace spaces and linked spatialization to a history of racism and class exploitation. Theirs was a narrative of collective struggle that not only crafted an identity constitutive of "the people" (Charland 1987) but was shaped by and grounded in firsthand experience with spatial marginalization that had a material impact, that is, an effect on physical well-being.

The grassroots narrative of collectivity emphasized two elements that contrasted with the myth of heroic individualism. First, the change agents in this rhetoric were "the people," not a singular hero. I wish to argue here the "people" in these examples comprised not only "rhetorical effects," "constituted," or "called into being" through discourse. They were individuals with lives impacted materially by restructuring plans and they frequently referenced their material experiences as a way to appeal for solidarity with other Detroiters. Certainly, appeals to "the people" as visionary, capable, and determined established the agent textually in a specific way, as empowered. Yet, the audience-member-as-change-agent is not wholly or only rhetorical, but is situated materially in a landscape demarcated by disparities in access to basic resources. These disparities comprise what Bitzer (1968) called the exigence. In the case of Detroit citizens, an exigence arose around geographical control over city spaces that affected their abilities to control their communities and keep a roof over their heads.

D-REM, DED, and MNOW websites described the change agent as a "coalition" or "community," and often referred to "Detroiters' interests,"

"Detroiters' voices," and "the vision of People" ("D-REM Objection" 2014; *People's Plan for Restructuring* 2014; "#PeoplesPlan Press Release" 2014). The rhetoric of collectivity was exemplified in a document, *People's Plan For Restructuring Toward a Sustainable Detroit*, created by D-REM, MNOW, and the National Action Network (NAN) and first published in February 2014. The *Plan* was created in opposition to Emergency Manager Kevyn Orr's Plan of Adjustment that proposed cuts to city workers' pensions in order to restructure the city's debt.

The *People's Plan* relied on contrast and juxtaposition to distinguish the power of the people to "misleading corporate schemes," an implicit reference to Gilbert:

> The restructuring and rebirth of Detroit will not be delivered by a state-imposed emergency manager, nor through chapter 9 bankruptcy proceedings, foundation contributions, closed door deals, or other devious and misleading corporate schemes. Detroit's rebirth will be the result of the people's unrelenting demand for democratic self-governance, equal access to and management of the natural and economic resources of the city. (*People's Plan for Restructuring* 2014)

The *Plan* provided a "people's analysis" proposed in opposition to the "deceit, misrepresentations and lawlessness" of the policies proffered by the Emergency Manager Kevyn Orr and Governor Snyder. The document described the "people's alternatives" to emergency management that were "rooted in the certainty of our capacity to envision and create a city culture in which human rights are protected" and offered a detailed "analysis of [the] current financial crisis" that contrasted with the dominant narrative proffered by Detroit leaders. The *Plan* also went beyond the immediate debt crisis to advocate specific proposals for "community life," "restoration of democracy and self-government," and "development and welfare of [Detroit] youth" (4).

In conjunction with the release of the *People's Plan*, D-REM, MNOW, and NAN organized an Emergency Town Hall Meeting on March 2, 2014, to discuss the *Plan* and to "seek more community input" on the document ("#PeoplesPlan Press Release" 2014). The groups emphasized the *People's Plan* was "created with the needs of residents, city workers and retirees at the center of the process" ("#PeoplesPlan Press Release" 2014). It is a "living document" that will "change and grow as our community responds to the political and social conditions of Detroit" (*People's Plan for Restructuring* 2014). MNOW's announced Emergency Town Hall Meeting referred to "mobilizing the people," and the twin needs to resist being "lulled by promises" made by Michigan's Governor Snyder, and "intensify" protest efforts ("Defend Detroit City Pensions," 2014). The appeal gained persuasive impact, in part, through references to a deteriorating city landscape in the form of run-down city buses, broken water mains, and street lights gone dark ("Defend Detroit City Pensions" 2014). The following month, the organizations sponsored a "We Object!" rally to "shift the paradigms from the needs of bankers to the needs of hundreds of thousands of Detroiters" ("'We Object!'" 2014). One goal of the rally was to encourage residents to "voice their opposition" to Orr's plans by filing an objection with Bankruptcy Judge Stephen Rhodes who was set to rule on the proposals for debt restructuring laid out in Orr's Plan of Adjustment ("'We Object!'" 2014).

Importantly, the rhetoric of collectivity established a people/coalition capable of acting in response to material needs existing outside of, but understood through competing public discourses concerning how to remake the city. These documents appealed to "the people" as visionary, as unified in opposition, and as capable of shaping and determining their city's landscape. But this appeal was attractive precisely because it resonated with audience members' experiences—with foreclosure, eviction, pension cuts—of physical well-being. Put differently, "the people" in these documents are not only (merely) a rhetorical construction or a "linguistic phenomena" (McGee 1975, 239), but they are also, to borrow from Marx (1844/1978), "real, corporeal" humans "with . . . feet firmly on the solid ground" (115). Humans are not only rhetorical "effects," interpellated, hailed, or recruited by discourses (Althusser 1984, 174). They are shaped and conditioned by needs of the body, that is, hunger, that can be fulfilled by an "object existing outside it, indispensable to its integration and to the expression of its essential being" (Marx, 1844/1978, 116).

In contrast to the myth of heroic individualism featuring a singular white male who dared to tame/redevelop Detroit, the scene described in the rhetoric of collectivity was a space with vast democratic potential but presently marked by race and economic exclusion. According to this narrative, the efforts of the change agent were directed at democratic placemaking aimed at challenging lived experiences of racist and market driven displacement. Their rhetorical efforts suggest the ways discursive placemaking was inseparable from their material experiences, similar to Kaplan's (2008) findings of homeless campers who created meanings around "home" and "work" that facilitated their struggle to survive on the streets. Ordinary Detroiters' efforts at placemaking represented "spatial counterstrategies" (Kaplan 2008, 275) that challenged hegemonic rhetorics of development and changed the meanings of city spaces.

The *People's Plan* devoted considerable print to suggesting legislation to improve "community life," with policies geared toward "self-governance," "open decision making," and control over city spaces. In contrast to "blight removal," the program of tearing down old structures and clearing land for (re)development (supported by Gilbert and other city leaders), the *Plan* promoted "support for urban homesteading" that would enable "people to legally move into abandoned structures and restore them." The *Plan* criticized blight removal as a waste of "massive resources" that did not provide "adequate plans for community-based economic redevelopment." To ensure development in the best interests of the "whole community," the *People's Plan* demanded Community Benefit Agreements that would ensure the needs of residents came before the interests of "corporate economic development."

"The people's" efforts at placemaking specifically pointed to the racial politics shaping city geographies. Articles on D-REM's website and direct actions organized by local resistance organizations repeatedly pointed to the racism underlying economic redevelopment. D-REM organizer Thomas Stephens criticized *Detroit Future City* for ignoring the "racial [and] economic realities that have put Detroit in the crisis that it's in" ("D-REM Statement on 'The Albert,'" 2014). In another article, Stephens asserted "democracy and the rule of law were suspended by a brutal white supremacist, neoliberalizing corporate patriarchal takeover" (Stephens 2014). Along with MNOW, the Coalition for an International People's Assembly Against the Banks and Against Austerity organized a rally on October 5, 6, 2013, to bring together "the people of this city under siege" to demand a moratorium on foreclosures and evictions and an end to the "racist emergency management of our cities and schools" ("Oct 5 & 6: International People's," 2013).

Residents also questioned the economics of exclusion in their efforts to control their own domestic spaces. In March 2014, MNOW organized an event, "Housing Truth," wherein residents were invited to share their stories of experience with foreclosure and/or eviction ("Defend Detroit City Pensions," 2014). Asking the question, "Do you live where you want to live, or where you have to live," the flyer encouraged readers to question the market-driven logic that directed the control over domestic spaces and often determined who would have a roof over their heads and who would be forced from their homes. The event name, "Housing Truth," suggested a lived reality outside of the myths proffered in redevelopment rhetorics celebrating a rebirth of Detroit. The flyer invited residents to "hear testimonies from those affected by practices of the Federal Housing Administration long ago, current practices of racial steering, foreclosures, predatory lending and other systemic issues designed to keep our region segregated" ("Defend Detroit City Pensions," 2014), suggesting that an epistemic advantage (Alcoff 2006, 96) or keener perspective came from firsthand experience as shared through testimony; hence, the telling title of the event, "Housing Truth."

In May 2014, Detroit Eviction Defense invited 20 officials from Fannie Mae and Freddie Mac to attend a "People's Hearing" in Detroit where they would hear the testimonies of persons faced with eviction. Over 200 residents attended the hearing to listen to 22 people tell their stories of struggles against eviction. Although the Fannie Mae and Freddie Mac representatives backed out at the last minute, the hearing went on as planned with empty chairs set up where the government officials were to have sat. S. Baxter Jones, one of the hearing's testifiers had this to say as he faced the empty chairs: "I really wanted you to view me and acknowledge me as a living breathing, human being and not just another statistical casualty.... I guess when you don't have to face me it makes it easier for you to not feel compassion for me or to account for your actions towards me" ("Why Are the Feds?" 2013). This testimony is significant for the way Jones establishes his subjectivity in contrast to the ways that statistics tossed around by government officials, city planners, and the like objectify/dehumanize real people thus facilitating policies of displacement. Jones was challenging hegemonic rhetorics of development that render poor, working-class, minority, elderly residents invisible and that legitimize processes (e.g., gentrification, foreclosure) that "screen off" non-white non-wealthy residents "from the eyes of real estate investors and tourists" (Susser & Schneider 2003, 8). The absence of Fannie Mae representatives prompted DED to videotape the hearing so that officials couldn't "hide from the truth" ("Why Are the Feds?" 2013). The testimonies got the attention of Fannie Mae who responded with settlements that prevented residents' evictions.

Another significant challenge to Fannie Mae and Freddie Mac came in October 2014 when the Federal Housing Finance Agency Director, Mel Watt, spoke at the Detroit Public Library to promote the Home Affordable Refinance Program (HARP), a program designed to lower interest rates for homeowners struggling to make mortgage payments. The program only covered homeowners who were current on their payment and who had Freddie Mac- or Fannie Mae-backed mortgage that originated prior to June 1, 2009 (MacDonald 2014). Residents expressed disapproval of the government program by crafting themselves as a community whose domestic spaces had been violated by greedy banks and government agencies. This narrative contrasted sharply with that of the heroic individual posited as the savior of Detroit's decline. A flyer distributed prior to Watt's talk declared, "We need principal reduction," "Save Our Homes!" and "To Stop Blight: Keep People in Their Homes!" ("HARP Isn't Enough!" n.d.). The flyer called out the processes of racist spatial exclusion when it asserted "Countrywide and other predatory lenders foisted" sub-prime loans on "African-Americans, Hispanics, the elderly, and homeowners with disabilities" ("HARP Isn't Enough!" n.d.).). And it affirmed the right of the people to control their own spaces by remaining in their homes. Similarly, Detroit Eviction Defense advocate, Steve Babson (2014), pointed out in an op-ed published by the *Detroit News* a few weeks after Watt's talk that "in many communities there has been no recovery, especially among people of color in urban neighborhoods targeted by predatory lending" (12A).

One hundred fifty protesters greeted Watt outside the library, while inside residents interrupted the director's talk in order to instigate a "real dialogue" with Watt on "specific proposals that could bring real relief" to struggling homeowners, in contrast to HARP, which they saw as too little too late ("Fannie Mae Head," n.d.). Residents recommended keeping "people in their homes by cutting loan principal on Fannie Mae/Freddie Mac mortgages" and letting "foreclosed families and community non-profit groups buy back their homes at distressed market value" ("Fannie Mae Head," n.d.).

NOTES

1. The comments of a planner involved in the Gratiot Redevelopment project reveal the racially charged motivations underlying site selection. He noted the east side where the development was to be located was primarily black while the west side—another potential site location that was similarly blighted—was "predominately white," presumably making it less acceptable for neighborhood upheaval (Thomas 1997, 58).

2. Astrid Monson acknowledged the plan would "increase congestion in the already over-populated areas" of Detroit (Sugrue 1996, 50).

3. Safety violations at Chrysler's Eldon plant were rampant. In one month alone, the plant "admitted to 167 separate safety violations" (Georgakas & Surkin 1975, 102). The fate of James Johnson, an Eldon worker who shot and killed two foremen and a job setter, spoke to the egregious nature of the plant's violations. The jury in Johnson's case toured the plant where the murder occurred and determined Johnson's working conditions were so deplorable that he was "not responsible for his actions" (102). Further, a separate case was launched against Chrysler and Johnson was awarded worker's compensation.

4. Sugrue (1996) explains this process with historical detail as it began in the 1920s when "New England textile towns were ravaged by the flight of mills to the Piedmont South" (p. 127). By the end of the 1950s, the "flight of industry and the loss of jobs reconfigured the landscape" of northern industrial cities, in essence creating a Rust Belt across the north and Midwest.

5. I put the word, crisis, in quote marks to indicate that the circumstances surrounding Detroit's bankruptcy were not as dire as city officials rhetorically constructed them. A report released by Dēmos, a public policy organization, asserted that the $18 billion in long-term debt cited by Orr as the reason for filing for bankruptcy was "irrelevant to analysis of Detroit's insolvency and bankruptcy filing, highly inflated, and, in large part, simply inaccurate" (Turbeville 2013, 1).

6. After nearly a year of fighting against pension cuts, Detroit's public-sector retirees reluctantly agreed to have their retirement funds cut by as much as 4.5 percent (Davey 2014b).

7. The issue of how much money would go to bondholders including pensioners eventually went to mediation with bondholders receiving 74 cents on the dollar (Lessenberry 2014).

8. "Live It Up in the D" appears on the website, Opportunity Detroit, a large-scale promotional and development effort "backed by Quicken Loans Inc." ("'Opportunity in Detroit'").

9. Post-bankruptcy Detroit's a bargain for corporations. Marketplace. Aired January 29, 2015.

10. The declaration was published on the group's website, D-REM.org, and was reprinted in the *Michigan Citizen*. Similar observations were provided in other articles appearing on the group's website (Stephens 2014; Wylie-Kellerman 2013).

11. The success and wealth of the Ilitch family was mentioned, as well, but less frequently than the heroics of Gilbert. The *Detroit Free Press* compared the "Ilitch and Gilbert contributions" to "corporate benefactors Andrew Carnegie and Andrew Mel-

lon." Their heroic status was unequivocal: "when the annals of the late 20th and early 21st Century downtown Detroit are written, [their] two names will likely stand out as paramount" (Gallagher 2014a).

THREE
Rationality vs. Demystification

In the book, *The Mysterious Benedict Society* (Stewart, 2007), four bright, orphaned children—Kate, Sticky, Reynie, and Constance—are sent to investigate a curious place called the Learning Institute for the Very Enlightened, whereupon they come across a group of students engaged in a memorization exercise called the "Free Market Drill," which goes like this:

> The free market must always be completely free. The free market must be controlled in certain cases. The free market must be free enough to control its freedom in certain cases. The free market must have enough control to free itself in certain cases. The free market ... (170)

Despite reassurances from one of the "Executives" of the Institute who told the quizzical children the drill was "very basic stuff" and that they would "pick it up in no time," the astute Constance asserted plainly, "Sounds like nonsense to me" (170).

The "Free Market Drill" might be seen as a metaphor for the ways discourses explaining capitalist processes often rely on mystification to confuse and obscure the economics of urban growth. I suggest a market logic provides a "veneer of common-sense" (Harvey 1989, 205) and evokes an apparent naturalness to prevailing social ideas concerning spatial uses and urban development. Despite the widespread acceptance of such discourses, some people, like the precocious Constance, see the discourse as "nonsense," or perhaps more specifically, as an unfit explanation for persistent spatial injustices. This chapter explores hegemonic rhetorics of *rationality* that rely on a market logic to elide the contradictory nature of development in the contemporary city. I also examine counterhegemonic discourses that rely on *demystification* to draw back the curtain and expose the economic motives underlying the seemingly detached rhetoric of the market. Before analyzing these competing narratives, I begin with a background on studies of capitalism's influence on urban development and then turn to communication studies for an overview of the rhetoric of economics.

CAPITALISM, ECONOMICS, AND RHETORIC

Goldsmith (2000) noted that "racial segregation is an essential feature and a leading cause of the bizarre spatial form the U.S. metropolis has taken . . . since World War II" (38). Not only is spatial development "bizarre," it is fraught with contradiction as when we see homelessness in an area characterized by a boom in housing construction or when we uncover "accumulation by dispossession" (Bailey 2013; Harvey 2009); "development of underdevelopment" (Soja 2010b, 40); creative destruction; and manufactured crises. My interest throughout the chapters in this book lies in the ways that discourses legitimate, justify, and normalize, or, in contrast, challenge, disrupt, and expose such contradictory processes as "nonsense," or more pointedly, as racially motivated and unjust.

Throughout his writings, David Harvey (1989; 1998) emphasized the centrality of contradiction and instability within capitalist processes. Conveying the link between space and capitalism, Harvey explained, "spatial practices derive their efficacy in social life only through the structure of social relations within which they come to play. Under the social relations of capitalism . . . the spatial practices . . . become imbued with class meanings" and may also be shaped by relations of "gender, community, ethnicity, or race" (Harvey 1989, 223). I approach the study of urban renewal discourses from a Marxist perspective that entails an understanding of and appreciation for the capitalist processes of accumulation, creative destruction, underdevelopment, and crisis on city spaces.

The overriding premise of capitalism is accumulation, sought through the never-ending expansion of labor and raw materials in order to achieve greater surplus value (Marx 1867/1906, 634).[1] Marx (1906) explained:

> the development of capitalist production makes it constantly necessary to keep increasing the amount of the capital laid out in a given industrial undertaking, and competition makes the immanent laws of capitalist production to be felt by each individual capitalist. . . . It compels him to keep constantly extending his capital, in order to preserve it, but extend it he cannot, except by means of progressive accumulation (649).

Elsewhere, Marx and Engels (1848/1965) pointed to the spatial dimensions of capitalism's imperative when they noted "the need of a constantly expanding market for its products chases the bourgeoisie over the whole surface of the globe. It must nestle everywhere, settle everywhere, establish connections everywhere" (63).

The process of accumulation is complex, driven by competition, fraught with contradiction, and marked by crises. According to Harvey (2006b), a "fundamental problem (or contradiction, if you will) for capitalism is a tendency towards overaccumulation" (162). One way that capital manages overaccumulation is through dispossession, what he defines as the "on-going cannibalistic and predatory practices occurring even within the advanced capitalist countries under the guise of privatization, market reforms, welfare withdrawals and neoliberalisation" (158; see also Harvey 2003, 2005).[2] These processes were touched upon in chapter 1 but bear reiterating here. Privatization entails the "transfer of assets from the public and popular realms to the private and class-privileged domains" (153). Financialization refers to the predominance of money as a commodity, exchanged and redistributed often through "speculation, predation, . . . [and] asset stripping through mergers and acquisitions, the promotion of levels of debt incumbency" that has led to "debt peonage" (154). A third characteristic of accumulation by dispossession is the "manipulation of crises," often provoked through forced bankruptcies or the "deliberate creation of unemployment" (154).

We see these processes with resounding clarity in the remake of Detroit between 2008–2014. Downtown buildings containing Section 8 units were scooped up by private investors such as Dan Gilbert at bargain prices and quickly transformed into market rate or upscale apartments. Financialization through predatory lending targeted low-income and minority residents who lost their homes to banks who then sold them to out of state investors for as little as $500, who then flipped them for a profit. And Detroit's declaration of bankruptcy in July 2013—deemed an unnecessary, indeed manufactured move by the public policy organization, Dēmos (Turbeville, 2013)—provided justification for the Mayor and the state-appointed Emergency Manager, Kevyn Orr, to privatize a host of city services, including lighting and garbage collection (Bukowski, 2015; Campbell, 2014; "Detroit Streetlight," 2014). Indeed, Detroit's economic renewal may be aptly viewed as a "spatial fix," or the effort to address the "overaccumulation problem" (Harvey 1989, 21) by "rejuvenating" or more precisely, restructuring city spaces in ways that favor profit-driven processes (Soja 2010b, 90).

The capitalist imperative toward accumulation also results in processes of "creative destruction" and "uneven development" (Harvey 1975; Smith 2002). Building on Marx's and Engels's ideas, David Harvey (1975) explains, "Capital . . . comes to represent itself in the form of a physical landscape created in its own image, created as use values to enhance the progressive accumulation of capital on an expanding scale" (13). Harvey continued, the "geographical landscape which fixed and immobile capital comprises is both a crowning glory of past capital development and a prison which inhibits the further progress of accumulation because the very building of this landscape is antithetical to the 'tearing down of spatial barriers' and ultimately even to the 'annihilation of space by time'" (13). We see this process laid bare in Detroit where hollowed out buildings that once housed auto manufacturing and parts facilities and the adjoining neighborhoods where tens of thousands of auto workers lived are now "blight" that will require an estimated $850 million dollars to tear down (Davey 2014a) to make room for profitable uses of the land. The related concept of uneven development references the cyclical processes of (de)valorization whereby fixed capital (e.g., sprawling auto manufacturing complexes) become outdated and/or profitability declines, the property is devalued, lies fallow, then is bought up by investors seeking cheap but potentially profitable investments, thus jump-starting the process of valorization once again (Harvey 2006a, 155; Smith 2002, 147).

Neoliberalism should be seen not only as a set of practices but as a confluence of hegemonic discourses that relies on rationality to explain away the deleterious effects of the free market. Here I must distinguish between rationality in argumentation, rational choice theory, and rhetorical appeals to rationality. In terms of public debate, rationality may be considered the process by which arguments are assessed for validity and cogency and either upheld or "demolished" (Johnstone 1973, 384). The German scholar, Jürgen Habermas (1984), also forged links between debate and rationality in his study of the emergence of a public sphere comprised of rational individuals who met and debated relevant social issues. Habermas offered the concept of communicative rationality whereby participants assess arguments according to the "validity claims of truth, moral rightness, and sincerity" (Gunaratne 2006, 96). Walter Fisher (1984) reconstituted the concept of rationality in narrative terms whereby human communication is deemed "rational" when it meets the twin demands of narrative probability and narrative fidelity (2). Fisher described rationality as the "logic of good reasons" (Fisher 1980, 121) and an "essential component of rhetorical competence" (122).

References to rationality in economic theory often appear in "rational choice" theory, which states that in decision making, people weigh the pros and cons and opt for the course that maximizes benefits to themselves. Scholars have explored the rhetoricity—the social construction—of economics by exposing the underlying motives driving rational choice theory and the field of economics, more generally (Aune 2001; Escobar 1995; McCloskey 1985; Williams 1991). Rather than view economists as disinterested observers of economic processes, they are more akin to literary writers (McCloskey 1995) in their uses of rhetorical strategies and appeals. Like the novelist that spins a reality, economists' "use[s] of economic terminology involve more a *deflection* than a reflection of reality" (Aune 2001, 24). Economists construct a "cultural discourse" (Escobar 1995, 58) in which rationality is a "dominant value" (Escobar 1995, 103). McCloskey (1985) calls out the "error" in thinking the "economist is engaged in mere making of propositions, about which formal logic speaks when in fact she is engaged in persuasive discourse aimed at some effect about which rhetoric speaks" (24). James Arnt Aune (2001) explores the "dominance of free market rhetoric" seeking to "unmask the strategies used by apologists for capitalism" (4). Both he and McCloskey examine how rationality operates rhetorically in discourses of economics. Appeals to rationality are attractive insofar as they reduce complexity, rely on quasi logical and quasi statistical argument, and convey a disinterested objectivity (Aune 2001).

Rational choice theory and other market-based logics are made attractive (i.e., persuasive) through appeals to rationality, which serve as an apt handmaiden to neoliberal discourses and practices. The idea of rationality is seated in the liberal tradition, which suggests that individuals are rational creatures who act in accordance with their needs. According to this theoretical construct, "a free, rational agent's selection from among a range of options constitutes the basic unit of economic behavior and social existence" (Shakow & Irwin 2000, 54). The state functions only to facilitate individual freedom, opportunity, and entrepreneurialism. Neoliberalism "emphasizes the maintenance of conditions that are amenable to the liberalization and privatization of economies, so as to maximize individual entrepreneurial freedoms" (Sastry & Dutta 2013, 23). Within this framework, rationality codes itself as disinterested and decontextualized, thus obscuring systemic racism and perpetuating the invisibility of whiteness. Appeals to rationality justify neoliberalism's laissez-faire attitude toward government and its support of a color-blind meritocracy (Jones & Mukherjee 2010, 406) that constructs opportunity as open and available to anyone, regardless of economic position, race, or gender.

THE FUTURE OF DETROIT: RATIONALIZING MARKET PROCESSES

Discourses of rationality are awash with appeals to common sense, they carry a sense of reasonableness that closes further discussion regarding their origins, underlying motives, or material consequences. With regards to Detroit's redevelopment in the post–Great Recession years, city leaders such as the Emergency Manager, Kevyn Orr, and city planning documents relied on appeals to rationality to frame a direction for the city's growth and development that appeared intuitive, in line with commonsense values, and thus a closed case.

Detroit Emergency Manager Kevyn Orr's "Plan of Adjustment" for lifting the city out of bankruptcy—rendered effective December 20, 2014, by the United States Bankruptcy Court—relied on the terminology of rationality to lend credibility to the Plan and justify pension cuts to city workers. A February 2014 statement released by Orr's office upon release of an initial draft of the Plan asserted it was the "most effective and efficient method to reorganize the City's financial affairs [and] provide an opportunity for the City to revitalize itself" ("Statement from Orr's Office," 2014). The statement noted the "Plan will continue its momentum toward reaching agreements with its key creditors" and that Orr "and his advisers intend to continue their commitment to the federal mediation process" ("Statement from Orr's Office" 2014). Terms such as "effective," "efficient," "opportunity," and "commitment" connote a level-headed, commonsense approach to city revitalization with which no one would take issue.

In November 2014 when the Plan was confirmed by the Bankruptcy Court in the Eastern District of Michigan, Orr's office publicly asserted: "With Judge Rhodes's historic decision, Detroit moves further along the path toward financial stability and success as a viable and attractive plan to live, work and invest" ("Detroit Emergency Manager," 2014). The statement associated the Plan with the measure and good sense of a judge and threaded a market logic throughout by underscoring the viability and investment potential of the city. The Plan called for active and retired police and firefighters to accept an approximate 10 percent cut in their pensions and for non-uniform city workers to take a near 30 percent reduction ("Detroit Bankruptcy Exit Plan" 2014; "Statement from Orr's Office" 2014) and suggested the privatization of city services such as lighting and garbage collection. The *Detroit News* couched the Plan's proposed cuts as "cost-saving" moves, associating the Plan's market logic with responsible leadership (Ferretti, 2014a). Orr defended his Plan stating, "I happen to think reasonable people would look at that and say 'that's pretty modest'" ("Detroit Bankruptcy Exit Plan" 2014). His reference to the obvious reasonableness of the Plan resonates with remarks made earlier in 2014 when he noted the Plan was "feasible and allows the city to . . . live within its means" (Snell & Livengood, 2014). He also observed, "I think the bargain is so good that it would be madness for it to fall through. . . . I don't know how anybody could walk away from almost $1 billion" (Helms, Gray, Egan, & Spangler 2014). His statement implied that those in disagreement with the Plan were unreasonable and thus not worth engaging in debate. Describing the cuts as "modest" also connotes a sense of measure and thoughtfulness that no reasonable person would take to task.

In addition to Kevyn Orr's Plan of Adjustment, the document, *Detroit Future City* (DFC), also conveyed a commonsense notion of rationality through the construction of a market driven worldview and the cultivation of an ethos of objectivity. These twin emphases made the DFC document easy to accept on its face, granting legitimacy because of the widespread cultural acceptance of the neoliberal values of growth, productivity, and opportunity.

Detroit Future City is a nearly 200-page document billed as a "blueprint" (Ramirez, 2014) for the city and a "framework for moving forward" (Ferretti, 2014a). The report was released in January 2013, after three years of planning and discussions among leaders from local businesses, faith, and philanthropic organizations, as well as members of the government and Detroit residents. As a "strategic framework," DFC proposes recommendations and actions based on the city's status and approach to the following areas: "public land disposition policies and procedures; urban and regional economy; urban agriculture and food security; neighborhoods, community development, and housing; landscape, ecology, and open space; land use and urban form; environmental remediation and health; city systems, infrastructure, transportation, and sustainability" (7). The document is motivated by a sense of urgency—as in the outline of "12 Imperative Actions" on page 9—tempered by an emphasis on the need for a methodical approach to long-term planning. Goals and objectives center on "quality of life" and "quality of business." DFC identifies 5 "planning elements"—economic growth; land use; city systems; neighborhood; land and building assets—that figure into an "integrated approach to transforming the city and its neighborhoods" (18). The remainder of the document is devoted to elaborating on the "transformative ideas" and "implication strategies and actions" pertaining to each element.

Rhetorically, *Detroit Future City* relied on a neoliberal trust in growth and enterprise. The document is replete with the terminology of economic stability and prosperity draped with an optimism of "clear vision" (*Detroit Future City* 2012, 12) and "innovation," a word frequently used in the plan. The document noted the importance of "re-energizing" the city's economy, using "innovative approaches to transform" land use, increasing the "value and productivity" of the land (8). DFC described "productive landscapes as urban catalyst" and putting "vacant land to productive use" (127). DFC confidently projected that by 2030, "Detroit will lead the world in developing landscape as 21st century infrastructure to transform vacant land areas into community assets . . . that elevate adjacent land values" (13). The city planning document seamlessly weaves market terms or the terminology of capitalism (e.g., "assets," "land values," "infrastructure") situating the ideas as "unquestioned presuppositions" (Sastry & Dutta 2013, 23), and suggesting an intuitive credibility and desirability that any rational person would accept. Once associated with seemingly universal values such as growth and innovation, market terminology becomes axiomatic, one with doxa, or widely accepted public opinion (Pal & Dutta 2013; Sastry & Dutta 2013; Shakow & Irwin 2000).

Detroit Future City benefited from the detached nature of a market logic to euphemistically talk about spatial transformations rooted in a history of racial exclusion and resulting in continued spatial marginalization. Politically divisive issues like unemployment, resident displacement, and privatization resulting from capital accumulation and growth were framed so as to elide the long-standing roles that racism and capital flight played in transforming the city geography. For instance, the document referenced "geographic and strategic alignment of existing assets" (35), "sizing ... networks," and the need to "realign city systems in ways that promote areas of economic potential [and] encourage thriving communities" (8). In a section called "Strategic Infrastructure Renewal," the document advocated a "differential level of investment across the city, aligning infrastructure capacity to Detroit's future form" (158).

Alignment suggests an indifferent/unbiased process whereby systems are coordinated or synced to work more efficiently. "Mapping," "cluster strategies," "sizing," and "differential investment" provided a sanitized way to talk about divestment, displacement, and privatization of once public city services. *Detroit Future City* leaves unmentioned the history of deindustrialization and white flight that left city infrastructure and services hollowed out and without a tax base. In neoliberal fashion, the document disappears race, upholding a "privatized discourse that erases any trace of racial injustice by denying the very notion of the social and the operations of power through which racial politics are organized and legitimated" (Giroux 2003, 192). In contrast, residents were quick to call out the biased nature of these processes, that is, the ways proposals for growth impacted people materially and in disparate ways according to race and economic status.

City planning discourses were also suffused with references to "opportunity," a key term supportive of neoliberal practices that reward the seeming self-reliance of the rational individual. Opportunity operates as shorthand for an unspoken argument that assumes individuals are autonomous beings who have an equal shot at obtaining social and economic success. Opportunity assumes free and uninhibited mobility throughout city spaces. References to opportunity rely on the common-sense of seemingly universal values of hard work and innovation and short circuit the ways entrenched systems (e.g., institutionalized racism) act as barriers to success.

In March 2014, as Detroit was muddling through bankruptcy and Orr's Plan of Adjustment was on the table, the Manhattan Institute sponsored a roundtable discussion, Detroit: The Next American City of Opportunity, throughout which opportunity was framed as forward-looking and universally beneficial. Michael Allegretti of the Manhattan Institute described Detroit as an "incubator of innovation," and a place "brimming with opportunity" (Allegretti 2014). Allegretti pointed to Detroit's opportunity due to "low real estate prices," a "resurgent auto industry," and because of an "entrepreneurial class which is emerging" (2014). Governor Rick Snyder highlighted $6 billion in investment, the creation of 10,000 jobs, and the fact that the city has "run out of housing in midtown and downtown for young professionals" as proof that "Detroit is poised to be one of the great value opportunities in the country and in the world" (2014). In these examples, opportunity served as the linchpin justifying urban programs and policies that render city spaces, Detroit in particular, ripe for capitalist expansion. The term opportunity codes success in the city (a la "young professionals") in terms of a white, economically well-off worker untouched by systemic racism, displacement, and job loss and employment restructuring due to capital flight.

Opportunity was similarly a key term in the planning document, *Detroit Future City*, which referenced "opportunity" nearly 60 times throughout the document. As in the Manhattan Institute roundtable, DFC deployed opportunity in a celebratory manner even as it operated in tandem with capitalist discourses of commodification. In DFC, opportunity was most often associated with jobs and business, access to education, and aligning assets. The document conceptualized the city landscape as a bridge linking people to opportunity. DFC (2012) painted the city "landscape" as an "urban catalyst" offering "job opportunities" and "places of innovation, where new ideas are tested and imagined" (127). DFC supported "economic growth 'pillars'" — education and medical; industrial; digital/creative, and local entrepreneurship — that "can create jobs, foster economic opportunity and social equity, and best utilize the city's land assets" (p. 51).

In a move to make neoliberal market terminology seemingly universal, DFC leveraged a post-racial notion of opportunity through a language of inclusivity that connoted a multicultural Detroit. The document portrayed the city as one that "supports minority business enterprises" (p. 41) and emphasized "Detroit should work to attract and retain all residents, regardless of race, gender, lifestyle, or household need" (217). The section, "A City of Equitable Economic Growth," asserted "Detroit's economic growth must be based on fairness and equity" and the city's economy "should be cultivated for people with a variety of educational backgrounds, skills, and interests" (37). In these examples, the capitalist imperative undergirding opportunity is tempered by acknowledgment that all must be given an equal chance to succeed. This sketch of opportunity gives the semblance of a complete picture even as it absents recognition of barriers to success rendered invisible by the appeals to universal good evoked when we read about opportunity, fairness, and equity.

Detroit's renewal leaders, with Dan Gilbert seated front and center, made opportunity synonymous with Detroit (Segal 2013). Gilbert and his company Rock Ventures were behind the Opportunity Detroit efforts, which manifested in a "mega plan" called Opportunity Detroit: The Blueprint for Downtown (Aguilar 2014b) and became a full-blown public relations campaign called Opportunity Detroit, which has its own website (opportunitydetroit.com), radio show, and YouTube channel. The *New York Times* called "Opportunity Detroit" "both a rescue mission and a business venture" (Segal 2013, 1) "Opportunity Detroit" is stamped on buildings owned by Gilbert up and down Woodward Avenue (see figure

2.1). The website, Opportunity Detroit, transforms opportunity into a neoliberal spatial concept that connotes physical and economic mobility. Clicking on the link, "Work," takes the viewer to a site extoling "Detroit's urban core" as "bursting with new businesses providing a plethora of opportunities for professionals." Detroit provides an "environment that inspires productivity and growth!" At the "Live" link, opportunity is tied to "urban energy," "residential options," and the "influx of new residents." At work in discourses of opportunity is a justification of neoliberal privatization that has resulted in the displacement of hundreds of longtime, minority residents in downtown Detroit. References to "urban energy," "opportunities for professionals," the availability of "architecturally charming" lofts and condos, access to "green space" and "artistic décor" code urban spaces as exclusive and exclusionary, as spaces for a new kind of Detroit resident suggestive of a white, professional normative ideal.

In these instances, opportunity works ideologically to undercut the city's history of blue-collar manufacturing and a black majority. In its seeming neutrality and association with neoliberal assumptions concerning the de facto rationality of "free" trade and unfettered growth, the term opportunity celebrates spatial potentialities while rendering invisible spaces where marginalized others live and work. Sassen (1996) suggests the ways corporate urban culture casts resident "others"—immigrants, minorities, low-wage workers—as having "no place in the economy . . . as only marginally attached to the economy" when in fact most workers in the city center are "low-paid secretaries, mostly women, many immigrant or African-American women" and at night "a whole other work force installs itself in these spaces, including the offices of the chief executives, and inscribes the space with a wholly different culture (manual labor, often music, lunch breaks at midnight)" (193).

As city leaders such as Dan Gilbert and Kevyn Orr were deploying appeals to neoliberal values of growth and opportunity, grassroots organizations were mounting a rhetorical opposition that relied on demystification to undo or expose the motives underlying seemingly universal appeals.

COUNTERING RATIONALITY THROUGH DEMYSTIFICATION

Marx (1867/1906) described the "mystical character of commodities" as a "fetishism" wherein the "social character of men's labour appears . . . as an objective character stamped upon the product of that labour" (83). Marx explains, "There is a definite social relation between men, that assumes, in their eyes, the fantastic form of a relation between things" (83). Marx's writings on the fetishism of commodities act to demystify the capitalist processes of production by pulling back the veil to expose the social relations of commodity production. Within Marxist theory more broadly, mystification refers to the ways social conflicts and structural contradictions are suppressed (Eagleton 1991). Mystification is "embedded in the very character" of the capitalist system (Eagleton 1991, 86). A task for critical scholars then has been to engage in demystification, a process of critique whereby the underlying motives or hidden ideologies of economic systems, political platforms, or cultural products are exposed, laid bare, or made transparent. Critics use demystification to show that "surface level claims . . . were not what they claimed" (Streeter 2013, 493), to "draw attention to the ideologies out of which texts are produced" (Giroux 1997, 137). The communication scholar Raymie McKerrow (1989) proposed a critique of domination aimed at "demystifying the conditions of domination" (91). Others (Brookfield, 2003; Giroux, 1997; Harris, 2004; Ott & Burgchardt 2013) have drawn parallels between demystification and goals of critical pedagogy, both of which necessitate going "beneath surface meaning, first impressions, dominant myths . . . received wisdom, and mere opinions, to understand the deep meaning, root causes, social context, ideology, and personal consequences of any action, event, object, process, organization, experience, text, subject matter, policy, mass media, or discourse" (Shor 1992, 129). Above all, demystification is an instrumental critical process with transformation or empowerment of marginalized groups as its goal. The process is central to "building a counter-hegemonic movement" (Cloud 2003, para. 15).

The ability to employ demystification grows out of development of a critical consciousness, which I argue, is rooted in material experience of marginality. Earlier chapters presented the concept of standpoint as a politicized viewpoint derived from firsthand experience with oppression and that lend[s] greater critical insight on relations of power, oppression, and exploitation. To talk of demystification and epistemic advantage is not to suggest a perfectly knowable and transparent truth underlying the lies and distortions of the media and the economic/political elite. It does suggest, however, that certain social positions grant one a better understanding of the dynamics of power. Occupying a marginalized position may grant a person double consciousness (DuBois 1903) or an outsider-within viewpoint (Collins 1986) that grants a unique and critical perspective on power. Other social positions—say, that of a white male—benefit from whiteness's strategic invisibility and thus have nothing to gain—indeed, something to lose—from demystification of racism and class privilege. Demystification is accompanied by deliberation where groups "seek out and entertain multiple positions on a given event . . . weigh competing evidence and reasoning" and take action based on sound argument (Cloud 2003, para. 37). In sum, through demystification, marginalized groups expose underlying motives and contextualize and historicize seemingly disparate, individualized actions and events so as to create a counternarrative of resistance that points to democratic potentials.

Residents offered alternative explanations of Detroit's development through involvement with Detroiters Resisting Emergency Management (D-REM), Moratorium NOW! (MNOW), and Detroit Eviction Defense (DED), and through the alternative media sources, *Voice of Detroit* and the *Michigan Citizen*. For these longtime residents, demystification provided a tool for countering the ideologically imbued neutrality and rationality of neoliberal market discourses and for countering a post-racial narrative of development that disappears race from the politics of geography.

Residents on the spatial margins of Detroit—that is, those rendered invisible through discourses celebrating the new availability of high-end lofts, exclusive eateries, and streetscapes—used demystification to contextualize development processes and to render visible what they viewed as the racially and economically motivated basis of city planning decisions. A symbolic touchstone for such arguments was 1214 Griswold, a downtown historic building located across the street from Capitol Park. The building, purchased in early 2013 by a shell organization calling itself 1214 Griswold, LLC, housed seniors, many of whom were disabled and/or minority residents who received Section 8 housing vouchers to pay for their apartments (Ellis 2013; Gallagher 2013, McGraw 2013). The Griswold building was one of a handful of apartment buildings downtown that housed residents with no income (Ellis 2013). With the purchase of the building, 1214 Griswold LLC announced the transformation the building's units into market rate apartments renting for a minimum of $1,123 a month. Current residents were given one year to find alternative housing.

In response to their eviction notices, residents, whose perspectives were aired in the *Voice of Detroit* and the *Michigan Citizen*, called out the racially and economically motivated nature of the building's proposed redevelopment. For them, the purchase of Griswold was not simply a seizing of opportunity a la Dan Gilbert, but an unfair, discriminatory move that was made easy by a spatial politics—justified by rhetorics of market rationality—that disregarded the needs and rights of poor people, people of color, and seniors. Griswold resident Willie Griffin explained urban space and exclusion this way: "The senior citizens that helped build this country should be entitled to stay down here [downtown] among the wealthy. This [forcing residents to leave] is nothing but financial discrimination. The tenants don't want to move, they resent it with a passion. If all [b]lacks and poor whites would get together . . . we can shut them down" (Bukowski 2013c). James Johnson, a 19-year resident of Griswold, observed developers are "only doing this because we're poor. They think they can get away with anything" (McGraw 2013). Another resident minced no words in stating the project to transform Griswold was "white supremacy to the max" (Ellis 2013).

The *Michigan Citizen* gave credence to these perspectives by explaining processes of development and resettlement in racialized terms. A July 2012 article explained that corporate interests "intend to drive people off the land so it can be 'cleared' for development. . . . Corporations, foundations and the governments they put into office plan a smaller, whiter, wealthier city" ("Reimagine [R]evolution," 2012). Another *Michigan Citizen* article framed gentrification as "apartheid" ("Gentrification Is Apartheid," 2014). The article explained, black residents are "experiencing the pain of removal while whites are moving into the city. Gentrification equals accommodating white people's desire for dog parks and bicycles."

In contrast to rhetorics of opportunity that summon a commonsense understanding of market growth as beneficial for the city, evicted residents of Griswold and other nearby buildings such as Alden Towers, Henry Street, Berwin, Claridge, and Bretton Hall Apartments gave lie to opportunity talk by pointing out the ways market opportunities played out in disparate ways and rendered some groups obsolete and/or invisible (Jeffries 2013). Resident Vanessa Hicks noted the economic motivation underlying the residents' evictions. "'Nobody invests in poverty,'" she pointed out (McGraw 2013). Hicks observed, some people, notably the poor get crushed "when the market changes for the better" (McGraw 2013). Jamaica Watts, a soon-to-be displaced Griswold resident, put the matter this way: "They [developers] want to remodel this building for somebody else. They have made it pretty clear that they don't care about us. All they care about is the money" ("Griswold Tenants Speak Out" 2013). Similarly, resident Betty Scruse, recently evicted from the newly renovated Alden Towers, noted, "They're [the well off] going to have the best and we're going to have what's left" (Jeffries 2013). Although not in so many words, Griswold resident Bill Williams pointed out the geographical impact of capital's chase for profit and the way the never ending process of accumulation (re)shapes city and suburban spaces: "During the energy crisis of the '70s they [the middle and upper classes who followed jobs] all left. Now they want to come back [downtown] and kick us out" ("Griswold Tenants Speak Out" 2013).

A rhetorical flashpoint for the ways opportunity and redevelopment was framed stemmed from a promotional video and window advertisement for the newly renovated 1214 Griswold, which the developers renamed The Albert. The video situated The Albert in a "new, energetic" and "exciting downtown" and explained the renovation would bring the "1929 classic Albert Khan historic building . . . back to its original glory . . . [and] to the beauty it once was when it was first created" ("Welcome to The Albert"). Viewers received a video tour of the updated units as the narrator extoled the classic hardwood floors and state of the art kitchens with "stainless steel appliances, quartz countertops . . . [and a] custom made rollaway island that will suit any renter's needs." According to the voiceover, the end result of the renovation will be "127 Class-A apartments in downtown Detroit . . . the resident is going to feel like they're living in a 5 star hotel." The video cued viewers to elements that marked the building and surrounding neighborhood as a space for young, white professionals. The video panned across the nightlife skyline of Detroit featuring bars and eateries, and focused on daytime shots of young, white people drinking coffee, playing ping-pong, looking at outdoor murals, and doing business over lunch at a café. These behaviors suggest a new association with "urban"—a term long allied with "crime," "underclass," and "black." Urban living a la The Albert is now tethered to lifestyle and consumptive behaviors fitting for a well-off professional class. A large advertisement placed in the window of the former 1214 Griswold supported this new stylized version of downtown life with a rendering of the new residents of the Albert conversing in the building's new lobby.

The *Voice of Detroit* and D-REM responded to these ads by revealing what is often concealed in discourses of city growth and renewal: the ways whiteness remains at once all-encompassing and pervasive yet invisible and unremarkable. To paraphrase George Lipsitz (2002), symbolic renderings of the new Detroit were replete with whiteness but it was very hard to see. Whiteness retains its invisibility by occupying a normative position that places it beyond mention. Regarding the window ad, the *Voice of Detroit* pointed out what many may not have noticed: the residents in the picture were all white (Bukowski 2014). The paper sent photos of the ad to the Executive Director of the Fair Housing Center of Metropolitan Detroit who confirmed that ads depicting all-white individuals violate the Federal Fair Housing Act.

Detroit Resisting Emergency Management posted an official response to the Albert's promotional video on its website describing the document as "heavy-handed and over-the-top in its sense of entitlement and obliviousness" ("DREM Statement," 2014). D-REM took aim at the way the video narrated a story of a new Detroit that disappeared longtime residents and relied on appeals to a white professional class. "The blatant injustice of kicking fixed income elderly people of color out of prime realestate to make way for, if we are to believe the promo video, young affluent whites is outrageous" ("DREM Statement," 2014). Like the *Voice of Detroit*, D-REM offered a counternarrative to challenge the seeming neutrality of opportunity via luxury living. These groups inserted what was not, in fact, missing, but only unspoken: the "centrality of race" (Keith & Cross 1993, 8).

Residents also addressed the politics of market growth by calling out the ways opportunity played out unevenly when it came to access to urban spaces. On their view, opportunity was not a neutral, open invitation but a prerogative exclusively exercised by an elite. Some noted the ways tax abatements afforded an unfair "opportunity" to corporations and developers at the expense of the city and its residents (Bukowski

2011; Jordan 2013). In a public statement given to the 36th District Court in July 2013, the Detroit Public Schools Board Member Elena Herrada explained the "rich do not have to pay taxes and are able to evict residents from their apartments and homes without a hearing. Sports arenas and casinos take precedent over schools. Privately-owned party buses roam the streets while Detroiters wait for public busses that never come. Taxes are waived for the rich while the poorest are left holding the bag" (Herrada 2013).[3]

Some observers drew on descriptive terminology provided in Naomi Klein's 2007 book, *The Shock Doctrine: The Rise of Disaster Capitalism*, to reframe popular understandings of opportunity and urban renewal. D-REM's website posted articles exposing the ways opportunity operated in ways that favor those already holding power. A March 2013 article framed the "manufactured" "financial crisis" as a "ploy . . . to consolidate power and privilege into the hands of a smaller and smaller and richer and richer corporate aristocracy" (Telford 2013). Another article similarly casts Detroit's "adjustment" plans in terms of "disaster capitalism," a process by which city elite use "devastation" as "opportunity" to buy up cheap land and privatize city services (Wylie-Kellerman 2013; see also Newsome 2013). The article retold the story of Detroit's path to emergency management and bankruptcy showing how Governor Rick Snyder exacerbated the city's cash flow problem and concluding, "emergencies are made not just found" (Wylie-Kellerman 2013). Glen Ford, the Editor of the Black Agenda Report, echoed this view noting that "Detroit's state-imposed bankruptcy has dramatically quickened the pace of the land rush" on the part of wealthy developers (Ford 2014). Ford framed the restructuring of Detroit as "disaster capitalism" at work or the "manufacture of phony 'crises' to divert government revenue directly to banksters and sell government assets off to privatizing looters" (Ford 2013). Elsewhere, Ford described the city's efforts at blight removal as the "'orderly' destruction of the nation's largest Black metropolis, to clear the way for a 'new' city—one in which marginalized people like the [blight task force] surveyors themselves will be relegated to the shadows" (Ford 2014).

These counternarratives contrasted markedly with dominant stories of urban growth (discussed in chapter 2) that celebrated the commodification of urban spaces stylized by billionaire urban pioneers whose "urban visions" and "massive plans" updated city spaces for a new elite (Aguilar 2014a, 2014c; Hicks 2014). While the *Detroit News* (Aguilar 2013c) explained the Ilitch family (owners of the Red Wings) would receive $250 million in tax dollars to fund the renovation of the Red Wings stadium and build a surrounding entertainment/residential district to replace the "desolated" and "blighted" area between Woodward and Cass Avenues (Aguilar 2013a), the *Voice of Detroit* called out the unfair advantages given to wealthy developers in the form of tax abatements, and state and federal tax funds (Bukowski 2013a; Howell 2014; Jordan 2013). The paper racialized development processes explaining that city leaders were "in bed with developers," their dealings were "destroying black Detroit" (Bukowski 2013a) and tax abatements amounted to a "deal with the devil" (Bukowski 2013c).

Willie Griffin, who worked with fellow Griswold residents to oppose their evictions, challenged the seeming neutrality of a market logic by calling out the ways development occurs unevenly and at the expense of certain groups. Griffin noted, "It's a new Detroit being built for the rich minority wealthy people. We're not considered wealthy, we're considered a lower class" (personal interview, March 23, 2014). He pointed out the politics of exclusion and the processes by which certain groups are rendered materially and symbolically invisible. "A minority . . . is going to own downtown. They're pushing us back to the west side, east side, away from downtown" (personal interview, March 23, 2014). When asked what "Opportunity Detroit" meant to him, he replied "A lie. It's unfair opportunity. [It's] not for the senior citizens" (personal interview, March 23, 2014). Fellow Griswold resident, Recardo Berrien echoed Griffin's views: "I was born and raised in Detroit. For us not to be part of this 'new Detroit' is absurd. We don't see 'us' in none of this. No elderly and poor. We are nowhere in the plans of anyone down here" (McGraw 2013).

In February 2014, when residents had about four weeks remaining to find alternative housing, Griffin wrote a letter addressed to Dan Gilbert and the "current owner of 1214 Griswold Apartments," which was signed by eight other residents (Griffin 2014). The letter spelled out eight demands centered on controlling the nature and length of their stay in the building they called home. Residents requested that "thirty of the renovated units . . . be reserved for current 1214 Griswold residents." They requested "lowering the rent on these thirty units to where they equal the HUD vouchers amount." And, calling attention to the disregard held by the current owner for low-income and senior residents, the letter demanded clean-up of the building for the present residents including clearing the air ducts, [and] removing asbestos, lead paint and bed bugs." Notably, the letter spoke out on the hot button issue of racism in the ad for the newly designated "Albert": "We want to make clear that the display on the front of the Griswold building is in violation of the Federal Fair Housing Act and the Fair Housing Center of Metropolitan Detroit is opening an investigation" (Griffin 2014). The letter gave voice to residents whose very existence in the Griswold was rendered invisible through celebratory market discourses that recast the downtown residential building as a site of a newly styled urban chic.

At times residents made a straightforward appeal to their rootedness in downtown Detroit as their home space, which contrasted with the rhetorics of transformation and references to luxury lofts emanating from city planning public relations. For those who had lived in downtown apartments, attended churches downtown, volunteered and worked downtown, the city space was not a blank slate awaiting the neutral processes of development as suggested by *Detroit Future City*. Isabella Butler, who lived at 1214 Griswold for 24 years stated, "A lot of us don't know anything but downtown. I went to school here, I worked here.... I'm a cancer patient and have had triple bypass surgery. I've had to stop going to my doctors to find a place that will accommodate my hopes and dreams" (Bukowski 2013c). Twenty-four-year-old resident Avery Chambers, who had lived at Griswold since he was 13 years old noted, "I've grown up here, and now they're taking it all away from me. I don't know where I'm going to move" (McGraw 2013). Likewise, Jacqueline McCoy pointed out, "I have no idea where I'm going, and I am too crippled to get on a bus and go look for a place. We thought this was our home. The rug has been pulled out from under us" (McGraw 2013). Willie Griffin detailed how the Griswold residents supported each other like family (personal interview, March 23, 2014). His view was backed by others such as Johnny Watts who said he "love[d] living in this building [Griswold] because everyone tries to help each other. We have good communication and some of us have common interests. Where else am I supposed to find that?" ("Griswold Tenants Speak Out" 2013).

In addition to demystifying the market process of urban renewal and urban opportunity, residents took great strides to unravel the racial politics underlying Emergency Management. Emergency Managers (EMs) such as Kevyn Orr in Detroit are appointed by a state's governor and given authority to take over the duties of that city's democratically elected mayor and city council. In Michigan, EMs have the power to "dismiss elected officials, abrogate labor contracts, sell off public assets and impose new taxes on residents" (Abbey-Lambertz 2013). In an article posted on D-REM's website, Bill Wylie-Kellerman called the takeover by Emergency Management "urban fascism" and drew parallels to forms of political takeover occurring in the global south. It was no coincidence, residents pointed out, that Emergency Management was instituted in a majority black city, thus disenfranchising primarily black voters. "Emergency management is racism," the *Michigan Citizen* stated (Wischusen 2013). The document, *People's Plan for Restructuring Toward a Sustainable Detroit*, described Orr's appointment as a "ruthlessly racist maneuver" that has "disenfranchised 55% of African American voters in Michigan" (*People's Plan*). D-REM, a primary drafter of the *People's Plan*, submitted a court objection to Orr's Plan of Adjustment in March 2014, stating the institution of EM over Detroit "Violates the will of the people expressed in the last election; Insults the legacy of all those who have fought and died for democratic rights; Destroys the right to vote for and hold accountable elected officials; . . . Benefits wealthy Wall Street bankers and bondholders . . . ; Is used primarily against African American communities; [and] Removes from power 75% of the elected African American officials in Michigan" ("D-REM Objection" 2014; see also "Call to Action" 2014; "People's Forum" 2014).

To further sound the bell and motivate residents to resist what they perceived as a racist takeover of their city space, members of D-REM and MNOW canvassed in various neighborhoods in the summer of 2013 to "talk about the attack on the city and the role of the banks" in leading the city into bankruptcy (Grevatt, personal interview, March 26, 2015). The repeated slogan "Make the Banks Pay!" "struck a chord" with residents who had firsthand experience dealing with recalcitrant banks who made it difficult for residents to remain in their homes despite owners' good faith efforts to make payments. Martha Grevatt (2014), an MNOW and UAW local 869 activist explained, "Detroit was the epicenter of the foreclosure crisis, we felt its impact first. [It] started in the city and radiated out . . . [to the] suburbs, so there was widespread hatred of the banks" (personal interview, March 26, 2015).

Grevatt and others also participated in campaigns to keep individual families faced with eviction in their homes. Members of MNOW and DED often stood watch and on the ready outside threatened homes prepared to form a physical blockade if need be. Activists also thwarted the dumpsters sent by banks to houses scheduled for eviction. In some instances, Grevatt and others parked their cars alongside the residential street so that the dumpster would not have a place to park. In one case, activists filled a parked dumpster with leaves so that there was no room left for disposing of the family's belongings. As they packed the truck, activists shouted, "Dumpsters are for leaves not the banker thieves!" (Grevatt, personal interview).

In October and November 2013, grassroots organizations including MNOW and D-REM organized community events that provided space for ordinary people to reframe Detroit's bankruptcy and recovery in their own terms. The events were well publicized on D-REM and MNOW's websites pointing to the potential for the online activism to complement social change projects (Downing 2001; Joyce 2010; Klein 2000; McCaughey & Ayers 2003; van de Donk et al., 2004). Notably, event organizers unraveled the discourse of market rationality that cloaked the race and economic politics of city redevelopment. A flyer for the International People's Assembly Against the Banks and Against Austerity demanded cancelation of the "debt to the banks which is strangling our schools, cities, states and countries"; ending "undemocratic, racist emergency management of . . . cities and schools" and a "moratorium on all foreclosures and . . . evictions" ("A Call" 2013; see figure 3.1). These demands focused attention on ordinary people's rights to control public, educational, and domestic spaces and called into question the ways market discourses were used to justify austerity measures such as those proposed in Orr's Plan of Adjustment.

Additionally, the People's Assembly garnered international attention and participation providing a way for Detroiters to draw parallels between their city's austerity measures and those imposed on other nations. Event organizers billed the event as an "international tribunal against the

Figure 3.1.   Flyer for the International People's Assembly Against the Banks and Against Austerity. *Source:* Used with permission from Moratorium NOW Coalition, Detroit, MI.

banks" and pointed out that neoliberal models of privatization and austerity imposed on nations in the global south were now being tested on Detroit. Their framings were a far cry from market rhetorics that lauded development and espoused opportunity. Employing demystification, ordinary Detroiters drew historical parallels, elaborated on policy preferentials granted to corporations and banks, and exposed the racist outcomes of emergency management. In short, they dug "beneath dominant myths [and] official pronouncements" to articulate a counternarrative more resonant with their own experiences.

Such demands were repeated in subsequent mass actions, including a November 2013 forum and May Day 2014 rally and march. In November 2013, D-REM organized a day-long People's Forum, attended by over 200 people (Furay 2013), which included discussion of the "roots and effects of Emergency Management," "FIGHTING displacement and colonization in our communities," and "ILLUMINATING the path to dignity and self-determination of all generations" ("People's Forum" 2013). D-REM's website announcement of the event noted "Over half of Michigan's African-American population is under dictator rule by Governor appointed Emergency Management" ("People's Forum" 2013). Event organizers encouraged participants to use social media to disseminate information about the injustices of emergency management (Furay 2013), and invited artists, poets, musicians, MCs, and "media makers of all ages" to contribute pieces that told the "true stories of resistance, resilience, and visionary community-led solutions happening in Detroit and across the state of Michigan" ("People's Forum" 2014). Social media provided a space for oppositional perspectives and enabled a virtual rooting that transcended the physical spatial limitations imposed by exclusionary development (see Landzelius 2006, 2). And telling "true stories" through alternative media (e.g., film, hip-hop) provided a way for residents to counter discourses of development that framed opportunity as a universal good, available to anyone who would but seize it. Through participation in the People's Forum and the International People's Assembly, residents provided a new way of understanding Detroit's road to renewal; to them it was a narrow path of exclusion that rendered invisible those unable to afford luxury lofts—in Recardo Berrien's words "we are nowhere in the plans of anyone down here"—and resulted in spatial inequality and displacement in the form of widespread evictions and foreclosures.

NOTES

1. Marx elaborated on the capitalist processes of accumulation in chapter 27 of *Capital*. It is beyond the scope of this book to explain accumulation in detail except to note the ways the imperative to expand and accumulate give rise to contradictions that impact spatial uses and (in)justices.

2. Harvey's (2005, 2006a) broad-reaching definition of accumulation by dispossession has been criticized for casting a net too widely and thus missing the "distinction between the workings of the capitalist economy in its quest for profit and the . . . ways in which the state uses extra-economic compulsion to augment and accelerate the process" (Bailey 2013, 9).

3. Herrada and Reverend Bill Wylie-Kellermann were arrested at a city council meeting for protesting the city's contract with Jones Day. Her statement was made during her court appearance on July 28, 2013.

Part II: Race and Health in Harlem

FOUR
Mapping Race

In a March 2014 speech given in Detroit to the Michigan Roundtable for Diversity and Inclusion, Reverend Jeremiah Wright emphasized the importance of ordinary people—the "dry long so"[1]—telling their own stories, of "hearing . . . their own voices and being exposed to the power, the pathos, and the pain of a lived experience, not an outsider's observations and interpretations of somebody else's experience but the actual experience of the person who lived it and the persons who are still living it" (Wright 2014). Wright (2014) continued, "Africans survive and thrive in spite of the toxic system. Ain't nothing wrong with the canary [in the coal mine]. Fix the toxic system you have trapped the canary in."

Black residents continue to face issues of segregation and discrimination in housing, limited mobility, and fewer and less desirable neighborhood options (Bullard 2000; Bullard & Wright 2009; Glink 2012; Rugh & Massey 2010; Westra & Wentz 1995). Thus do issues of race, place, housing, and health come together. Just as particular city spaces become marked as "ripe for development" and lead to displacement of longtime residents, spaces may be deemed "disposable" leading to the toxicity of long-standing communities. As black residents in urban locations were uprooted to suit the needs of economic expansion as detailed in the previous chapters, they were often relocated to sites deemed less desirable and targeted for toxic dumping. Just as development and displacement align with race so too do issues of toxic dumping and waste disposal.

Bullard and Wright (2009) point out that "race tracks closely with social vulnerability and the geography of environmental risks" (1). Their observation resonates with the experiences of poor and minority communities from Coal Run, Ohio, and Flint, Michigan, to post-Katrina New Orleans to indigenous communities in Central and South America whose access to clean drinking water and safe housing has been compromised by political and economic processes of spatial exclusion (Bullard & Wright 2009; Haglund 2010). Residents in these and countless other areas have faced contaminated water, toxic housing, and polluted air. Chapters 4 and 5 focus on the ways specific locations become contested sites of profit and pollution, with dominant and vernacular discourses competing over understandings of race and the right to a healthy living space. In these chapters I focus on the experiences of residents in West Harlem who have acted on numerous fronts to challenge toxic dumping and pollution in their neighborhood.

Many of the same forces affecting Detroit residents such as gentrification, financialization, and development are at play in Harlem and other areas of New York City prompting residents to form organizations and engage in community building around the issue of health. In this and the following chapter, I focus on how the body figures in to discourses of race, place, and toxicity. For oppressed groups who bear the scars, diseases, ill diets, and damaged organs stemming from targeted toxicity, deindustrialization, or neighborhood/nation-state neglect, to say "space matters" goes without need for abstruse theorizing.

Bodies matter, too.[2] Sojourner Truth spoke of bearing thirteen children most of them sold to slavery; Frederick Douglass revealed the scars on his back when on the public platform; and garment factory workers in New York City in 1911 and Dhaka, Bangladesh, in 2012, suffocated, were burned alive, or jumped to their deaths from ten or more stories up in sweatshop factory fires and accidents. Throughout history, marginalized "others" have emphasized the physical impact of the economic, political, ideological environments on their bodies. All of this is not to say that bodily experiences are open to straightforward interpretation; experience is always mediated, our interpretations partial. Yet, I argue that physically endured experiences (of hardship, etc.) can serve as a political awakening, prompt critical reflection on the dynamics of power, and often result in an "aha" moment where one develops keener insight on the politics of inequality (Collins 1991; Hallstein 2000; Triece 2003, 2013).

This and the following chapter explore how discourses of environmental justice promoted by the organization WE ACT rely on the body as a trope for conveying the interrelated nature of race, place, and health. In the present chapter, I focus on vernacular rhetorics of recognition that map the black body to specific city spaces. Chapter 5 looks at rhetorics of "street science" (Corburn 2005) that grant the physical body an epistemological function bolstering the knowledge claims of black residents in their debates with powerful polluting corporations. I also examine dominant narratives addressing toxicity that render bodies invisible through rhetorics of technology that depoliticize processes of location and mapping. First, however, it is important to understand the rhetorical situation—the exigencies, audiences, and constraints—facing black residents whose communities have so often been viewed as sites for dumping out of sight.

RACE AND DEVELOPMENT IN NEW YORK CITY: A BRIEF HISTORY

Harlem began as an enclave for Dutch immigrants, a quiet, uptown haven away from the bustle of the city core. In 1904, a proposal to build a new subway line connecting downtown Manhattan to the upper areas spurred land grabs, which in turn led to inflated land prices. Real estate speculation based on the prospect of the new transportation line led to a glut of housing and high prices. To recoup losses, some realtors became willing to rent to black residents, but this move did not come without a backlash (Freeman 2006). As the number of Harlem's African American residents expanded, white tenants fought what they called the "Negro invasion" (Taylor 2003, 5). White residents formed the Hudson Realty Company in order to pool their resources to buy properties in order to evict black tenants. Other white owners urged banks not to lend to African Americans seeking home ownership (Chinyelu 1999, 18). The development of Harlem as a symbol and space of black culture, life, and identity thus came about through the flight of racist white residents and was further enhanced by the migration of southern blacks to northern states like New York. Harlem provided a choice location in Manhattan for black residents excluded from other areas through white violence and redlining.[3] Pre–Great Depression Harlem was "not just another ghetto; it truly was a physical and spatial manifestation of the new Negro" (Freeman 2006, 22).

But Harlem as a community and clearly demarcated space for African American life was particularly vulnerable to the forces of urban renewal and development that swept through cities in the 1940s and 1950s. In New York, no less than any other location, "health and illness have historically been stratified by race and class through the spatial organization" of the city (Sze 2007, 28). Urban life—geographical layout, community development, housing, and health—is rooted in and contoured by an economic and political history that has never been race neutral. Just as Detroit's housing and employment history was key to understanding the present-day rhetorical situation facing the Motor City's residents, New York's past urban planning projects bear on today's environmental justice advocates in West Harlem.

Much more than a simple question of location, then and now, debates in New York (and cities across the country) over growth, development, and placement of controversial facilities have been situated within and contoured by prevailing racialized discourses of morality vs. degeneration, health vs. disease; and these debates have been directed by the economic imperative of urban planners and developers. In the early

1900s, reformers took the approach that "remolding the city's physical environment" would provide a "means of elevating its moral tone" (Boyer 1978, 175). Presidents and mayors, preachers and moral crusaders extolled the benefits of outdoor exercise and the installation of parks and green spaces throughout cities as a way of ameliorating the effects of drunkenness, prostitution, gambling and the like (Boyer 1978). These reform efforts, termed "positive environmentalism" (233), dovetailed with the sanitary movement, which focused on improving city cleanliness and health through the implementation of public water, sewage, and garbage systems.

New York City's reform efforts have been historically associated with Jacob Riis, the journalist whose muckraking-style tract, *How the Other Half Lives*, exposed life in the tenements from a moralizing perspective and laid the groundwork for an approach to urban renewal employed throughout the twentieth century (Schwartz 1993). Fluctuating between pity and blame, Riis described the tenement inhabitants as corrupted, degraded, loose in morals, and at the mercy of unscrupulous landlords. His writings provided a springboard from which to pass legislation stipulating minimum standards for tenement construction (Schwartz 1993, 7). City uplift programs, well intentioned as they may have been, were attempts at controlling and socializing the masses of European and Russian immigrants who were settling in tenements in large cities. In their wake, reformers often left residents homeless and/or displaced, as was the case in New York's Mulberry Bend area, which was leveled to build Columbus Park (Schwartz 1993, 8).

As African Americans migrated from the south to northern cities between 1940s–1960s, their experiences were shaped by city planners and developers who used federal and local policies to undergird large-scale renewal projects that "decimated older black neighborhoods, forcing relocation in rapidly ghettoizing areas, or in some cases creating physical barriers that confined African Americans to certain areas" (Kusmer 1996, 325). Real estate agents, developers, and neighborhood associations evoked racist ideologies linking black residents to disease, violence, and disorder in order to justify housing discrimination, neighborhood segregation, lynchings, and physical and sexual assaults (Massey & Denton 1993; Gregory 1998; Sugrue 1996).

As the twentieth century progressed, public health and city planning centered less on social concern and beautification, relying instead on science and rationality, ideological hallmarks, I would add, of contemporary urban planning language. Sze (2007) notes that "by the 1920s, the reformers had lost the sense of crisis that had bound them together as the turn inward manifested in many ways: health workers focused on individual pathology, social workers discovered casework, and city planners focused on zoning" (36). Far from neutral, city planning and zoning discourses tapped racist ideologies linking black residents with moral and physical degradation and thus justifying segregation and other forms of spatial exclusion (Sze 2007, 43; Wailoo 2001, 30). Miller, Hallstein, and Quass (1996) note how zoning policies "set the stage for an unyielding process of disinvestment and environmental racism which ultimately permitted the construction of the North River Sewage Treatment Plant" in Harlem, an issue taken up later in the chapter (64). Terms such as "ghetto" and "slum" and references to the black family as a "tangle of pathology"[4] permeated popular and political discourses and acted as racially coded markers that stigmatized black individuals and the places they occupied (Sampson & Raudenbush 2005, 7). Efforts to avoid such places and thus contact with the racialized Other are assisted by the Sketch Factor app, discussed in the Introduction, wherein users can report or learn about places that are deemed "sketchy." Unspoken but palpable is the ideological linkage between black and sketchy, that is, criminal, violent, drug-ridden, or undesirable (Sampson & Raudenbush 2005). In this example, the racial politics of space plays out through place-based images of danger—"sketchiness"—and, in a coded manner, secures the connection between black and dangerous. Race, stigma, and place conjoin with discourses of the environment in the image of the polluted space. Through stigmatizing racist images, black people have been socially segregated. The historical association of black as "lazy, undisciplined, and prone to the pleasures of the flesh"—a foil for the white supremacist, capitalist imperative to work within the given economic system—gives rise to the idea the areas populated by black residents are "socially polluted" and thus appropriate places for "environmental pollution" (Higgins 1994, 259, 262).

Like Detroit, New York City galvanized urban renewal efforts funded by the 1949 Federal Housing Act, which resulted in the widespread displacement of low-income and African American residents. A key figure in New York's renewal was Robert Moses, who used Title I of the 1949 Housing Act to see through massive highway and building projects that displaced tens of thousands of black residents throughout the 1950s. "With Title I, the city that led the nation in racial decency would lead it in the fine art of 'Negro removal'" (Schwartz 1993, xv). Under Title I, Moses created his own Committee on Slum Clearance to control what areas would be defined as "blighted" and thus ripe for renewal. Moses curried favor with realtors and manipulated votes on the City Planning Commission thus denying local residents a say in the development of their neighborhoods (Schwartz 1986, 155). By the 1960s, nearly 100,000 residents throughout Manhattan, including Harlem, were forced from their homes (155).

As an example, the redevelopment of Manhattantown on New York's Upper West Side became "synonymous with Negro removal" as black residents were twice displaced by development projects, such as the one for West Park described as a "'prime residential community' menaced by 'malignant' forces" (160).[5] As a member of the New York City Planning Commission, Moses devoted millions of dollars to the improvement of Riverside Park while neglecting the section between 125th and 155th Streets, an area populated by black residents (Miller 1993). The decision making of Moses and his fellow Commissioners laid bare a pattern of improvement and neglect that tracked with the racial composition of identifiable areas along the Hudson River (Caro 1974; Miller, Hallstein, & Quass 1996).

In the 1940s and 1950s New York City leaders debated where to locate a new waste treatment plant to keep up with the needs of a burgeoning population. Moses sat on the City Planning Commission that rejected the Department of Public Works' request to situate the plant between West 70th and 72nd Streets along the Hudson River. Instead, in 1962 during a closed-door meeting and without the knowledge of West Harlem residents, the Planning Commission proposed a site upriver between West 137th and 145th Streets in West Harlem, despite the fact that this location was deemed less scientifically sound ("A Neighborhood Fights Back"; Miller 1993).

Perhaps the most notable chapter in New York City's history is the fiscal crisis of 1975, a budgetary debacle that parallels the experiences of twentieth-century Detroit in striking ways. Once again, the vagaries of capitalist expansion, divestment, and uneven development created social, political, and economic crises in cities across the nation. Like other older cities, New York City was impacted by the flight of manufacturing jobs, a shrinking tax base, and reductions in federal aid to fund state social programs and services. In 1974–1975, the city faced a shortage of credit as it was unable to sell its short-term securities in the bond market (Bailey 1984; Moody 2007: Sites 2003). In June 1975, a group of business and political elite formed the Municipal Assistance Corporation (MAC), a state agency tasked with restructuring the city's debt, monitoring the city's budget, and protecting creditors (Bailey 1984, 27). Essentially, MAC did the bidding of businesses by initiating austerity through wage freezes; salary and pension cuts and lay-offs; transit fare hikes; and a newly instituted tuition at City University of New York (CUNY) (Moody 2007, 37). The New York state legislature assisted MAC in its efforts by passing the Financial Emergency Act in September 1975, which created the Emergency Financial Control Board to oversee the city's budget and ensure the repayment to investors.

New York City's Emergency Act did not constitute a bankruptcy along the lines of 2013 Detroit, but the city's moves to restructure its debts set in place a "crisis regime" that formalized political and economic practices favoring the business elite (Bailey 1984; Moody 2007; Sites 2003). As was the case in Detroit, the pretext of a financial crisis enabled political and business leaders to define both problem and solution in ways that favored a neoliberal agenda. City leaders blamed financial insolvency on the usual suspects—bloated welfare rolls, funding of public housing and hospitals, and the seeming unreasonable demands of unionized city employees (Moody 2007, 49). Low-income and black and brown communities became convenient scapegoats while an important chapter in the history of city growth went unnoticed; namely, the capital flight to places south and overseas and white flight to the suburbs. With these moves city revenues plummeted and urban neighborhoods were left without an adequate tax base.

The solution, then, according to the crisis logic was to rely on market mechanisms to lure businesses back to the city core. New York City was not alone in providing tax subsidies, tax expenditures such as exemptions, and abatements that benefited corporations. One study "estimates that American cities and states gave corporations some $50 billion a year by the early 2000s to attract or retain their business, with little to show for it in terms of jobs" (Moody 2007, 101). Throughout the 1980s–1990s, cities focused on developing finance, insurance, and real estate industries (referred to as FIRE) that moved money around but did not produce goods or social services needed by a majority of the population. Cities like New York in 1975 and Detroit in 2013 use financial crises to "institutionalize the agenda of the corporate headquarters complex and business elite" (Moody 2007, 61). In contrast to the democratic impulse characterizing urban policies of the 1940s–1960s, neoliberal policies and practices paved the way for austerity budgets, retrenchment of social services, neighborhood gentrification, and corporate growth.

The specific framing of urban financial crises—e.g., as caused by city dwellers that suck social services dry—racializes public debates over the uses and users of city spaces. Roger Starr, New York's Housing Administrator under Mayor Beame, proposed "planned shrinkage" in 1976, which was a thinly veiled strategy for ridding the city of its low-income and minority residents (Fried 1976; Starr 1976). His suggestion for cutting essential city services to areas where population has already declined would "accelerate" losses in "certain slum areas" (Fried 1976). "Better a thriving city of 5 million than a Calcutta of seven," Starr wrote in the *New York Times*. Fast forward to 2014 when the county executive of Oakland County, a suburb of Detroit, asserted the way to help Detroit get back on its feet fiscally is to "turn Detroit into an Indian reservation, where we herd all the Indians into the city, build a fence around it, and then throw in the blankets and corn" (Williams 2014). Either way—forcing residents out or fencing them in—the proposed plan creates spaces of exclusion marked by race and class. Spaces become demarcated, attain a symbolic status along race or class lines, making them vulnerable to capitalist strategies of (de)valorization. African American communities have disproportionately borne the brunt of toxic waste disposal and other polluting facilities.

New York City of the 1980s and 1990s continued on the neoliberal path of development, with policies favorable to the FIRE industries (e.g., tax incentives and exemptions), cuts to social services, and neighborhood gentrification and "quality of life" programs that established spaces of upward mobility, leisure, and upper-class consumption (Hyra 2008; Moody 2007; Sites 2003). All of these processes held implications for the racialization of urban spaces, for determining who/what services were unwanted/disposable/excluded (e.g., the homeless, street vendors) and who/what services were invited/welcome.

The process of spatial ex/inclusion played out in a number of high profile housing cases that revealed how easily race, crime, and welfare become conflated in the popular imagination. In 1971, the city proposed a "scatter-site" or low-rise housing project to be built in the Jewish community of Forest Hills, Queens. The proposal was motivated by efforts to integrate black residents who had been relegated to high-rise public housing in areas with deteriorating schools and services. Residents of Forest Hills opposed the plan through a newly formed Forest Hills Residents Association that called the project a "welfare project" and warned residents their neighborhood would be "invaded by hordes of vandals, addicts, [and] muggers" (Newfield & Barrett 1989, 117). Forest Hills residents protested with signs bearing racial epithets. Their efforts paid off, in part, with the final housing plan built on a scale smaller than originally proposed.

Racist assumptions and stereotypes which influence the spatial practices of African Americans, including their mobility, housing options, and general presence in specific urban areas, have always been undergirded by the threat, or actual practice of white violence to enforce exclusion. In the 1980s, in the Howard Beach neighborhood of Queens, a group of white youths armed with baseball bats chased two African American men from their neighborhood. One of the African American men died as he tried to cross a freeway to escape the violent young men. In Bensonhurst, a neighborhood in Brooklyn, a group of white men shot and killed an African American man who had come to the area to examine a used car for sale (Brecher, Horton, Cropf, & Mead 1993). These examples reinforce the observation that spaces are "filled with ideologies" (Lefebvre 1976, 31); in these cases racist assumptions and beliefs that support exclusionary processes identifying who belongs and who does not.

The growth and development of New York City, and Harlem more specifically, was facilitated not only through overt racist practices and ideologies but also through "laissez-faire racism," defined as a hands-off approach where "modern racial inequality relies on the market and informal racial bias to re-create, and in some instances sharply worsen, structured racial inequality" (Bobo, Kluegel, & Smith 1997, 17). Two political initiatives—Mayor Rudolph Giuliani's "quality of life" program (discussed in chapter 5) and the 1994 Empowerment Zone project—can be understood as playing a role in laissez-faire racism.

Harlem and Detroit were two of six urban areas designated "empowerment zones" in the 1994 legislation passed by Congress and signed into law by President Bill Clinton. The Upper Manhattan Empowerment Zone (UMEZ), which covered Harlem, sought to develop the area's economy by bringing in businesses and developing a workforce geared toward tourism, retail, and health care. One of the UMEZ's mega-projects was Harlem, USA, a mall that opened in 2000, and included Old Navy, Modell's Sporting Goods, K&G Superstore, and Chase Manhattan Bank. The UMEZ supported these and other corporations such as the Walt Disney Store, Toys R Us, and HMV Records, with a $100 million grant and $250 million in federal tax credits (Chinyelu 1999, 48). The empowerment zone legislation stipulated that seventy-five percent of jobs created go to local residents, but this requirement expired after ten years. To be sure, the UMEZ highlighted benefits to local residents including a $1 million grant and a $1 million loan to assist locally based start-up businesses; a $125,000 grant to the National Jazz Museum; and, a $6 million grant to the Work Development Initiative (Chinyelu 1999, 51).

Another way to view the UMEZ is through a lens that magnifies the dynamics of race and space. In addition to "empowering" traditionally marginalized or neglected urban spaces, empowerment zones can be seen as a means for legitimating and subsidizing corporate entry into previously under-tapped markets. Mamadou Chinyelu (1999) is more explicit in his assessment of the racist implications of the UMEZ. He describes the policy as a "beggar-thy-neighbor policy [that] intentionally establishes a trade imbalance in favor of one group over another. In this case, corporate America, in the embodiment of regional, national and transnational retailers, will give a few jobs to Harlemites (and the other Upper Manhattan residents) in exchange for having access to the $6 billion those 520,000 residents spend annually" (47). Chinyelu describes the UMEZ as a "'foreign' aid program for Harlem, designed to create a few jobs for African-Americans, while simultaneously creating profit for corporate America" (47).

AFRICAN AMERICAN URBAN RESISTANCE

Black residents of New York City did not passively accept racist spatial practices. Black communities have thrived and exercised agency in the face of Jim Crow segregation and other less formal means of enforcing urban marginalization (Goings & Mohl 1996, 3). Through collective efforts referred to as "geographies of resistance" (Keith & Pile 1993, 14) or "spatial justice" (Soja 2010b), residents struggle to control the shape and quality of urban spaces, including the places they live, the air they breathe, and the water they drink.

In the early 1900s, New York City residents in the Bronx and Harlem, among other neighborhoods, formed tenants' rights groups to protest rising rents and dilapidated living conditions. Residents held strikes, blocked evictions, and demanded legislative actions, which came to fruition in the form of "rent laws" (Spencer 1986). African American residents played a leading role in tenants' rights actions through the first few decades of the twentieth century. The Harlem Tenants League, formed in 1928, protested the expiration of the Emergency Rent Laws, held protest meetings, and marched alongside members of the Communist Party who were deeply invested in tenants' rights actions. Richard Moore, the first president of the Harlem Tenants League, framed Jim Crow as a tool of spatial control enacted by the "capitalist caste class." He explained, this system "segregates Negro workers into Jim Crow districts [which] makes these doubly exploited black workers the special prey of rent gougers. Black and white landlords and real estate agents take advantage of this segregation to squeeze the last nickel out of the Negro working class who are penned in the black ghetto" (Naison 1986, 97).

Significant rent strikes and tenant agitation occurred between 1930 and the late 1960s throughout New York City and in Harlem specifically (Naison 1986; Schwartz 1986). In 1930, the Communist led Harlem Unemployment Council assisted residents facing eviction by organizing "interracial defense squads" that returned belongings to the apartments of evicted tenants (Naison 1986, 41). In 1934, when the racial makeup of residents at 291 Edgecombe Avenue changed from white to black, the landlord doubled the rent and stopped making routine repairs. Inspired by the success of on-going strikes and boycotts, Harlem residents living at 281 Edgecombe Avenue initiated a wave of strikes with tenants demanding lower rents and more consistent building maintenance. "By mid-September 1934, the movement, helped by near-unanimous tenant support and intimidating mass picketing . . . won victories in all the buildings it had organized; owners agreed to reductions of three to ten dollars a month plus repairs" (Naison 1986, 115). These strikes led to the formation of the Consolidated Tenants League, which worked primarily through the local court system to establish the legitimacy of tenant rights.

To fight against the bulldozing engendered by Robert Moses and Title I of the Federal Housing Act, Manhattantown residents, whose neighborhood had been marked "blighted" by Moses' Committee on Slum Clearance in 1951, gathered signatures and demonstrated at city hall. The Manhattantown residents garnered support from folks living in Harlem to form the United Community to Save Our Homes, an organization that challenged Title I projects in court. Although they lost in court, the efforts of Save Our Homes was significant for creating solidarity among black residents across neighborhood lines (Schwartz 1986, 156).

Harlem residents' efforts during the 1960s were often led by Jesse Gray of the Community Council on Housing. Gray and Harlem residents used mass rallies, eviction blockades, and court proceedings to protest deplorable building conditions. Gray's organizational tactics "inspired direct action throughout Harlem" during the 1960s (Schwartz 1986, 177). The East Harlem Tenants Council, formed in 1962, used rent strikes in 1964 to successfully force landlords to make building repairs. Another East Harlem group, the Metro-North Citizens Committee provided "rent clinics," tenant counseling, demonstrations, and strikes to win housing rights.

The experiences of residents in the primarily African American Corona-East Elmhurst neighborhood in Queens were instructive in pointing to the ways official city planning documents (e.g., surveys, studies, maps) — seemingly neutral in content and intention — act hegemonically to reinforce racist assumptions and practices surrounding urban growth/decline. The Federal Housing Act of 1961, like its 1949 legal predecessor, authorized $2.5 billion for urban renewal efforts and jump-started city efforts to locate areas defined as "blighted" and in need of uplift. New York's City Planning Commission crafted a decidedly race-neutral understanding of Corona-East Elmhurst's geographic challenges and "renewal needs," obscuring the "impact of institutional racism" on the living conditions of the area's residents (Gregory 1998, 88–89).

In 1994, Corona residents fought against the placement of an elevated rail system through their neighborhood on the grounds the massive transportation project posed an environmental risk to their community (Gregory 1998). To appease concerns of the environmental impact on the Corona neighborhood, Queens officials reframed the project in scientific terms, drawing on the logic of technology as a means for addressing the issues (Gregory 1998, 222). Further, in public debates with Corona residents, the New York State Department of Transportation circumscribed the debate over the transit system by "shielding wider issues of urban development and environmental justice from public disclosure and scrutiny while funneling opposition into insulated pockets of technical expertise and problem solving" (222). Gregory (1998) reveals how residents' broad-based critique focusing on environmental justice was undermined and/or ignored through a combination of maneuvers that ensured public officials maintained control over the nature and content of the public debate (218–247).

Another example of collective resistance against the encroachment of industry on a predominately black neighborhood is embodied in the efforts of Peggy Shepard, Chuck Sutton, David Paterson, Hilton Clark and three others who put on gas masks, held large signs, and blocked morning traffic on the West Side Highway in January 1988 to protest the foul air in their neighborhood created by the North River Sewage Treatment Plant. The plant, originally set to be constructed at 70th Street along the

Hudson River in Manhattan, was moved for political reasons "upriver to 137th Street after key developers lobbied to stop construction at the first location" (Shepard 1993, 741). West Harlem residents became aware of the location of the plant in their neighborhood after the deal had been brokered (Miller, Hallstein & Quass, 1996). In order to meet a federally mandated deadline for completion, the plant opened in May 1986 before it was "fully constructed and operational," accompanied by a host of environmental concerns including a noxious odor that permeated the homes of nearby residents (Miller, Hallstein & Quass 1996, 67; Shepard 1993, 741). When residents such as Peggy Shepard received no help from city leaders to address the problems stemming from the plant, they took matters into their own hands, using direct action and forming the West Harlem Environmental Action group (WE ACT). Struggles with the "health disparities created by the (mis) operation of the North River Sewage Treatment Plant" prompted the group's formation in 1988 ("WE ACT—Dedicated," 2009, 1). But "what was initially an isolated assault on quality of life was reassessed as one which was not only environmental in nature but also social and political and could not be separated from the broader issue of quality of life in West Harlem" (Miller, Hallstein & Quass 1996, 73). The group explicitly notes that "institutionalized racism . . . has led to the siting and mismanagement of toxic facilities uptown [Manhattan] and that black and low income communities have been excluded from the political process" ("WE ACT—Dedicated," 2009, 1). These efforts sit squarely within the larger movement for environmental justice.

URBAN RESISTANCE AND ENVIRONMENTAL JUSTICE

When it comes to race and city spaces, environmental justice is about the economics and politics of location. It is no accident that the communities most at risk for removal/toxicity are communities of color (Bullard 1994; Krauss 1993; Walker 2012). In response to deaths and illnesses resulting from corporate dumping, air pollution, and waste disposal, communities of color have fought back. In 1982 Warren County, South Carolina, residents were jailed as they attempted to prevent a PCB landfill from being located in their rural community (Bullard 1994, 5). Their efforts marked the birth of the environmental justice movement and "led to the racialization of environmentalism" (Pulido 1996, 151; see also Pezzullo 2001).

Observing the link between toxic dumping and black and brown communities, the United Church of Christ Commission for Racial Justice and its executive director, Rev. Benjamin Chavis, conducted a study that indeed uncovered a "systematic" connection between location and race. In fact, the study found that "although socio-economic status appeared to play an important role in the location of commercial hazardous waste facilities, race still proved to be more significant" (Grossman 1994, 277). The Commission's study led to the 1987 publication, *Toxic Waste and Race in the United States*, which concluded, "nonwhites are disproportionately exposed to pollution" (Pulido 2000, 12). The study also found that 40 percent of the country's "landfill capacity is concentrated in three communities—two that are 80–90 percent African American and a third that is nearly 80% Latino" (DiChiro 1992, 99). Insights from the study prompted Chavis to coin the term environmental racism, which he defined as "racial discrimination in environmental policy making and the enforcement of regulations and laws, the deliberate targeting of people of color communities for toxic waste facilities, the official sanctioning of the life-threatening presence of poisons and pollutants in our communities, and the history of excluding people of color from leadership in the environmental movement" (Di Chiro 1992, 99, 100). An updated report, *Toxic Wastes and Race at Twenty, 1987–2007*, found that "host neighborhoods with commercial hazardous waste facilities are 56% people of color whereas non-host areas are 30% people of color" (Bullard et al., 2007, 52) and that throughout the 1990s, the percentage of people of color living near hazardous facilities actually increased (53).

Broader than environmentalism—a movement centered on preservation and dominated by white, middle- and upper-class individuals—the environmental justice movement focuses on issues of health, community survival, workplace safety, and economic sustainability, from a racialized perspective (Di Chiro 1992; Pulido 1996). Bullard (2001) defines environmental racism as "any policy, practice, or directive that differentially affects or disadvantages (whether intended or unintended) individuals, groups, or communities based on race or color" (160). Environmental justice efforts draw the dots between corporate practices—often subsidized by tax breaks and government funding—and the experiences of low-income families and communities of color that bear the brunt of health hazards stemming from corporate dumping and disinvestment ("Environmental Justice in the United States" 2002). More than a concern with protecting ocean life and endangered species, the agenda of people of color in the environmental justice movement is "holistic" (Pulido 1996, 165) encompassing safe housing, mobility, and health as they are linked to location. Environmental justice efforts center people in the environment by examining how issues concerning air, water, and housing quality impact people's abilities to live healthy, dignified lives (DiChiro, 1992). Often, environmental justice advocates align their efforts with those of civil rights, labor, welfare rights, and farmworkers (DiChiro, 1992, 97). And importantly, Pulido (2000) suggests understanding environmental racism as more than the malicious acts of various and unrelated toxic sitings to a view that situates environmental concerns vis-á-vis structural racism, white privilege, and "larger urban processes" (13).

In 1991, activists came together to hold the First National People of Color Environmental Leadership Summit in Washington, D.C. Summit attendees adopted a 17-point statement, "Principles of Environmental Justice," that included numerous demands concerning the intersections of spatial inclusion, race, and health. Principles included the "right to ethical, balanced and responsible uses of land and renewable resources"; expressed opposition to "military occupations, repression and exploitation of lands, peoples and culture"; and called "for universal protection from nuclear testing, extraction, production and disposal of toxic/hazardous wastes and poisons and nuclear testing that threatens the fundamental right to clean air, land, water and food" ("Principles" 1991). Notably, principles also encompassed issues of labor and housing emphasizing the "right of all workers to a safe and healthy work environment," and the "need for urban and rural ecological policies to clean up and rebuild our cities and rural areas in balance with nature, honoring the cultural integrity of our communities, and providing fair access for all to the full range of resources" ("Principles" 1991).

Environmental justice efforts have also been associated with women's activism (Krauss 1993, 1994). DiChiro (1992) asserts the "vast majority of activists in the environmental justice movement are low-income women and predominantly women of color" (93). One of the earliest and most recognizable names associated with environmental advocacy is Lois Gibbs, who became involved in environmental health issues when she learned her community in New York, Love Canal, was built atop a toxic waste dump. In their positions as caretakers and mothers, women have developed perspectives and interests that predispose them to the health-centered efforts of environmental justice. The alignment of womanhood and environmental issues is enveloped in the organizational document, Empowering Ourselves: Women and Toxics Organizing, which was an outgrowth of the Women in Toxics Organizing conference in November 1987 (Peeples & DeLuca 2006, 62). In their arguments for healthy communities, women often tapped traditional tropes of motherhood and family (Krauss 1993), which is not surprising given the sexual division of labor that positions women as primarily in charge of the health and well-being of their children and homes (Krauss 1994, 260). West Harlem Environmental Action, the organization whose efforts are the focus of this and the following chapter, was shaped by "women's interests, concerns, experiences, and knowledge" (Miller, Hallstein, & Quass 1996, 62). The organization's success can be attributed, in part, to black women's community networks and their common concerns for the health and well-being of their children. When the North River Sewage Treatment Plant began operation in 1986 and noxious odors began to emanate from the facility, "women and seniors came to the forefront" and remained for a decades long community struggle (69).

To advance their arguments, working-class women and women of color often eschewed bureaucratic language in favor of storytelling, centering particularly on their experiences as mothers (Krauss 1994, 259). Activists referenced their experiences dealing with their children's illnesses, diseases, even deaths and miscarriages due to toxic exposure. They used their stories to justify and lend credibility to their arguments (DiChiro 1992; Krauss 1994; Peeples & DeLuca 2006). Their emphasis on family and community survival sits within a long tradition of militant motherhood (Tonn 1996) and motherwork (Collins 1994) that used the family as a springboard for efforts and arguments of economic and political justice. Motherwork refers to the efforts of women of color to ensure the "physical survival both of their own biological children and of those of the larger African-American community" (Collins 1994, 61). Similarly, militant motherhood refers to a rhetorical strategy combining nurturance and confrontation to promote/protect the interests of marginalized communities, including one's immediate family. Together motherwork and militancy provided the entry point for women of color to the environmental justice movement. The African American environmental justice activist, Cora Tucker, explained the matter this way:

> This white woman from an environmental group asked me to come down to save a park. She said that they had been trying to get Black folks involved and that they won't come. I said, "Honey, it's not that they aren't concerned, but when their babies are dying in their arms they don't give a damn about a park." I said, "They want to save their babies. If you can help them save their babies, then in turn they can help you save your park." And she said, "But this is a real immediate problem." And I said, "Well, these people's kids dying is immediate." (Krauss 1993, 256)

Likewise, Aurora Castillo, a member of Mothers of East Los Angeles, drew on the urgency of motherhood as she explained her environmental justice efforts, "you know, if one of [her] children's safety is jeopardized, the mother turns into a lioness" (Gutierrez 1994, 223).

Women's reliance on personal stories aligns with a "feminine style" of communicating characterized by "personal tone, disclosure of personal experiences, reliance on anecdotes and analogies as primary forms of evidence ... and encouragement of audience identification and participation" (Peeples & DeLuca 2006, 65). This rhetorical approach was instrumental at convincing "women to believe that they are capable of changing their circumstances," an important goal given the socialization of women and mothers to remain sequestered in the home and focused on domestic affairs (68). Importantly, women's mothering experiences offered not only an argumentative but an epistemological location—a standpoint (described above and in the Introduction)—from which to ground and position an understanding of the world, specifically one in which race and neighborhood location often determined quality and longevity of life. To invoke the standpoint of African American women as mothers does not require a flattening of the differences among women but rather enables us to understand the common experiences of toxicity and illness as inseparable from black women's social location within a larger set of structures that privileges the interests of a largely white corporate class. Explaining the role of women in the formation and sustenance of the West Harlem Environmental Action, Miller, Hallstein, and Quass (1996) point to the "supportive networks of black women" who came together "to preserve their quality of life" (63).

SPACE, RACE, AND THE BODY: SOME THEORETICAL CONSIDERATIONS

The concept of standpoint suggests the importance of exploring the ways that the body works in tandem with spatial configurations to create nodes of both oppression and resistance. For oppressed/disenfranchised/marginalized groups, issues of the body and space have figured prominently. The bodies of women, slaves, the disabled, and the poor have always been open to scrutiny, disciplining, displacement, toxicity, and control. In Honduras, pro-union and pro-democracy bodies/activists are disappeared and entire community bodies are vulnerable to evictions at the hands of transnational corporations that have the support of the government. Migrant farmworkers in the United States who pick our grapes and lettuce live in dirty camps and are exposed to pesticides that have made their children vulnerable to childhood cancers (Moses 1993). Historically, space has also aligned closely with the gendered body, as women have been ascribed their place "in the home," while primarily white men of privilege have controlled access to, and the workings of public spaces (Massey 1994). And scholars have noted the ways that race correlates with environmental vulnerability and the placement of toxic dumping (Bullard & Wright 2009). This observation resonates powerfully with black residents of New Orleans struggling to rebuild in the wake of the toxic disaster left by Hurricane Katrina (Bullard & Wright 2009; see also Bullard 2000; Cole & Foster 2001; Collin & Harris 1993).

For disempowered groups, establishing a bodily/physical presence in politics, the workforce, or in the broader culture has always been a central task. For campesinos in Honduras, establishing a firm physical presence on their land is central for sustenance and cultural survival. For industrial workers in the United States and abroad, the body is the instrument by which one sustains oneself and is also the site of exploitation. Collective bodies located in a strategic place, for example, factory floor or public park, have provided a vocal and material presence (e.g., United Auto Workers' sit-down strike of 1936-1937 and Occupy Wall Street) and have often been effective at forcing the hand of those in power (Simons 1972; Triece 2001, 2007). Certain bodies—standing on the public platform—have made compelling arguments simply through their physical presence, referred to as "enactment" (Campbell & Jamieson 1978). Thus do issues of the body and space come together.

When it comes to studies of space, communication scholars have often entered through the postmodern/poststructuralist door to engage what has been termed the "spatial turn" that, according to Denis Cosgrove (1999), corresponds to the postmodern/poststructuralist skepticism toward unified narrative and authentic voice (7). Notably, the spatial turn recognizes that "position and context are centrally and inescapably implicated in all constructions of knowledge" (7). What is curious about many communication studies influenced by the spatial turn is the absence of real bodies in physical locations, particularly given what we know about the imprint that physical location leaves on the body. Mediation and materiality are collapsed through "texturality" (Conley & Dickinson 2010, 4). Focus on biopower and articulation has replaced capitalist critique (Stormer 2010). And "clinamen" and "aleatory style" unseat collective action instigated in strategic public spaces (Conley 2010, 25).

In earlier chapters I suggested a return to the work of Marx and Engels for understanding issues around capitalist accumulation and city growth/abandonment and displacement. Likewise, Marx and Engels' writings on the laboring body and the geographical movement of capital provide an apt starting point for understanding the nexus of bodies and space. At a historical moment marked by exploitation of bodies in sweatshops, human trafficking, and land evictions, it is hard to ignore Marx's (1844/1978) understanding of the body as experiential, laboring, and motivated by physical needs. Marx set his view of human experience against his contemporaneous philosopher, Hegel, who posited that "mind is the true essence of man," that the "humanness of nature and of the nature begotten by history . . . appears in the form that they are products of abstract mind and as such, therefore, phases of mind" (111). In contrast, Marx and Engels (1845/1970) understood consciousness not in a pure form but as a "social product" (51)—"life is not determined by consciousness, but consciousness by life" (47).

A Marxist theory of human relationships and the production of life opens the door to understanding the connection between body and space, evoking the way the body is grounded within a particular historical location and the ways sites are shaped by human behavior. Marx (1844/1978) conceived of humans as "natural, corporeal, sensuous, objective" beings "conditioned and limited" by needs (115). Above all, humans are connected through "sensuous activity," that is, "labor and creation" (Marx & Engels 1845/1970, 171). Human sensuous activity is not static, nor a given for all time, but is the "product of industry and the state of society" in a given epoch (170). Put differently, physical bodies are not abstractions or mere affect but are "corporeal." Humans stand with "feet firmly on the solid ground, . . . exhaling and inhaling all the forces of nature" (Marx, 1844/1978, 115).

Importantly humans' sensuous experiences shape perspectives on relationships and society. Standpoint refers to the knowledge gained from one's position within the larger system of human activity contributing to the meeting of physical needs. The concept of standpoint—developed by Georg Lukács and Nancy Hartsock, among others—stems from an understanding of society as fundamentally rooted in the production of society's basic needs (Marx & Engels 1845/1970, 48). Production positions humans within social relationships that have a material, that is, corporeal/physical, impact on bodies in space. One example is the way industrial pollution and dumping manifests on the bodies of marginalized groups in systematic ways. Black communities have responded by demanding recognition of the black body in neighborhoods and asserting the body as a point of departure for social critique.

This chapter and the following one draw on Marxist thought in order to reseat the sensuous body within space(s) contoured by historical change. I examine vernacular discourses of environmental justice for the ways "geographical knowledge" shapes common understandings of the organization of spaces "that provide the material basis for the reproduction of social life" (Harvey 1984, 1). Conducting rhetorical analysis within a framework of historical materialism prompts us to recognize that space is marked above all by material systems and structures—for example, geographical layout, neighborhood infrastructure, industrial or service economies—that constrain and enable bodily movement and physical/mental well-being in ways that often fall along the lines of race, class, sex, ability, etc. This observation regarding the link between bodies and space is made clear by the fact that one's zip code is a determinant of one's health and mortality (Arrieta, White, & Crook 2008; Benson 2009).

MARKET DYNAMICS VS. COUNTERMAPPING

Grossberg (1993) notes, "power and resistance are defined by the spatial relations of places and spaces, and the distribution of people and practices within them" (15). Even as cultural meanings attached to specific locales vary and change over time, "cities are also material spaces with relative stability and rigidity that shape and bound people's lives and determine the types of encounters possible in public spaces" (Caldeira 1999, 102).

Patterns of toxic dumping are significant, indeed may be mapped, even as they remain invisible to and unspoken within popular imagination and discourse. In what follows, I examine how environmental justice advocates used mapping to highlight the politicized process of location and placement. Rhetorically, mapping draws on the topoi of relationality creating an "ecology of place" (Armstrong & Shumack 2011) that drafts/draws localities in relation to other variables, for example, asthma, lead, air pollution, waste facilities. The WE ACT website provided a counter-space for developing a resistant "geographic imaginary" (Ewalt 2011, 337) through countermapping.

Walker (2012) has observed the ways city leaders, economists, and industrialists utilize a discourse of "market dynamics" to explain and justify facility placement. According to this narrative, siting is "explained as a consequence of the decision-making of rational actors operating within a market system" (92). This market driven framing is similar to the rhetoric of Detroit's urban planners who bolstered their arguments for city growth by referencing the neoliberal appeal to rationality, opportunity, and individualism. The inequalities resulting from urban renewal, whether in the form of gentrification or toxic facility expansion/siting, are justified as "natural" outcomes or consequences of progress and growth and the processes remain unquestioned and commonly accepted as "good" (who doesn't want "progress"?). Additionally, the racial implications of such a logic are obscured and/or remain invisible.

The racist dimensions of mapping are not always hidden. Chapter 1 discussed how the government agency, the Home Owners' Loan Corporation (HOLC), mapped and color-coded areas in order to demarcate and separate racially coded "good" areas from "bad." "Residential Security Maps," developed by the HOLC and circulated among lending institutions (Massey & Denton 1993, 52), rated black neighborhoods "hazardous" and outlined them in red, leading to the practice of redlining which facilitated the wholesale disinvestment in black neighborhoods (Massey & Denton 1993; Sugrue 1996).

Of interest here is the way mapping operates hegemonically—as a form of common sense that remains unquestioned—and how organizations may utilize mapping as a form of resistance. To call out the political intersection of race and space, WE ACT promoted mapping, both graphic and verbal, as a rhetorical strategy to counter neoliberal appeals to rationality that obscure the biased and interested ways that markets operate. Mapping enabled advocates to highlight the centrality of race and space in the lives of West Harlem residents. The use of mapping on the part of environmental justice advocates sheds light on the ways maps may be used as a mode of resistance to counter the more traditional uses of maps, which have been employed to assert spatial hegemony (Sparke 1998). That is, maps have more commonly been viewed as official documents that simply display location and topography; maps present as neutral, as a "scientific or objective form of knowledge" (Harley 2011, 56), and thus instill a fixity to prevailing understandings of the spatial layout of a given area. As such, maps often elude dispute or contest; they purport to merely describe even as they are deployed hegemonically to fix space and place, to label, control and colonize, to identify nation-state.

Although traditionally viewed as attempts to fix place through representation, maps are better understood as a "site of social contest," a battle "over the power to label space-time, to impose the meaning to be attributed to a space" (Massey 1994, 5). Mapmaking may operate persuasively as social control or social change (Barney 2009, 413). Wood and Fels (2011) articulate the rhetoricity of mapping as they point out maps are a "cultural artefact, a cumulation of choices made among choices every one of which reveals a value: not the world but a slice of a piece of the world; not nature but a slant on it; not innocent, but loaded with intentions and purposes" (51). Mapping is a "process of constant re-territorialisation . . . maps are transitory and fleeting, being contingent, relational and context-dependent" (Kitchin & Dodge 2011, 109; see also Black 1997; Harley 2001). As rhetorical artifacts—contingent and up for debate—maps hold participatory and democratic potentials and may lay the ground for organizing "collective action around spaces of injustice" (Ewalt 2011, 334; see also Barney 2013; Bauer 2009; Corburn 2005, 173–199). Labor activists, particularly those in farming, have employed workplace-risk mapping to chart exposure to toxins where they work (Mujica 1992).

Environmental justice advocates have drawn on the authority of mapping—its reference to a material location—to overlay *bodily*, that is, physical, experience, in essence creating epistemologies of race and health located in larger systemic economic and political processes and decision making. In this way, mapping serves as an "evidential weapon" (Barney 2013, 317), a way to challenge dominant knowledge claims (e.g., those of city planners and corporate polluters) that negate or minimize the claims of black residents advocating for the health of their homes and communities. Mapping offers one way for organizing and presenting locally generated knowledge to a wider audience. Scholars have referred to this cartography effort as "participatory mapping" (Bauer 2009) or "counter-mapping" (Ewalt 2011). Participatory mapping refers to the vernacular uses of ordinary mapping or GIS technologies for the purpose of "breaking down entrenched power structures" supported by dominant maps (Bauer 2009, 234). Likewise countermapping refers to the use of maps to "resist social, economic, or global oppression" (Ewalt 2011, 334). Counter-mapping may support "collective action frames" (Benford & Snow 2000, 614), which offer a representation/understanding of city toxicity and race that contrasts with dominant framings and that mobilizes environmental justice supporters. That is, in contrast to the rhetorics of city planners and engineers who focused on function and design when it came to the issue of waste plant emissions, environmental justice advocates advanced frames that mapped—and thus repositioned—the problem and solution onto a space and, importantly, tied in the issue of race.

Environmental justice advocates utilized both verbal and visual maps to assert knowledge claims about race and health. Residents deployed "spatial narratives" (Dickinson 2006, 214) alongside graphic mapping to advance an argument that revealed the connections between race, health, and location. In this way, mapping represented an important rhetorical tool for environmental justice advocates in West Harlem. Verbal and visual mappings offered a "place-frame" that "highlight[ed] the potential relationship between activism based on an idea of neighborhood and the material experiences of that place" (Martin 2003, 733). Black residents in West Harlem challenged traditional understandings of urban planning and toxicity that denied a connection between race and the placement of toxic facilities.

The WE ACT website contained links to 31 maps created by WE ACT member Carlos Jusino. The maps used color gradations to depict differences in various health indicators according to location in and around Manhattan, Queens, Brooklyn, and the Bronx. For example, the map, "Asthma Hospitalizations Rates by ZIP Code," illustrated asthma rates among children in Manhattan (see figure 4.1). The darkest shade of brown—representing hospitalization rates of 257–505 per 10,000—clustered around neighborhoods in Northern Manhattan, such as Harlem. Zip codes were placed on the map to underscore the relationship between asthma rates and spatial location, giving credence to studies that indicate the single biggest determinant of one's health is the zip code in which one resides, what one doctor called "almost death by zip code."[6] The map positioned icons representing the location of various polluting facilities, including MTA bus depots, DOT diesel truck depots, marine waste transfer stations, and sewage treatment plants. The color clusters, zip code labels, and icons translated into "data visualization" that enabled viewers to detect important patterns that otherwise may go unnoticed (Davisson 2011, 115). The map relied on an overlay of icons and colors that functioned holistically to establish an argument about health, facility sitings, and resident location. WE ACT's maps established spaces as "experienced, as opposed to imagined" and thus connected the represented space on the map "to an idea of the real" (Cosgrove 1999, 12).

Further, the information on this map operated intertextually with the map, "MTA Diesel Bus Depots In Communities of Color," in order to seam race to health and location (see figure 4.2). "MTA Diesel Bus Depots" displayed the placement of bus depots with red dots and mapped the percentage of people of color residing throughout Manhattan and surrounding boroughs. Northern Manhattan and the Bronx were awash in brown, indicating a population consisting of 81–100 percent people of color. When viewed with other maps such as "The Asthma, Diesel Connection" and "The Diesel Bus Pollution Correlation" one gets a clear sense of the disproportionate number of polluting facilities situated in minority neighborhoods (see figures 4.3 and 4.4).

Figure 4.1. Asthma Hospitalizations Rates by ZIP Code. Created by Carlos M. Jusino, Information Systems and Technology Manager/GIS Mapping Specialist. *Source:* Used with permission from WE ACT For Environmental Justice, New York, NY.

The maps operated persuasively in at least four ways. First, maps promoted a politics of visibility that demystified the apparent neutrality and rationality associated with grids (Sassen 1996, 191). Broadly speaking, visibility politics "move individuals and collectives out and away from the shadows and margins . . . into the light of public spaces"

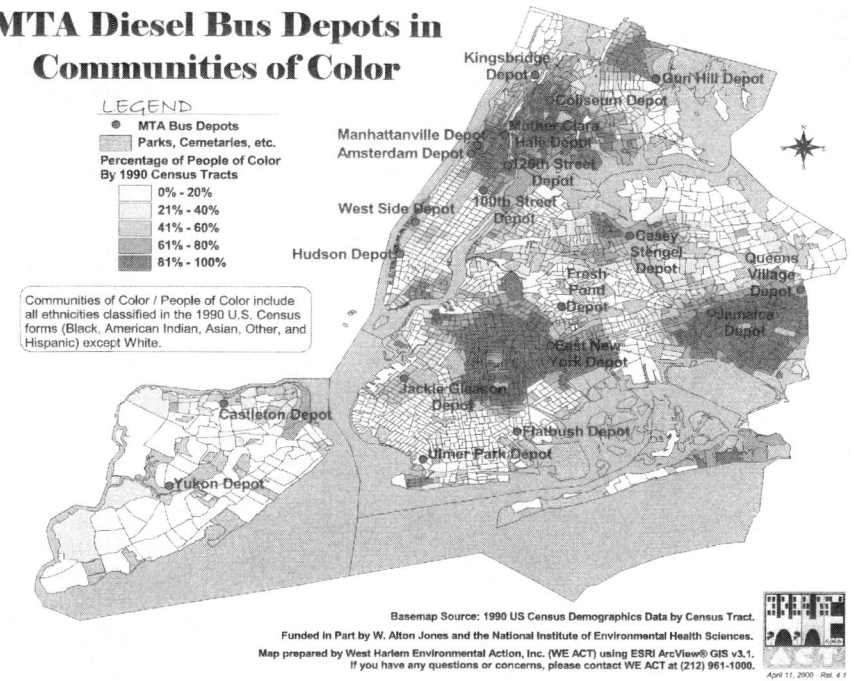

Figure 4.2. MTA Diesel Bus Depots in Communities of Color. Created by Carlos M. Jusino, Information Systems and Technology Manager/GIS Mapping Specialist. *Source:* **Used with permission from WE ACT For Environmental Justice, New York, NY.**

(Brouwer 1998, 118). Mapping offers one rhetorical option for "increasing the visibility of marginalized groups" and "can be used as a credible and graphic base from which to launch political campaigns" (Bauer 2009, 234). WE ACT's mapping demanded recognition of a community and that area's health experiences in a context in which those experiences were elided, ignored, or outright denied. To this extent, the organization's maps served an epistemological function, a visual representation of a body of knowledge based on statistical data but borne of firsthand experience.

Second, maps provide a way to distill data in a form that may be readily understood. As graphic representations maps are "used to place aggregate data . . . into a recognizably compressed and simplified emblem" (Barney 2013, 322). Color-coding prompts the viewer to see the spatial connections between asthma rates, race, and residency at a glance. The clustering of dark colors in and around the Bronx and Harlem asserted an argument about the connections between race, health, and the

The Asthma, Diesel Connection

Diesel Fuel Polluting Facilities, MTA Depot Expansions, and 1996 Asthma Hospitalizations For Children 0-4 Years Old in Manhattan

Figure 4.3. The Asthma, Diesel Connection. Created by Carlos M. Jusino, Information Systems and Technology Manager/GIS Mapping Specialist. *Source:* Used with permission from WE ACT For Environmental Justice, New York, NY.

placement of various toxic facilities sitting above 96th Street, indicated by a dotted line on some of the maps.

Further, as visual displays, maps provided a way to render visible the racialized and systematic relationship between race, health, and location. Maps provided a useful tool for emphasizing patterns, in this case, those

Mapping Race 111

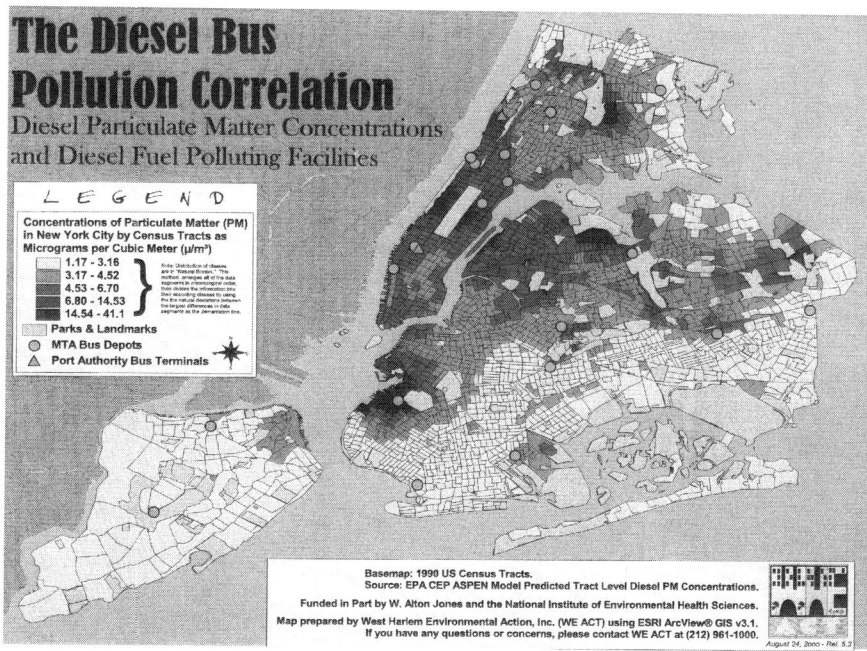

Figure 4.4. The Diesel Bus Pollution Correlation. Created by Carlos M. Jusino, Information Systems and Technology Manager/GIS Mapping Specialist. *Source:* Used with permission from WE ACT For Environmental Justice, New York, NY.

of illnesses and physical toxicity that clustered in specific racially marked locations. Maps offer an argument based on relationality; they provided a rhetorical tool for illustrating and underscoring environmental justice advocates' key point, that low-income, minority communities are disproportionately targeted as sites for toxic dumping and waste disposal. In this way, maps countered the arguments of city planners and engineers that emphasized functionality or how to render a toxic/waste facility a "friendly neighbor" by ensuring it is designed and operating correctly.

Finally, although the correlation between race and dumping has been verified by numerous studies,[7] mapping software and Internet technology afforded environmental justice advocates a way to localize the issue of toxicity by charting their health experiences in a quantifiable manner. Mapping software has been explored for its "ability to convey complicated messages through cartographic images without any formal training in cartography" (Davisson 2011, 106). For WE ACT supporters, mapping facilitated the organization's value of letting "communities speak for themselves" (Shepard 2008). We ACT's Environmental Health and Community-Based Participatory Research efforts provided lessons to residents on surveying and mapping "so that they can assess the risks of high concentrations of bus diesel fumes in their neighborhoods" (Mock 2009). In this way, mapping provided one tool among many that enabled residents to tell their own stories of health disparities. User-generated maps provide ordinary people a vehicle for inserting their experiences visually, "challenging traditional . . . maps" considered the domain of "experts"—scientists and cartographers— and even countering mainstream media representations that influence how the public understands race and health (see Davisson 2011, 102).

Notably, maps encapsulated quantifiable information that bolstered the credibility of narrative mapping, which verbally described facility sitings and the health issues experienced by citizens. Indeed, it was the racialized politics of location surrounding the North River Sewage Treatment Plant that jump-started WE ACT's formation. WE ACT's website explained the organization was founded

> as the result of local community struggles around environmental threats and resulting health disparities created by institutionalized racism and the lack of social and political capital, all dynamics that led to the siting and poor management of the North River Sewage Treatment Plant, the siting and operation of 6 out of 7 New York City diesel bus depots in Northern Manhattan, the operation in our community of the only 24-hour Marine Transfer Station in Manhattan, the use of Northern Manhattan communities as New York City's dumping ground. ("History of WE ACT")

Like the maps on the WE ACT website, this description visualizes the clustering of toxin-emitting facilities in and around primarily black and Latino communities residing in the northern section of Manhattan.

In contrast to the neoliberal construction of the body as autonomous and emboldened by free choice, mobility, and opportunity, environmental justice advocates located the body within a constraining physical location. The body was impinged upon by a host of factors, but as the next chapter shows, residents appointed the stressed/ill body as a knowing body, an epistemological point of departure from which to enact agency. WE ACT's primary campaigns centered on location and placement, vis-à-vis the black body. Through both design and content, the website for WE ACT reinforces the organization's spatial narratives. WE ACT's defining phrase displayed prominently on the home page—"The environment is where we . . . live, work, play, pray and learn"—links disparate physical locations together through reference to environment.[8] Further, each location—home, workplace, recreation area, church, school—is described in terms of the physical activity engaged therein. The website is organized into "domains" that register with different locations that chart everyday movements and physical (im)mobility. These include "clean air," "equitable transit," "pesticide reduction," "toxic free products," "food in schools," "sustainable land use," "open and green space," and "healthy indoor environments."[9] The website and the group's activities call attention to each of these locales, particularly as they are marked as "black" and/or "low income" and thus open to toxic exposure in ways other areas of Manhattan are not.

For instance, the website links seemingly personal health issues like chronic stress and asthma to "social stressors (like poverty)" to show spatial correlation and clustering in low-income neighborhoods ("Community Stressors and Susceptibility to Air Pollution in Urban Asthma"). The WE ACT newsletters, *Harlem Community Voices* and the *Uptown Eye*, rhetorically yoked location to health through articles that called out the raced dimension of spatial locations—the home, the community, the city—and the ways the body therein was impacted.[10] Articles regularly reminded readers that "residents of Harlem and Washington Heights are disproportionately exposed to environmental hazards, both within the home and out in the neighborhood" ("WE ACT and Columbia University," 2001). A *Harlem Community Voices* article pointed out how toxic "chemicals have silently invaded our [black and brown] communities" ("Are You Safe?" 2010; "Toxic Substance Control Act" 2011). One article cited a study from the Columbia Center for Children's Environmental Health that found "members of the communities of Washington Heights, Harlem and the South Bronx [predominately people of color and low income] are disproportionately affected by environmental toxins" ("Are You Safe?" 2010). An article appearing the following year asserted "there is undeniable evidence that communities of color and low income are most affected by the noxious chemicals that should be regulated under TSCA [Toxic Substance Control Act] ("Toxic Substance Control Act" 2011).

Articles rooting specific health issues in location also worked to rhetorically broaden an understanding of health/illness as not only a matter of the personal body but as shaped by more broad-reaching structures. A study published in the March/April 2004 issue of the *Uptown Eye* noted that polluted air "ubiquitous in Northern Manhattan" contributed to lower birth weights and smaller head size of infants born to mothers living in that area (Greaves 2004). A 2009 *Harlem Community Voices* article located lead-based paint and dust in "buildings and homes built before 1978" and noted that 89 percent of the housing in Northern Manhattan, an area dominated by black and Latino/a communities, was built prior to 1978 ("Lead Poisoning Remains" 2009). Two years later, *Harlem Community Voices* carried an article detailing the extent to which "New York City's immigrant population" is situated in "homes contaminated with indoor pollution and dangerous concentrations of lead" ("Preventing Lead Poisoning" 2011). And a 2011 article on lead poisoning in the homes of immigrants employed the spatial tropes of "foreign soil," "concrete jungle," and "land of opportunity" to point out immigrants often end up occupying the most deteriorated of dwellings in the city ("Preventing

Lead Poisoning" 2011). Another article raised the issue of food and health arguing "obesity, diabetes, and other diet related illnesses" are not a result of personal choices but "from the way our city is constructed and the way it is run" ("Faith Leaders" 2010). These descriptions represented spatial narratives, verbal mappings that provided vivid and personalized visualization of spaces and gave fuller voice to traditional maps generated by justice advocates. Importantly, spatializing health provided a way to illustrate patterned racist practices of neglect and development that refocused blame on broad based institutions and political processes as opposed to personal decision making.

One of WE ACT's most significant campaigns focused on the placement of bus depots throughout Manhattan. Transit issues resonate with the history of the U.S. civil rights movement marked by the Montgomery Bus Boycott and the Freedom Rides, both of which linked issues of geographic mobility and race. Transit discrimination—placement, development, accessibility—exposes the "significant racial, class, and geographical biases embedded in all forms of public planning" (Soja 2010b, xiii). The WE ACT website explained that "some New Yorkers—particularly low-income residents, communities of color, the disabled, the elderly, and children—are disproportionately burdened by the inadequacies of our transportation system" ("New York State Transportation Equity Alliance (NYSTEA)"). Taken-for-granted, widely accepted, and thus normalized urban planning practices such as those explored in chapter 3 also impact issues surrounding mass transportation.

For WE ACT, the issue concerned the ways mass transportation pollution disproportionately impacts black and brown communities through the placement of depots. In 1997, WE ACT launched a Dirty Diesel Campaign with the slogan, "If you live uptown, breathe at your own risk," cinching the connection between race, place (uptown), and health. The campaign sought, among other things, to encourage the Metropolitan Transit Authority (MTA) to follow through on its promises to replace dirtier diesel buses with clean burning buses and to renovate depots to equip them for receiving clean burning buses (Shepard, Corbin-Mark, & Foster 2006). The campaign—funded by an EPA Pollution Prevention grant—utilized a variety of communication outlets to map the relationship between asthma, polluted air caused by buses, and black communities. WE ACT used bus shelter advertisements, a 30-second public service announcement aired on a Spanish language cable station, brochures, buttons, and stickers to inform residents of the air quality in their community (Shepard 2005/2006). Advocates also distributed maps charting depot locations and asthma rates in Northern Manhattan (Shepard 2005/2006). And in 2006, WE ACT Executive Director Peggy Shepard and WE ACT Deputy Director, Cecil Corbin-Mark, and Sheila Foster of Fordham University Law School provided testimony to the New York City Council on transit pollution in Northern Harlem.

The message repeated throughout the campaign concerned the patterned placement of bus depots in ways that disproportionately impacted the health and well-being of Northern Manhattan residents, especially children. WE ACT documents recounted a spatial narrative that visually clustered depots in black and brown neighborhoods giving credence to claims of environmental racism. In testimony to the New York City Council, Peggy Shepard, Cecil Corbin-Mark, and Sheila Foster pointed out "over 82% of Manhattan's entire diesel bus fleet—more than 1,000 buses—is presently housed, maintained and traveling into and out of NYCT depts. located north of 96th Street, even though this section comprises less than 31% of Manhattan's total land area" (2). Articles carried in the *Uptown Eye* and on WE ACT's website provided similar observations noting even depots servicing routes that "never travel to Northern Manhattan" were located in the area, further underscoring the dubious planning of depot location ("The Greenest, Cleanest"; "The MTA Accountability Campaign"). The campaign also visualized the impact of air pollution on Harlem children, which corresponded to the visual mapping described earlier that depicted asthma hospitalization rates clustered around neighborhoods in Northern Manhattan. WE ACT's testimony to City Council noted "25% of all children living in Central Harlem suffer from asthma—almost three times the national average" (Shepard, Corbin-Mark, Foster 2006, 2). WE ACT Board of Directors Chair Dennis Derryck said of the polluted air in and around Harlem, "you know it's an epidemic when you get into a classroom and it's no longer a crisis if a kid leaves his or her inhaler at home because they can borrow one from anyone in that class" (Solomonow 2001, 4).

In 2000, WE ACT filed a complaint with the Federal Department of Transportation under Title VI of the Civil Rights Act, charging the Metropolitan Transportation Authority (MTA) with "siting diesel bus depots and parking lots disproportionately in communities of color in Northern Manhattan" (Solomonow 2001, 1). In 2004, the Department of Transportation's Federal Transit Administration found "'the MTA is not, on balance, in violation of Title VI'" but it stipulated the MTA perform "impact analyses in construction . . . of bus depots . . . curtail the practice of idling buses . . . provide appropriate opportunities for public participation . . . and give due consideration to environmental justice principles in siting decisions" (Shepard, Corbin-Mark, & Foster 2006). The campaign resulted in "heightened public awareness" of the links between diesel buses and residents' health, and provided "increased visibility of WE ACT" (Shepard 2005/2006, 52). Importantly, the group's efforts demonstrated the "willingness and eagerness of community residents to become involved in structured efforts to improve the quality of life in their neighborhoods" and showed that "community-based organizations are sophisticated enough to conduct an effective media campaign. . . . The people most affected by the disproportionate siting of these hazardous facilities have become their own best advocates" (53).

NOTES

1. Wright referenced the "dry long so" as the "ordinary" people. Dry long so (or drylongso) is an expression used in the blues and within African American communities to mean so poor ("dry") as to not be able to go on any longer. *Drylongso* is the title of a book by John Langston Gwaltney that gives voice to ordinary black men and women and their views on black culture.

2. Feminist scholars have theorized the body from a number of perspectives. See Grosz, *Volatile Bodies*; Horner & Keane, *Body Matters*.

3. In some neighborhoods such as San Juan Hill, "mobs of whites" were known to attack any black person in their neighborhood (Freeman 2006, 18). In one riot in the early 1900s, white residents dragged black residents from streetcars and beat them.

4. In his 1965 report, *The Negro Family: The Case For National Action*, Daniel Patrick Moynihan sounded the alarm over the female-headed black family, which he described as a "tangle of pathology" and the eventual "source of most of the aberrant, inadequate, or anti-social behavior" among black youth (Moynihan 1965, 76).

5. Schwartz's study, *The New York Approach*, provides a detailed historical analysis of New York's urban renewal projects led by Robert Moses. In this sentence, Schwartz is quoting from "A Report on an Important Section of West of Central Park submitted by the City Planning Committee of the West of Central Park Association, Inc." (338, fn 32).

6. See Stuckler and Basu (2013) for a well-supported argument showing the connections between health and one's zip code. The phrase, "death by zip code," was used by NBC's Chief Medical Editor, Dr. Nancy Snyderman, in reference to a report on the health of Americans released in July 2013 (Raab 2013).

7. In addition to the study conducted by the United Church of Christ Commission for Racial Justice described earlier in the chapter, the U.S. General Accounting Office published *Siting of Hazardous Waste Landfills and their Correlation with Racial and Economic Status of Surrounding Communities* (1983). See also, Bullard (2000).

8. Di Chiro (1992) noted that the activists she interviewed similarly defined environment as "the place you work, the place you live, the place you play" (95).

9. Since the time of this writing, WE ACT has revamped its website. The tabs indicating the organizations primary areas of work are "climate justice," "clean air," "healthy indoor environments," and "sustainable land use."

10. At the time of this writing, the WE ACT website provided links to *Harlem Community Voices* issues from June 2009–August 2011.

FIVE
Citizen Science
How we come to know what we know

Explaining how she got involved in the effort to fight the siting of the North River Sewage Treatment Plant in West Harlem, WE ACT cofounder Vernice Miller-Travis (2013) countered the "standard thinking that you have to be an expert . . . in order to be an environmentalist. That's not the case. . . . People can absorb information, can learn it, and can become extraordinarily sophisticated advocates on their own behalf once they realize what the challenge is." Miller-Travis went on to explain the history of land use, zoning, and urban development that negatively affected the health and well-being of people of color, public planning that gave rise to abnormally high rates of asthma and asthma-related deaths in her own community. As Miller-Travis worked with the United Church of Christ Commission for Racial Justice to create the extensively researched and widely cited report, *Toxic Waste and Race in the United States*, her grandmother pointed out the work she was doing "was documenting something that everybody who lived in Harlem could tell you" (2013). This observation suggests a relationship between knowledge and experience rooted in a specific location.

Environmental justice advocates have often relied on the testimony of those experiencing physical symptoms and sensations (e.g., coughing, asthma, lead poisoning, odors, eye irritations) stemming from home and community location in order to establish arguments pertaining to environmental racism. This chapter explores the use of community-based participatory research, otherwise known as street science as a rhetorical tool that, in conjunction with mapping discussed in chapter 4, facilitated a politics of recognition to counter neoliberal rhetorics of market rationality proffered by city leaders and planners.

This chapter argues that epistemological claims to knowing based on physical experience, that is, street science, offer a rhetorical option (among others explored in earlier chapters) to justify claims of environmental racism. Harlem residents' claims to health and well-being is best understood against the larger context of Mayor Rudolph Giuliani's "quality of life" initiative that scripted urban well-being in racially coded ways. After detailing that discursive backdrop, I overview the concept of community-based participatory research in order to establish how this form of knowledge contrasts with the rationalist framework found in discourses of experts (e.g., scientists, engineers) that shape city planning and growth. I then turn to an examination of the ways New York City planners and engineers relied on technology-based reasoning emphasizing form and design in order to justify the operation of the North River Sewage Treatment plant in West Harlem. Finally, I examine the uses of street science on the part of West Harlem residents who based their arguments on firsthand experience shaped by spatial location in order to counter dominant narratives of facility placement and to establish the credibility of their claims of environmental racism.

BROKEN WINDOWS THEORY AND "QUALITY OF LIFE" CAMPAIGNS

Rudolph Giuliani served as mayor of New York City from 1994–2001. His urban policies were influenced, in part, by the "broken windows" theory, a view on crime and crime prevention developed by George Kelling and James Q. Wilson and popularized by the conservative Manhattan Institute. Alarmed by the rise in crime rates and perceived disorder of urban areas, these scholars posited the presence of unchecked, relatively minor signs of crime—such as broken windows—created fertile ground for larger, more insidious social breakdown. Writing in the *Atlantic* in 1982, the two explained "'untended' behavior," such as rowdy teens, abandoned property, panhandling, public intoxication, "leads to a breakdown of community controls" (Kelling and Wilson 1982). They elaborate:

> The citizen who fears the ill-smelling drunk, the rowdy teenager, or the importuning beggar is not merely expressing his distaste for unseemly behavior; he is also giving voice to a bit of folk wisdom that happens to be a correct generalization—namely, that serious street crime flourishes in areas in which disorderly behavior goes unchecked.

Putting aside, for the moment, their confusion of correlation and causation, Kelling and Wilson's article is almost single-minded in its focus on the binary, order/disorder, with all of its moral implications.

Importantly, the broken windows theory created a framework for understanding public spaces that tapped racist imagery and upheld a notion of moral order. Broken windows theory is important for understanding how urban spaces take on bifurcated meanings—moral/immoral; generative/ degenerative; orderly/disorderly—in racially coded ways. The report's authors offered a seemingly race- and class-neutral narrative of urban decay and crime that begs many questions that may otherwise have led to an exploration of the history of racism in urban renewal policies and their impact on physical and mental health and well-being in the city.

Broken windows theory provided an underpinning for a host of "quality of life" programs in cities across America throughout the 1990s. Vitale (2008) summarizes "quality of life" programs as a "set of concrete social control practices united by a political philosophy that explained the nature of homelessness and disorder as one of personal responsibility and established punitive methods for restoring social order and public civility" (1). Quality of life programs elided the ways broad based structures and long-standing policies impacted people's lives and the opportunities available to them. Additionally, "quality life" represented a vague reference to well-being but in practice spoke to the tastes, perceptions, and experiences of middle- and well-off city dwellers. Squeegee men, street vendors, and subway graffiti may have represented a threat or been perceived as "uncivil" to the average New York City tourist or Lower Manhattan banker, but for the window washer or vendor, their public presence was part of an effort to make a living.

References to "quality of life" can be found in the rhetoric of New York City Mayor John Lindsay, who used the term through the late 1960s–early 1970s to include concerns and fears of the middle class as well as the interests of local businesses. Lindsay's use of the term encompassed urban aesthetics, amenities, and pollution. But for Lindsay, the primary cause of urban problems "was not racism or social inequality but a failure to deal adequately with the consequences of growth and prosperity through planning and infrastructure investment" (Vitale 2008, 38). During his own tenure as mayor in the early 1990s, David Dinkins attempted to refocus "quality of life" on to the needs and concerns of the city's poor (Vitale 2008). But even Dinkins made use of the moralizing and stigmatizing rhetoric inherent in quality of life discourses when he promised to rid New York City's streets of the "squeegee pest" (Clines 1993). In 1994, Dinkins lost his bid for reelection to Rudolph Giuliani who recast "quality of life" in moral tones and shaded his rhetoric with appeals to order, safety, and civility. Along with his appointed Police Commissioner William Bratton, Giuliani used the "broken windows" theory to shape policing tactics and urban policies. The Mayor's "Reclaiming the Public Spaces of New York" planning document promoted a crackdown on minor crimes such as prostitution, loud music, graffiti, fare beating, and panhandling (Vitale 2008, 45). During Michael Bloomberg's tenure as mayor, the New York City Economic Development Corporation produced a pamphlet detailing how the city's "quality of life" program benefited businesses. "Quality of life initiatives . . . help designated areas to become safer, cleaner and more viable business environments" ("Quality of Life Program" n.d.).

On the surface, "quality of life" policies appear universally appealing. But when understood vis-á-vis the concerns of marginalized New Yorkers, the policies become troubling for ways the term "quality of life" hijacks public discussions of urban living and well-being. "Quality" is selectively defined and the emphasis on binaries (e.g., order/disorder; moral/immoral) short-circuits a deeper understanding of urban development and decay that must be enhanced through a historical lens. African American residents in West Harlem understood quality of life in terms of the ways the city—infrastructure, housing, health—acted on the body. And their public efforts to shape urban policy linked quality of life to larger social issues, such as racism, that have always guided—in more or less explicit ways—urban layout and policies targeting development.

LOCAL KNOWLEDGES VS. PROFESSIONAL EXPERTISE

Earlier chapters have engaged the fundamentally epistemological question of how we come to know, that is, how we generate claims to knowledge. Each chapter has then explored what rhetorical strategies have been used by city residents to argue and give credence to knowledge claims. Historically, marginalized groups have drawn on firsthand experience with a given issue say, poverty or segregation, in order to back a host of claims concerning definition (corporate subsidies constitute public assistance), value (black women who work outside the home are good mothers), and policy (the government should provide poor mothers a living wage to support their families) (Triece 2003, 2013). Acting collectively, these groups then use a host of rhetorical and extra-discursive strategies to convince others of the soundness of their knowledge claims.

Given a contemporary society characterized by rapid technological development and increasingly complex issues (e.g., climate change, drone warfare, genetic mapping), scholars (Corburn 2005; Fischer 1990, 2000; Gaventa 1993) have been curious to explore the challenges faced by ordinary citizens as they seek to understand and participate in public deliberation and decision making. How might citizens meaningfully participate in public deliberations heavily steeped in technical and scientific knowledges and embedded in a broader social context that celebrates and reinforces a neoliberal logic focused on rationality? This question has come to the fore in explorations of citizen engagement in environmental issues.

Fischer (2000) criticizes the traditional positivist approach to the study of social issues such as environmental degradation, which privileges the insights of experts and professionals who apply a "rationalist worldview" to generate valid principles that may "predict and manage . . . the persistent conflicts and crises that plague modern society" (17). Positivism erroneously posits a separation of fact and value thereby neglecting the ways human choices, social values, and beliefs bear upon and shape the nature of scientific inquiry. Importantly, the positivist approach represents an epistemological position (among others) that conceptualizes social problems in abstract, technical terms supposedly "freed from the cultural, psychological and linguistic contexts that constitute the lens of the social tradition," in short, a mode of inquiry that masks its own biases (17). Just as mapping hides its rhetorical dimensions, so too does scientific inquiry.

The positivist approach to understanding social issues such as sources of and solutions to toxic waste holds much in common with the discourses of market logic examined in chapter 3, which were employed as a frame for understanding the course and nature of urban development in Detroit. Free market rhetorics supporting urban regeneration gained credibility by donning a neoliberal cloak of rationality that appeared as common sense, natural, as the only apparent way to conduct urban planning. Similarly, the positivist framework that overlays discussions of social issues linked to scientific inquiry is rooted in instrumental rationality and technocratic modes that mask the political dimensions inherent in deliberation and decision making, instead presenting technological questions as in need of objectivity and disinterestedness (Fischer 2000, 14).

In contrast to the positivist approach that ignores the insights of ordinary citizens, scholars propose an approach to the exploration and assessment of social issues variously called citizen participation (Fischer 2000), participatory action research (PAR), community-based participatory research (CBPR), popular epidemiology (Brown 1992, 1993), or street science (Corburn 2005). Although they differ somewhat in theoretical pinnings, each of these methods emphasizes the centrality of "firsthand experience . . . [or] local knowledge" (Corburn 2005, 4) in the process of identifying and exploring a problem "in its particular context" and then, in a pragmatic fashion, deciding the appropriate response to that specific issue. This sort of "practical deliberation" brings together the insights of citizens, experts, and politicians alike as a community makes policy decisions concerning a host of pressing social issues within specific contexts.

Participatory action research sees the views of professional and laypeople as "complementary" whereas street science emphasizes a "coproduction" of knowledge that can occur when science and technology experts engage openly with laypeople and allow residents to speak for themselves on issues that impact their own lives (Corburn 2005, 9). Popular epidemiology refers to the process "by which laypersons gather scientific data and other information, and also direct and marshal the knowledge and resources of experts in order to understand the epidemiology of disease" (Brown 1992, 269). Importantly popular epidemiology "emphasizes social structural factors as part of the causal disease chain" (269). These approaches emphasize the interdependence of science and politics and suggest the importance of finding "new ways of fusing the expertise of professional practitioners and scientists with the 'contextual intelligence' that only local residents possess" (Corburn 2005, 4).

Theoretical parallels may be drawn between the notion of street science or community-based knowledge and that of standpoint, a concept discussed at length in the Introduction. The idea of "local knowledge" in community-based research is rooted in the anthropologist Clifford Geertz's definition, which describes a body or set of ideas derived from firsthand experience and "strongly rooted in a particular place" (Geertz, 1983, p. 75). Standpoint is more pointedly grounded in a Marxist theory that emphasizes the ways one's position within a capitalist economic system shapes material experience (e.g., food scarcity; workplace exploitation; neighborhood toxicity) and suggests that one's position or place within the larger economic system shapes one's understandings of social systems and related issues of inequality and power disparities. The ideas of standpoint and local knowledge similarly refer to an "epistemological device" (Hartsock 1983b, 118) or way of knowing that privileges knowledges that come from positions on the margins.[1]

Standpoint differs, however, in that it resists a parochial politics that ignores patterned discrimination rooted in broad based and entrenched systems. An emphasis on local knowledge at the expense of systematic injustices may lead to an understanding of environmental degradation as the result of "malicious, individual acts" (Pulido 2000, 12). Pulido (2000) suggests incorporating the notion of white privilege into studies of environmental racism in order to point to "structural" and "deeply historicized understanding[s] of racism" (13). Although local knowledge is just that—localized and grounded in a specific place—it need not elide the ways structural systems and institutions create disparities *across localities* based on race, class, or sex. Indeed, the report, *Toxic Waste and Race in the United States*, represents one such example of documentation of patterns of discrimination across the United States that impact communities of color in similar ways. Of interest from a communication perspective is what rhetorical strategies are available to citizens holding little formal power to back their arguments that connect environmental harm, facility placement, and systematic, institutionalized racism.

THE DIS-PLACING RHETORICS OF TECHNOLOGY AND FUNCTION

The positivist approach to scientific inquiry is imbued with a "technocratic ideology" that assumes technology exists in order to "serve our needs and desires" and only "requires an amoral, objective process of evaluation and adjustment" (Fischer 2000, 14). The technocratic ideology obscures the presence of moral judgment in scientific inquiry; presents technology as transcending "partisan interests," as "value neutral" (17); and dismisses as unreliable the knowledge claims generated by laypeople who hold firsthand experience with the given issue at hand (18). Technocratic ideologies inform and delimit public debate and deliberation across a variety of public speaking forums, including the mass media. For instance, a May 18, 2015, story on National Public Radio's All Things Considered probed the process of crop dusting used as part of the U.S.-backed War on Drugs in Colombia. A small scale coca farmer, Franklin Canacuan, spoke of the indiscriminate spraying of crop dusting planes that not only hurt his plants but made local residents, including his 8-year-old daughter, sick ("Colombia Will End" 2015). The interviewer followed Canacuan's statement saying, "It's impossible to verify Canacuan's claims," but then noted, later in the story, the World Health Organization has concluded that glyphosate [the active ingredient in the chemical used in crop dusting] is probably carcinogenic to humans" ("Colombia Will End" 2015). This brief story on the issue of crop dusting, herbicides, and public health illustrates how technocratic ideologies permeate public discussions in subtle ways. The interviewer's dismissal of Canacuan's claims of illness was prompted by the widely accepted and largely unspoken assumption that local knowledge—understandings generated by ordinary people from their firsthand experience—is not reliable and thus not a valid source of information. Instead, the interviewer placed credence in a study of the World Health Organization, an organization that relies on the expertise of scientists and professionals who utilize traditional methods of scientific inquiry to establish claims to knowing.

Communication scholars have long recognized the value-laden, interest-driven—that is to say, rhetorical—dimensions of scientific and technological inquiry (Gross 1990; Harris 1997; Prelli 1993).[2] The rhetorical scholar Kenneth Burke (1969b) wrote eloquently about the links between rhetoric, motives, and science. It is not enough, according to Burke, to explore technology and science as merely "good" or "bad" but we should attend to the ways these enterprises "could become identified with motives good, bad, or indifferent, depending upon the uses to which it was put" (30). Of concern, from a rhetorical standpoint, are the underlying motives and attendant consequences resulting from languages of science and technology. The "impersonal," technocratic language of scientific expertise is often used to justify "professional killing" (30). Burke explains, "Possibilities of deception arise particularly with these ironies whereby the scientists' truly splendid terminology for the expert smashing of lifeless things can so catch a man's fancy that he would transfer it to the realm of human relations likewise. It is not a great step from the purely professional poisoning of harmful insects to the purely professional blasting and poisoning of human beings, as viewed in similarly 'impersonal' terms" (34).

Technocratic ideologies function as a frame or a "terministic screen" (Burke 1966) that directs how a culture or society may come to understand a host of social issues, including environmental degradation. Terministic screens frame and delimit our understandings of events, people, experiences, etc. Burke (1966) explains, "Not only does the nature of our terms affect the nature of our observations, in the sense that the terms direct the attention to one field rather than to another. Also, many of the 'observations' are but implications of the particular terminology in terms of which the observations are made" (46). In *A Grammar of Motives* Burke (1969a) noted, "Men seek for vocabularies that will be faithful *reflections* of reality. To this end, they must develop vocabularies that are *selections* of reality. And any selection of reality must, in certain circumstances, function as a *deflection* of reality" (59).

In this section, I examine how technocratic ideologies served as a terministic screen filtering information about toxicity in West Harlem in ways that minimized the claims of local residents and instead privileged the arguments of city leaders and engineers who focused on the form and design of polluting facilities such as the North River Sewage Treatment Plant. If, as Aristotle (1954) pointed out, "The use of persuasive speech is to lead to decisions" (128), city leaders' emphasis on plant design encouraged the public to see the North River plant as essentially unproblematic, merely in need of the applied knowledge of engineers who could diagnose and address design flaws. As city leaders and plant engineers focused on sanitation technology and potential plant design flaws, they simultaneously deflected information concerning race and the politics of location, two issues that nearby residents had been calling attention to since 1968 when the plant's location became public (Miller 1993, 711). Further, the focus on design flaws led logically to design-based solutions, again diverting attention from issues of race and place.

The placement of the North River Sewage Treatment Plant was a point of contention from the beginning of city planning discussions in the 1960s (Miller 1993; Sze 2007). Situated in West Harlem at 137th Street, the plant began operation in 1986 and from the get-go generated anger from nearby residents who were immediately exposed to noxious fumes. Initially city leaders—including Mayor Koch, Joe Miller, chief engineer for the NYC Department of Environmental Protection, and Harvey Schultz, Commissioner of the Department of Environmental Protection—skirted or outright denied residents' claims of noxious plant emissions. Plant supporters relied on a technology-based rhetoric that focused on the plant's design and possible design flaws in order to displace the issue of location and its impact on the health of black residents.

New York Times coverage of the North River Sewage Treatment Plant facilitated the focus on design by initially relying almost solely on the insights of individuals whose jobs were to oversee the design and operation of the plant. City officials and plant experts represented "legitimate" news sources speaking for "legitimated institutions" (e.g., the city's political system; a body of scientific information) and thus adhered to the institutional norms of the newsroom (Tuchman 1978, 91). Frequently used sources included an "odor control specialist," a regional water engineer for the state of New York, a "sludge operations official," New York City's Environmental Protection Commissioner, and the chief engineer for New York City's Department of Environmental Protection (Gold 1991b; Severo 1989).

In 1986, the North River plant began primary treatment processes and immediately nearby residents began complaining of the foul odors coming from the plant and resultant respiratory problems ("History of WE ACT"). City engineers responded three years later by attempting to locate the source of the stench and a way to minimize it. A November 1989 *New York Times* article acknowledged, "there is agreement that the odor is a telltale sign of hydrogen sulfide gas. But there is no agreement on its cause, and speculation ranges from a broken sewer line to the assertion that the plant is trying to handle more raw sewage than it was designed for" (Severo 1989). The chief engineer for New York city's Department of Environmental Protection, Joe Miller, suggested mounting fans below the West Side Highway along which the plant was situated in order to "blow unwanted fumes back into the plant" (Severo 1989).

Other "experts" such as Richard L. Newman, New York state's regional water engineer, explained how sewage plants can be turned into "friendly neighbors" by ensuring a "well-designed plant, good control of the treatment process and . . . strong morale among plant workers" (Gold 1991b). Newman explained, "if you have the right kind of esprit de corps, the plant is a good actor" (Gold 1991b). The odor-control specialist, Jim Joyce, explained that plants typically emit odors at two points, "where waste water enters and where sludge . . . is handled at the end" (Gold 1991b). Other articles similarly focused on design and function noting that solid wastes that are supposed to settle to the bottom are instead floating to the top (Gold 1991a) and that an "eight-block concrete roof" is trapping "foul air" (Specter 1992b). Graphs of the plant's design accompanied these articles in order to illustrate problems in the plant's construction. The graphs, along with quotes from "experts" and "government officials" created a terministic screen suggesting a specific understanding of both the problem and solution to the plant's odors as centered on design, that is, function, skirting the original controversy surrounding the plant's placement in a historically black neighborhood.

City leaders and plant engineers also justified the North River Plant's operation through a refutative "yes-but" strategy wherein a brief acknowledgment of the smell was followed by a minimizing statement that undermined the initial complaint. When residents pressed for an independent review board to research their claims of foul odors, a spokesperson for the city's Department of Environmental Protection claimed that such a move was "totally unnecessary" given there were only eight complaints the previous year, only one of which was directed at the North River Plant (Dunlap 1989). In a similar spirit, Harvey W. Schultz, Commissioner of the Department of Environmental Protection asserted the "amount of hydrogen sulfide gas produced at the North River is truly negligible" (Severo 1989). Joe Miller, the Department of Environmental Protection's chief engineer did not deny the presence of occasional odors but noted, "I am not aware of any odor back in the community" (Severo 1989).

Residents also expressed concern that the plant's odors were so strong they would render useless a park planned for the top of the plant. The Riverbank State Park was a 28-acre green space with a football field, a 400-meter track, basketball courts, a skating rink, and indoor and outdoor pools designed to sit atop the North River Plant. As residents persisted in their assertions of odors emanating from the plant, park planners minimized their concerns. Ted Flickinger, a member of the National Association of State Recreation Planners, wrote off the smell as a given consequence of living in an urban area: "In terms of odor, you get the smell from traffic and toxic gases at Central Park. It's part of the environment of the big city" (Holloway 1992). Others minimized complaints by emphasizing the infrequency of the odor (Holloway 1992; Rothstein 1993). Park planners asserted the "blasts of foul air occur only a couple of times a month" and pointed to a design flaw on the roof that caused "bad air [to] collect until gusts off the river blow it . . . out of the building" (Holloway 1992). Elizabeth Goldstein, the New York City regional director of the state's Office of Parks, Recreation and Historic Preservation asserted odors were "infrequent" and that "once people start using the park, the issue may fall away" (Rothstein 1993).

New York Times coverage of the controversy did not wholly ignore the issue of race and the placement of toxic facilities but rather shaped readers' understandings in ways that changed over time as the topic of environmental racism gained traction in the wider public.[3] In 1991, environmentalists held the First National People of Color Environmental Leadership Summit in Washington, D.C. (Ferris 1994). In the early 1990s, Congress debated legislation that would "eliminate disproportionate exposure to environmental hazards in communities of color and low-income communities" (Ferris 1994, 316). In 1992 WE ACT and other environmental groups filed a lawsuit against the city of New York that, in the context of political debates regarding environmental justice, shined a light on the issue of environmental racism and lent credibility to the long-standing claims of West Harlem residents.

During this time, the *Times* ran articles that provided more space to issues of race, place, and health in West Harlem. An April 1992 article gave voice to Peggy Shepard, one of the founding members of WE ACT who raised the issue of environmental racism. She asserted, "This plant has become one of the shining symbols of environmental injustice. . . . They [city leaders] dumped it [the plant] on us" (Specter 1992b). Another article detailed the lawsuit including charges that early studies showed the optimal site for the plant was not West Harlem but a location further south (Specter 1992a). The article pointed out that WE ACT "was organized to battle the [North River] plant" but also sought to call out "how often and unfairly environmental hazards end up in lower income communities" (Specter 1992a). Subsequent *New York Times* articles appearing between 1992–1999 gave greater space to the issue of place, race, and toxicity making connections between the location of waste management facilities and low-income, minority neighborhoods (Levy 1993; Pérez-Peña 1994; Siegal 1999) and the dearth of open green spaces and parks in low-income and minority neighborhoods (Winerip 1993).

COMMUNITY-BASED KNOWLEDGE OR "WE'RE SICK AND TIRED OF BEING SICK AND TIRED"

In contrast to the arguments of experts who relied on discourses of technology to explain and justify the workings of the North River Sewage Treatment Plant, Harlem residents drew upon the knowledge acquired from firsthand experience living in Northern Manhattan. Environmental justice advocates used narratives of the knowing body to connect the dots between bodily reactions and bodily location in the city vis-á-vis polluting facilities (e.g., bus depots, old homes containing lead based paint, etc.).

Studies of environmental justice efforts repeatedly demonstrate the ways people in elite positions, that is, planners, professionals, experts, have used claims of expertise to trump the assertions of ordinary residents who describe illnesses experienced from exposure to toxins in water, the air, the workplace, and home (Corburn 2005; Fischer 2000; Krauss 1989). In the early 1970s, a South Brunswick, New Jersey, man, Frank Kahler, started noticing a foul odor in his drinking water (Krauss 1989). Additionally, his family had been experiencing a host of health problems, including headaches, nausea, dental problems, and rashes. Suspecting infiltration from a nearby toxic waste dump, Kahler called the South Brunswick Department of Health to test the water his family was drinking. All tests indicated the water was safe for consumption. Kahler explained, "I couldn't believe their reports. I couldn't believe them because I smelled the stuff and it was vile. Without a PhD in chemistry, without knowing what was in the water, I knew something was wrong" (234). Kahler galvanized his neighbors and they engaged a six-year effort to close a local toxic dump site in their neighborhood. Kahler's group falls within the broader NIMBY (Not In My Back Yard) movement wherein residents band together and collect data based on lived experience in order to assert public arguments regarding the links between toxicity and dumping in their communities. One consequence of NIMBY efforts is that it may well be the backyard of a low-income and/or minority community that gets the dump, waste facility, or bus depot. Furthermore, communities using the NIMBY argument consist of homeowners who have relied on the tropes of private property and ownership to argue against toxic facilities near their dwellings. People of color, still up against housing discrimination (Rugh & Massey 2010), are less likely than white residents to be homeowners and thus cannot rely on that position from which to argue against toxic dumping ("Environmental Justice in the United States" 2002).

So a unique challenge faces neighborhoods such as West Harlem where residents seek to establish not only that nearby facilities are harmful to their daily lives but that city planning and decision making regarding such facilities sits on a foundation of (often tacit) racist assumptions. West Harlem residents engaged in narratives of the knowing body which, I suggest, provided a rhetorical strategy particularly apt for the environmental justice movement whose goal is to bring "to the surface the *ethical* and *political* questions of 'who gets what, why, and in what amount.' Who pays for, and who benefits from, technological expansion?" (Bullard 1994, 11). More specifically, their narratives interceded in discourses dominated by technocratic ideologies and references to "quality of life" that largely ignored the racialized political dimensions pertaining to the management and placement of toxin-emitting facilities.

Their narratives represented a "critical interruption" that destabilized the taken for granted assumptions embedded in urban policy formation and decision making (Pezzullo 2001). Residents used reports of physical discomfort/illness to justify knowledge claims about toxicity, location, and race. The body is not only (albeit importantly) a register of physical harms, pains, and stunted growth, it is a body capable of forming knowledge claims—that is, a body of knowledge—based on firsthand experience. My use of the phrase "body of knowledge" holds a double meaning. A "body of knowledge" may refer to a set of ideas, concepts, and/or theories relating to a particular field, industry, or profession. A "body of knowledge" can also refer to a physical body with knowledge or holding knowledge, that is, a knowing body. The notion of a knowing body relates back to standpoint, an epistemological device suggesting that "real sensuous activity" (Marx, 1844/1978), particularly that associated with "labor and creation" (171), shape how we understand social relations and structures that impact our lives.

WE ACT refocused public discussions of facility operation onto the issue of place and the politics of location in the larger context of city growth. WE ACT recognized the "interconnectedness of issues and the processes which created them" so that the example of the North River Plant was framed not as an isolated issue of function but as socially and politically imbued (Miller, Hallstein & Quass 1996, 73). Indeed, WE ACT for Environmental Justice, "one of the first environmental organizations in New York State to be run by people of color" ("History of WE ACT"), formed out of struggles against "health disparities created by institutionalized racism . . . and the exclusion of communities of color from democratic decision-making" ("History of WE ACT"). To advance arguments linking location, health, and systematic racism, West Harlem residents relied on community-based participatory research (CBPR), which served at least four functions that responded to the elements of the rhetorical situation, including the speaker, argument, and the audience. First, CBPR reclaimed "quality of life" to capture the ways race dovetailed with well-being in urban spaces. It was not a coincidence, according to many Harlem residents, death rates for those living in Harlem matched rates of people living in Bangladesh (Chinyelu 1999, 1). Second, CBPR crafted residents as experts in their own right, capable of speaking to "quality of life" issues on par with city elite. Next, CBPR lent credibility to residents' claims of knowing. Citizens gained standing in public debates by backing their claims with scientific evidence and aligning their arguments with studies conducted by respected institutions. And finally, CBPR motivated residents to act.

"Quality of Life" for Whom?

CBPR gained significance for its bottom up approach to defining health and well-being that contrasted with the ways New York City leaders referenced "quality of life" throughout the 1980s–1990s. Mayors referenced "quality of life" to address the perceived safety concerns of the middle class and issues such as the "right" to walk through the streets unencumbered by the presence of homeless individuals and rowdy teens or sit at a stoplight without worrying about the "menace" of "squeegee pests" who "extort" drivers (Clines 1993).

In contrast to the politically popular usage of the phrase, Harlem residents invoked "quality of life" in their own public discourses to refer to the health of minority residents (Shepard 2005/2006; Shepard, Corbin-Mark, and Foster 2006). West Harlem residents such as Peggy Shepard and Cecil Corbin-Mark of WE ACT drew on documented health experiences of poor and minority residents in Northern Manhattan to sketch a picture of "quality of life" that highlighted the ways racist planning practices shaped the well-being of some city dwellers. Shepard (2005/2006) explained how residents came to realize the ways environmental racism shaped their living spaces when the North River Sewage Treatment Plant opened in 1986. Harlem residents immediately noticed a foul odor emanating from the plant. As they fought to gain the attention of city leaders in charge of the plant's operations, they realized their "predominately African American and Latino community of West Harlem was being used as a dumping ground for noxious facilities and unwanted land uses" (51).

In publications and on their website, WE ACT made frequent use of the phrase "quality of life" to point out how "quality" was moored to race. For these activists, "quality of life" was not colorblind and its definition was political. The website explained the organization's founding as motivated by "local community struggles around environmental threats and resulting health disparities created by institutionalized racism and the lack of social and political capital, all dynamics that led to the siting and poor management" of numerous polluting facilities ("History of WE ACT"). Given that quality of life is determined by lived experience as an African American or Latino/a city resident, CBPR provided an appropriate means for demonstrating the well-being of one's living circumstances. WE ACT used "citizen participation in public policy making" in order "inform, educate, train and mobilize the predominately African-American and Latino residents of Northern Manhattan on issues that impact their quality of life" ("History of WE ACT").

As Mayor Michael Bloomberg threatened a crackdown on "quality-of-life crimes," such as prostituting, panhandling, and public urination (Nagourney 2001), Harlem residents were fighting Bloomberg's proposal to expand and reopen the Marine Transfer Station (MTS) on 135th Street in Northern Manhattan on their own "quality of life" grounds (Tulton 2004). WE ACT's program director Cecil Corbin-Mark referenced "quality of life" to explain how the MTS would negatively impact the community's health. At a meeting with Harlem residents, Samara Swanston of Organizations United for Trash Reduction and Garbage Equity (OUTRAGE) highlighted the "quality of life concerns Harlemites will encounter includes increased air pollution, odor, and property devaluation" (Tulton 2004, 8).

In their testimony to the New York City Council, Peggy Shepard, Cecil Corbin-Mark, and Sheila Foster (2006) explained how "bus depots diminish quality of life" (2). They pointed out, "because of the disproportionate siting of NYCT bus depots north of 96th Street and NYCT's historical and well-documented poor record of environmental practice, tens of thousands of residents for years have suffered diminished quality of life" (2). Shepard, Corbin-Mark, and Foster identified a "pattern" wherein "5 of 6 operating diesel bus depots are located in low-income communities and communities of color in Northern Manhattan" (Shepard, Corbin-Mark, and Foster 2006, 1). Their observations were grounded in the documented health experiences of Harlem residents. They note, "as a result of the high concentration of diesel exhaust from heavy bus traffic and depot emissions, Northern Manhattan children suffer some of the highest rates of asthma and asthma-related hospitalizations in the nation" (1). For these residents, "quality of life" had to do less with visual appeal—as in Giuliani's whitewashing of Times Square—as it did with the vitality of their children. Shepard explained their efforts to move or retrofit bus depots in Northern Manhattan "has never been a matter of aesthetics—pollutants are placing our kids at a significant developmental disadvantage and impacting their life chances" (Greaves 2004, 5). Shepard also noted, "25% of all children living in Central Harlem suffer from asthma—almost three times the national average . . . a significant portion of Harlem's asthma epidemic is attributable to or exacerbated by diesel exhaust from buses and the disproportionate placement of diesel buses in this community" (2).

For these residents, neighborhood and resident "vulnerability" was not due to unsightly graffiti or people sleeping on the sidewalks, rather it was the "toxic environment" created by the placement of bus depots. In a document, "The Greenest, Cleanest Depot Possible" (2010), WE ACT explained the "pollution load" produced by bus depot operations "detracts from quality of life . . . generally by making the outdoor environment uninviting for social and physical activity; thereby contributing to increased risk of being overweight, obesity, and diabetes" (4). Residents' efforts to relocate bus depots and thereby improve health and quality of life rested on their firsthand experiences.

Residents as "Experts"

WE ACT explained, "as a result of outcry from community members and our research into the disproportionate impact of diesel pollution on Northern Manhattan," they initiated the Dump Dirty Diesel Campaign ("The Greenest" 2010, 3). Thus a second function of CBPR was to deploy residents as experts in their own right. CBPR resisted the top-down definition of "quality of life" by embracing a "people first" philosophy, which meant "those most impacted by a particular problem are in the best position to develop solutions and take a frontline stance on implementing identified strategies" ("Northern Manhattan Garbage"). WE ACT's campaign materials identified Harlem residents as knowing bodies, as residents whose firsthand experience with and proximity to toxin-emitting facilities made them experts on related health issues. Here expertise consists of knowledge that is experiential in nature and borne of a specific physical location in the city. One of WE ACT's founding members Peggy Shepard noted "we value when communities speak for themselves. . . . Community residents are experts on their communities" (Shepard, n.d.). When it comes to the issue of protecting "their communities and families, people will talk their heads off" if given the opportunity, noted Vernice Miller (2013). According to WE ACT's Deputy Director/Director of Policy Initiatives Cecil Corbin-Mark, the organization placed a premium on listening to community residents who have "expertise" that the so-called "experts" do not have ("Environmental Justice Advocacy"). Corbin-Mark, a Harlem resident, explained that when the Harlem community worked with planners and developers, it was crucial to "train" these professionals to "listen to community residents . . . train them that community residents have expertise . . . and train them that their role is not about creating a vision but supporting those whose place it is to create the vision" ("Environmental Justice Advocacy"). Corbin-Mark's reference to "training" real estate developers and city planners fostered a new way of understanding the relationship between longtime city residents and developers. Corbin-Mark placed power in the hands of residents, a move that upended the long-standing dynamic between well-off developers and residents whose lives are profoundly impacted by city planning decisions. On this new view, residents, not developers, hold the power to shape vision and spearhead discussions; it is they who should lead and be consulted, rather than the individuals traditionally thought to be leaders.

Resident Credibility

CBPR relied on scientific evidence to lend credibility to residents' arguments. Over twenty years after Shepard and others blocked traffic to demand attention to the North River Plant, the facility remained a thorn in the side of nearby residents who turned to WE ACT to report sights, smells, and physical pain associated with their location near the plant. Folks noted the plant emitted "odors that range from methane to an 'eggy,' sulfurous smell . . . to an unidentifiable 'chemically' odor that causes headache and nausea" ("Residents Worry Worsening," 2010, 1). Others reported seeing "dark gray to black smoke emit from the plant's stacks" and "waste water that has a layer of white to yellow foam on top" ("Residents Worry Worsening," 2010, 1).

Residents' testimonies of physical discomfort established a body of knowledge generated by way of physical location in an urban landscape marked by spatial and racialized disparities. Their observations comprise a "popular epidemiology" (Brown 1993) that recognizes "people who live at risk because of toxic hazards have access to data otherwise inaccessible to scientists" and such information stems from "lay observation" (19). When organized and formalized in the form of CBPR, residents' observations may be joined with the efforts of scientists so as to "democratize" the development of environmental policies (Dotson Newman, personal interview, May 28, 2014). Dotson Newman's observation that CBPR helped "prove accurate and correct" the physical experiences of residents supports the notion that standpoint provides an "epistemic advantage" (Alcoff 1996) to those on the margins.

The drive to employ citizen science was motivated in part by residents' realization of the obstacles they faced as public speakers. Residents were well aware of the ease with which their expertise may be ignored or misdirected. In a 2008 community meeting discussing the reconstruction of a bus depot located near her apartment building, Millicent Reddick repeated the importance of voicing resident concerns. She "recalled previous experiences . . . where the community was totally ignored" and noted "we can't get anything if we are quiet" ("Mother Clara Hale Bus Depot" March 2008). Ogonnaya Dotson Newman similarly noted that historically when residents spoke up regarding their health experiences, their claims were ignored or labeled invalid. In response, residents deployed CBPR, or what Dotson Newman called "citizen science," to "convince authorities in power that what they [we]re experiencing [was] accurate" (personal interview, May 28, 2014). In other words, CBPR provided not only a tool of invention, that is, a way to create and establish an argument, but a means for validating claims that were often delegitimized, minimized, or marginalized by people in more powerful positions.

In order to create a body of knowledge that held credibility, local residents became involved in more formalized, but still localized, efforts—such as councils, and street teams—in order to accumulate information and establish patterns of toxicity and discrimination in their community. For example, beginning in 1997 and continuing through the 2000s, WE ACT and West Harlem residents engaged a "Dirty Diesel Campaign" (see chapter 4) wherein residents attempted to call attention to the disproportionate siting of bus depots in Northern Manhattan and exert control over the future siting and retrofitting of bus depots in their neighborhood.

As part of their efforts they formed a community Leadership Council ("New Uptown") in early 2004 and later that year a Resident Oversight Council (ROC) ("The MTA"). The purpose of the Leadership Council was to "develop residents' capacity to lead the struggle against dirty diesel in Northern Manhattan" ("New Uptown" 7). The Council's objectives were geared toward equipping residents with specific types of information that would facilitate their communicative agency when they engaged in dialogue with professionals. Objectives included "increasing understanding of the dangers of diesel and the racially disparate impact of the MTA's policies" among immediate residents and the wider city; "identifying and training leaders to spearhead recruitment efforts"; "organizing trainings and briefing sessions on how city agencies function and make decisions"; and "creating a glossary of MTA jargon and legalese to equip residents for dialogue with decision-makers" (7). These objectives spoke to a perceived need to create "informed participation," a mode of empowering residents as they entered into formalized discussions with local officials and the like.

Both the Leadership Council and the Resident Oversight Council (ROC) were comprised of residents who lived in close proximity to

Northern Manhattan bus depots. The ROC collected data based on their firsthand experience dealing with the "noise, particulate matter (soot) and nauseating fumes" that pervaded their homes on a regular basis ("The MTA"). The information gathered by ROC members was valued precisely because these individuals were "directly, and sometimes tragically, impacted by the depots' negative impacts" including "high bus traffic traveling in areas where children, seniors and pets gather, dirt and soot fallout settling" in homes and "emission of pollution such as PM [particulate matter] and nauseating fumes that contribute to their poor health status" ("The Greenest, Cleanest" 2010). Information from the ROC was then shared in meetings with the MTA in 2004 and at an October 2006 City Council meeting (Prakesh 2004; Shepard, Corbin-Mark, Foster 2006).

During planning for the rebuilding of the Mother Clara Hale Bus Depot, the ROC was extended into a taskforce to oversee the project. The Mother Clara Hale Taskforce served as a channel for expressing community "concerns about diesel and other noxious and toxic pollution that . . . has . . . translated into poor health status for a larger proportion of residents" living near the depot ("The Greenest, Cleanest" 2010). Pointing to the value placed on knowledge generated through geographic proximity, the taskforce relied on the observations of older adults—"elders"—in the community who were "perfectly situated to be the 'eyes and ears' of the neighborhood" because they "live or spend so much of their days near the depot" ("The Greenest, Cleanest" 2010).

The taskforce's efforts paid off. Information generated by the ROC helped build a campaign to "hold MTA accountable for its contribution to [the community's] disproportional burden of the City's pollution load" (The Greenest, Cleanest" 2010). Local resident, Millicent Reddick, who lived near a bus depot and sat on the ROC explained that the meetings with MTA officials were helpful because "it's perhaps the first time somebody from Transit has actually sat down and listened without dismissing our concerns. Just listening to each other is an important first step—if you can hear me, then we can get ready to move to the next level, which is hopefully correcting the problem" (Prakesh 2004, 5). Reddick's emphasis on the importance of listening resonates with Cecil Corbin-Mark's observation that ordinary residents have to "train" the so-called "experts" to listen to residents' concerns. Residents expressed confidence in the soundness of their claims but they were also well aware of obstacles to be overcome in getting their knowledge accepted as credible and then taken into account in a meaningful way when it came to city decision making.

WE ACT also utilized Street Teams and community collaboratives to document and give voice to experiences pertaining to health, race, and location. These efforts fall in line with community-based participatory research geared toward utilizing local knowledge for public policy transformation. The Street Team used "research, investigation, and peer-to-peer communication to build community capacity" ("Garbage, Pests" 2009, 5) and the Community Action for a Renewed Environment (CARE Collaborative) relied on "open meetings and community surveys" to "create profiles of specific environmental health issues and their suspected causes" and then "develop strategies for reducing the risk posed by hazards in the community" ("Northern Manhattan Garbage"). Street Teams and collaboratives provided a framework for organizing and formalizing knowledge gained through day to day experiences in one's community. Given the largely invisible process by which one is exposed to toxicity and the fact that such exposure often occurs in private settings such as the home, organizational efforts to give voice to these experiences was particularly important. Surveys, face-to-face communication, and community meetings opened the door to residents who may otherwise not have had an opportunity to share experiences of living with asthma, itchy eyes, and foul smells.

Community efforts to collect and synthesize health data proved important for at least two reasons. First, it enabled organizations such as WE ACT to establish *patterns* of spatial health discrimination, to make the case that health was implicated in issues of place-base racism. Additionally, collective efforts, including those engaged with formal institutions such as Columbia University, and state and city agencies, forced leaders to "see people" suffering from physical harm generated by their community location (Pezzullo 2001, 14). And notably, twinning community knowledge with the efforts of government agencies and academic institutions enabled local residents to overcome a rhetorical constraint associated with credibility. That is, historically, marginalized groups, including environmental justice advocates in West Harlem, have had to overcome the obstacle of perceived credibility. Once knowledge claims were generated, residents had to find ways to get those claims accepted as true and accurate and to get them incorporated into larger, more formal bodies of knowledge that informed public policy and decision making.

WE ACT partnered with a number of outside agencies including Columbia University, the University of Pittsburgh, and the Center for Environmental Health in Northern Manhattan with the goal of arming residents with scientific data and galvanizing them to act on their own behalf. Combined with their own narratives of health related, place-based suffering, data generated by academic institutions and state agencies resulted in a body of knowledge that could empower residents and influence the decision making of city leaders (Gonzalez n.d.). Data from the University of Pittsburgh was used to underscore the spatial correlation between poverty and pollution ("Community Stressors"); a study promoted by the Center for Environmental Health in Northern Manhattan shed light on the "environmental components of disease" ("Community Outreach").

In the early 2000s, WE ACT worked with the Columbia University Center for Children's Environmental Health (CCCEH) to understand the health-related experiences of mothers raising children in the Harlem area (Greaves 2004; "WE ACT and Columbia University" 2001). The "Healthy Home, Healthy Child" campaign launched in the summer 2001 relied on information generated through interviews and focus groups with women living in Washington Heights and Harlem. The goal of the campaign was to empower through education, to give residents the "tools they need to make their environments healthier and safer" ("WE ACT and Columbia University" 2001). Another study conducted through the CCCEH provided data less focused on the private sphere of home and more pointed to systematic, geographically based exposures in predominately African American neighborhoods. The 2004 study showed "women exposed to polluted air gave birth to underweight babies, with smaller head sizes—on average" (Greaves 2004, 5). Highlighting the connection to patterned environmental discrimination, the *Uptown Eye* article discussing the study noted "pollution from cars, trucks, buses and a host of other sources is especially ubiquitous in Northern Manhattan—due to the disproportionate presence of polluting facilities in the area" (5). WE ACT Executive Director Peggy Shepard underscored the purpose of the study was not only to raise awareness but to serve as "additional fodder" for the group's "ongoing effort to empower community residents to hold polluters accountable" (Greaves 2004).

Mobilization

Finally, CBPR was used to motivate residents to action. WE ACT framed its task as seeking knowledge from affected communities through citizen science then helping "organize residents around their vision." Dotson Newman called CBPR a "powerful tool to drive movement" (personal interview, May 28, 2014). WE ACT materials frequently referred to "empowering" and "galvanizing" residents to become a "proactive" force in their communities ("Community Outreach"; "History of WE ACT"; "Northern Manhattan Garbage"). West Harlem residents also utilized direct action near the point of exposure to demonstrate how toxic fumes in their communities affected their bodies and thus made them experts on the issue. In January 1988, a group of people known as the Sewage Seven donned gas masks and blocked morning traffic on the West Side Highway in front of the North River Sewage Treatment Plant ("History"). Local residents similarly wore gas masks and carried signs as they blocked nearby Riverside Drive. As an act of civil disobedience that inconvenienced morning commuters, the action intensified the two-year-long struggle to call attention to the Plant's noxious fumes. Additionally, the gas masks worked rhetorically to call out an issue (smelly, harmful air) that by virtue of its invisibility proved hard to verify and, as we saw earlier, was readily dismissed. The gas masks suggested residents knew something about the air that remained invisible to the eye but that remained sufficiently toxic to necessitate the use of protective wear.

Into the twenty-teens, WE ACT has continued to address issues related to air quality, equitable transit and land use, food justice, waste and pesticide reduction, and toxic free products. With growing international attention on climate change, WE ACT has recently turned attention to "climate resilience," an issue that recognizes climate change "exacts a disproportionate toll on the poor and working class people" ("The Northern Manhattan Climate Action Plan"). WE ACT's planning document on climate resilience draws a distinct connection between poverty, the growing wealth gap, and climate change noting that those with access to power and resources are better equipped to withstand the repercussions of global warming. Importantly, the organization emphasizes the need to "leverage . . . efforts to address other social crises, such as chronic unemployment, poor diets, mass incarceration, and low-quality education . . . otherwise we may prevent climate change from erasing NYC only to watch the slower erosion of gentrification swallow what's left" ("The Northern Manhattan Climate Action Plan"). Community-based participatory research continues to undergird WE ACT's approach to environmental justice as the organization works to ensure low-income and minority communities play a central role in the policy making[4] that directly affects their neighborhoods and families.

NOTES

1. See also the work of Harding (1993), hooks (1984), and Collins (1991).

2. The body of scholarship on the rhetoric of science is too long to cite here. A communication journal, *POROI: An Interdisciplinary Journal of Rhetorical Analysis and Invention* is devoted to the study. POROI stands for Project on Rhetoric of Inquiry.

3. Burch and Harry's (2004) study of news stories of pesticide use and farmworker safety concluded that newspapers relied on a variety of sources including activists, government, and industry, with papers favoring an anti-pesticide perspective. They argue that papers can promote a counterhegemonic perspective, whereby views that challenge the status quo can "make their way into news reporting" particularly in contexts involving conflict and opposition (571).

4. Although beyond the scope of this chapter, WE ACT has also sought to engage "participatory budgeting," a relatively new concept that allows ordinary citizens to play a part in the budgeting and allocation of monies at the government level.

Conclusion

Neoliberalism, Urban Spaces, and Race

In a 1951 survey of Detroit residents, 21 percent of black respondents, compared to 4 percent of whites, placed the police department in the top three "most important matters that needs attention in the city." Black residents pointed out the police "are too prejudiced. All Negroes look alike to them"; and "the police shouldn't be so quick to shoot and go into homes and wreck them as they do some Negro homes" (Thompson 2001, 21). Gallup polls conducted over 60 years later found much the same lack of confidence in the police among black citizens. In Gallup surveys conducted between 2010–2014, black respondents were more likely to "give police officers lower honesty and ethics ratings" and they have a "significantly lower level of confidence in the police as an institution" (Newport 2014). These findings fit squarely within the larger narrative of state imposed order and spatial politics that discipline the black body in the city and suggest an abiding link between race, space, and the neoliberal city.

The multiple deaths of unarmed black men at the hands of police—deaths spanning the twentieth and twenty-first centuries but gaining widespread attention since 2014—may be understood within the larger neoliberal scaffolding that imposes a racialized urban "order" that attends cycles of city growth and decay into the twenty-first century. The neoliberal city rests on tacit assumptions about race and urban areas. Tough on crime rhetorics—popular throughout the twentieth and twenty-first centuries—become a requisite part of a new "code of the city"—a partnership between repressive and hegemonic tactics that ensure the "rights of capitalism" over human rights.

Both then and now, a people's pushback has come in the form of urban unrest such as the 1964 Harlem Uprising that occurred in the wake of the police shooting of James Powell, a 15-year-old African American boy, and the Great Rebellion in 1967 Detroit. In the twenty-teens, in cities like Ferguson, Missouri, and Baltimore, uprisings responding to the police killings of unarmed black men may give way to understanding how racialized housing and city development policies have created an "architecture of segregation" that directly impacts the options and opportunities available to African Americans in the twenty-first century (Jargowsky 2014; Rothstein 2014). Jargowsky (2014) explains that neighborhoods with high concentrations of poverty are "not the value-free outcome of the impartial workings of the housing market. Rather, in large measure, they are the inevitable and predictable consequences of deliberate policy choices." My interest in the previous chapters has been to uncover the ways urban planning policies come to be understood as "value-free" through specific communication strategies and framings that cloud or mystify the exclusionary implications of such practices. And, on a more optimistic note, I've examined how ordinary residents—often poor and/or minority—fight back to save their communities, homes, and health against the encroachment of planning practices that have racist implications.

Specifically, I have attempted to draw a line connecting past processes of spatial domination to present day efforts to restore urban centers in the wake of deindustrialization. The book began by discussing how racist spatial practices have been woven into the fabric of the United States dating back to the displacement of tens of thousands of Native Americans, continuing through the twentieth century's codification of neighborhood segregation, and persisting today in the form of a colorblind neoliberal paradigm that justifies or naturalizes urban growth that in fact has led to crises in housing and health for hundreds of thousands of black residents. Each chapter drew extensively on urban studies and scholarship on geography but centered primarily on the communicative dimensions of urban growth and resistance. I was most interested in examining how language is used to promote growth as an unquestionable good and the ways ordinary residents—often those with little or no formal power—challenge processes of urban renewal through specific rhetorical strategies.

The contemporary relationship between urban planning and race may be fully understood by exploring how neoliberal assumptions and practices direct global and local economic policies and urban growth and decay. In this final chapter I describe three hallmarks of neoliberalism that create and delimit public understandings of users and uses of urban public spaces. I suggest understanding recent (2013–2016) highly publicized policing of black bodies in city spaces as shaped by the neoliberal context, which emphasizes an alleged colorblind moral order that upholds the logic and interests of the free market. A new "code of the city," steeped in neoliberal assumptions that facilitated the exclusionary growth processes detailed in previous chapters, has created a disciplinary urban environment that leads to the policing of the bodies of marginalized "others" in the city.

Chapter 1 discussed the concept of neoliberalism as a practice and a discourse. The remainder of the book explored what I suggest are the rhetorical hallmarks of neoliberalism in the contemporary American city and rhetorical strategies of resistance available to citizens hoping to retain control over the spaces where they live, work, and raise their families. One discursive characteristic or hallmark of the neoliberal paradigm is a *narrative of progress* marked by steady, unquestioned growth. This narrative is often conveyed via a socially constructed public memory that operates through selective amnesia or strategic forgetting, discussed in chapter 2. To accept the idea that the United States is on a road of progress and moral perfection one must forget anew the ways racism has consistently figured into urban policies. Rothstein (2015) points out how most Americans have forgotten the history of state sponsored segregation. He explains, the "major reason we have ghettos in very metropolitan areas in this country is because federal, state and local governments purposefully created racial boundaries in these cities. It was not the unintended effect of benign policies. It was an explicit, racially purposeful policy that was pursued at all levels of government." Not merely the result of the racist attitudes of white residents and real estate agents, urban residential and labor segregation have always been about legal and widely used practices that deliberately excluded African Americans from certain spaces. Restrictive covenants, eminent domain, and exclusionary zoning created segregated neighborhoods, pockets of concentrated poverty, and hampered the mobility of black families. Widely accepted and rarely scrutinized policies such as the federal income tax deduction of home mortgage interest and the federal subsidizing of highway construction disproportionately benefit homeowners and suburban dwellers who, due to the aforementioned racist housing policies, are more likely to be affluent and white (Jargowsky 2014; Rothstein 2014).

Especially in the contemporary twenty-first-century society where we sit amidst post-race claims, policies that are supposedly "colorblind," and celebrations of "diversity" and "tolerance," narratives that whitewash urban histories are central to arguments that claim the neutrality of urban policies. Additionally, public memory that supports the view of untarnished and consistent progress opens a door to assigning blame to individuals for present day urban problems. For instance, if we can forget how government policies led to the formation of urban ghettos, we can more easily cast blame on individuals—namely black males—for their own disenfranchisement and thus let policies and economic practices off the hook.

In contrast, residents such as those in Detroit recalled the *ongoing* history of racist displacement through the construction of countermemories that drew a line connecting past practices and policies with the present. Residents recalled the history of deindustrialization, widespread unemployment of black residents, and divestment of black neighborhoods in order to establish a parallel to the city's present day situation and to resist the idea that black neighborhoods are suffering because of the poor morals or lack of motivation on the part of their residents.

A second discursive hallmark of neoliberalism is the *emphasis on the individual* to the neglect of structures and systems. The concept of liberal individualism, influential in the formation of U.S. identity and social policies alike, promotes an understanding of personal agency as unconstrained by broader systems. According to this widely accepted viewpoint—embodied in bootstraps stories of people who succeed despite overwhelming obstacles—the individual operates on free choice and is able to take advantage of a wide range of opportunities as long as he/she works hard. The tenets of liberal individualism prop up public memories that situate urban histories on a line of steady progress and universally beneficial growth. Mainstream news accounts of Detroit's rebirth that centered on the good deeds of billionaire developers Dan Gilbert and Mike Ilitch served as a morality tale casting these men as heroes for saving the city and promoting progress. Narratives of heroic individualism obscure the ways economic and political policies tilt the playing field in ways that support wealth accumulation for an elite, primarily white, minority.

In contrast, longtime residents galvanized collective action in part through use of the Internet. Residents in both Detroit and West Harlem used websites to raise awareness, provide pertinent information concerning urban renewal and health-related issues, and importantly to organize groups to act. In these situations, grassroots websites, such as those of Detroiters Resisting Emergency Management, Moratorium NOW!, and WE ACT, may be viewed as "virtual public spheres" (Papacharissi 2002) or a "parallel polis" (Lagos, Coopman, & Tomhave 2014) wherein residents could disseminate information, create a collective identity, and organize on-the-ground struggles. The literature on Internet activism is extensive and was only briefly touched upon in chapter 1. Cyberprotest remains an area ripe for continued study as scholars may examine how this medium works in tandem with more traditional forms of communication.

A third rhetorical cornerstone of neoliberalism is a *market logic* that emphasizes rationality or the view that economic processes are disinterested, objective, and operate optimally when left uninhibited by government intervention. Discourses of rationality justified the consequences of urban renewal by promoting a market logic that assumes the unbiased nature of decision making and urban planning. So in the case of Detroit, city development decisions were framed by a language of economics, with terms such as "opportunity," "feasibility," and "cost-saving adjustments" that held commonsense appeal but obscured the race and class dimensions of market processes. In West Harlem, a technocratic language focused on function and design, which effectively elided the issues of race and placement of toxic facilities. Like individualism, discourses of rationality let structures and institutions off the hook by mystifying or obscuring the motives underlying public policy and economic imperatives.

In contrast, residents in Detroit and West Harlem used knowledge obtained through firsthand experience with hardships relating to housing and health in order to generate rhetorical strategies that challenged market rationality. In Detroit, residents relied on demystification, which operated in tandem with countermemories, to contextualize city development within a history of racial segregation. Demystification proved useful in challenging the invisibility of whiteness as it called out the ways market processes underwrote white privilege. In West Harlem, WE ACT advocates used countermapping and citizen science to reposition discussions of toxic facilities onto the salient issue of the racial politics of facility placement.

The analyses in chapters 2–5 suggest the importance of maintaining a critical eye on the ways neoliberal practices that lead to marginalization and exploitation worldwide are maintained through public discourses that often appear unremarkable but have profound influence on the ways we view urban growth and progress. The neoliberal paradigm is constructed through a selective public memory, sustained through stories of individual heroism, and justified by appeals to rationality. These three elements work together to form a consistent narrative that composes progress in terms of individual hard work and understands political and economic processes as unbiased and beneficial to all. This picture elides the ways capitalist structures and systems uphold white privilege and tacitly sustain racist assumptions and practices.

NEOLIBERALISM, DEVELOPMENT/DECAY, AND POLICING IN URBAN SPACES

The three hallmarks of neoliberalism operate hegemonically by appearing as commonsense understandings for the ways cities develop and take shape over time. It is hard to argue against such tenets as progress and growth until or unless one sets these processes on a trajectory that accounts for the violence, exclusion, and disenfranchisement exercised against minority citizens over the course of the country's history of (sub)urbanization. It is then that we may come to understand the race-, class-, and gender-inflection of city planning, growth, and decay. And it is then we may come to understand how an "architecture of segregation" signals a spatial environment of race exclusion supported by repressive tactics such as police violence and increasing control and regulation of the bodies of homeless, poor, and minority residents in urban locations.

The deaths of Michael Brown, Eric Garner, Tamir Rice, Freddie Gray, John Crawford, and Walter Scott killed at the hands of police over a short nine-month period have brought to the attention of white America what black communities have known for centuries: race based police brutality has always been present in the lives of black Americans. In 1971, Detroit Mayor Roman Gribbs formed Stop the Robberies, Enjoy Safe Streets (STRESS), an effort that became synonymous with police attacks on the black community (Thompson 2001). In the first nine months of 1971 alone, STRESS officers had killed 10 suspects, 9 of whom were black (82). In a similar move, New York City mayors throughout the 1990s and to the present have enforced "quality of life" and "broken windows" policing tactics that disproportionately target low-income minority men, whose bodies are culturally scripted as violent and disorderly (Jackson 2006; Peters 2014). Indeed, in the late 1960s, leaders in the Detroit chapter of the National Association for the Advancement of Colored People (NAACP) pointed out police "operate under the bigoted misapprehension that most Negroes are criminals" (Thompson 2001, 38).

Likewise, in the twenty-first century, there is an unmistakable connection between repressive police tactics, race, and the killings of Brown, Garner, Rice, Gray, Crawford, and Scott. Michael Brown was allegedly walking in the middle of the street when the white police officer, Darren Wilson, confronted him and shot him twelve times in an altercation. Eric Garner was selling untaxed "loosies," individual cigarettes, on a sidewalk in Staten Island when police officers approached him and placed him in a chokehold that resulted in his death. Tamir Rice was playing in a neighborhood park when police officer Timothy Loehmann shot him within two seconds of arriving on the scene and before the squad car had even come to a complete stop (McGinty 2015). John Crawford was shot by Beavercreek, Ohio, police while standing in an aisle at a Walmart. Police thought the BB gun he had gotten off the shelf at the Walmart was loaded. And Walter Scott, stopped by a white North Charleston, South Carolina, police officer, was shot in the back while fleeing from his car.

In each case, the *unarmed* African American man (or boy in the case of 12-year-old Rice) was perceived as chaotic, a danger to the urban space (e.g., street, park, store) and a threat to order. Police response coupled with the failure to indict officers in four of the six cases indicate persistent racist assumptions rooted in long-standing stereotypes of the black individual and black family. Media coverage of the killing of Eric Garner—on CNN and in local and national news outlets—repeatedly noted that Garner "weighed well over 300 pounds" (Goodman & Goldstein 2014), an inscription of the black body that tapped white fears of the African "brute" or "beast" (Jackson 2006).[1] Just three days after Tamir Rice was killed by a white Cleveland police officer, the local news outlet, Cleveland.com, published two stories that amounted to moral tales condemning Rice's alleged violent upbringing and violent neighborhood implying their connection to Rice's death. These articles drew on the trope of the black family as a "tangle of pathology" and the black ghetto as scary, dangerous, and morally bereft to situate Rice as guilty by association or corrupted by spatial location. One article explained that Rice's neighborhood was "long-plagued by gangs, guns and drugs" (Shaffer 2014). Conjuring the image of the "bad home," the article detailed the location and aesthetic surroundings where Rice lived:

> Tamir lived in a three-unit, brick apartment building off Madison Avenue, across from the park. Graffiti covers almost every surface in sight—a convenience store, a US Postal Service box, a "No Parking" sign, a used clothes and a shoe collection bin. A few block west, near Berea Road, a sign on a mechanic shop nestled between crumbling warehouses warns customers that the business is not responsible for vehicle fires, break-ins or smashed windows. . . . A few blocks east of Tamir's apartment, at West 98th Street, a once notorious gang wage a 'reign of terror.'" (Shaffer 2014)

This description, along with an article detailing Rice's father's "history of violence against women" and his mother's guilty plea to drug trafficking and assault (Blackwell 2014) amount to yellow journalism the likes of which were common during the Jim Crow era. Cultural codes ride alongside neoliberal assumptions of progress, individualism, and growth such that Rice became a synecdoche for the failed black family, Eric Garner's bodily presence represented a challenge to the sanctioned lines of commerce, and John Crawford personified the black threat to public safety in a Walmart where he held an unloaded BB gun retrieved from the store shelf.

The tenets of neoliberalism provide a contemporary and colorblind platform for upholding long-standing racist assumptions; the precepts underwrite a "script" that registers the black masculine body as "violent," "incompetent and uneducated," and "innately incapacitated" (Jackson 2006, 75), as a threat to progress, individualism, and productivity. The scripted black male body provides a ready pretext for neoliberal policing tactics carried explicitly in the broken windows theory (chapter 5) and less obviously in prevailing expectations and assumptions concerning appropriate behaviors in, and uses of public space, including what places are hip and which ones should be avoided. Broken windows theory of policing rests on a prevailing cultural investment in individualism that centers blame on individuals for their living circumstances rather than understanding the formation and persistence of the contemporary "ghetto" as a direct result of explicitly racist federal and local policies (Rothstein 2014). Militarizing the police as was the response to peaceful protesters in Ferguson,[2] punishing people without permanent homes through no camping ordinances, disciplining bodies out of line or out of place as in neighborhood "watch patrollers" such as the one who shot and killed unarmed black teenager Trayvon Martin, become part and parcel of a city code that rests on racialized binaries: white/black, order/disorder, moral/immoral, safety/danger, clean/unkempt.

In direct response to the 2012 killing of the unarmed African American teenager, Trayvon Martin, at the hands of a neighborhood patrol watch person George Zimmerman, three African American women—Alicia Garza, Patrisse Cullors, and Opal Tometi—formed the Black Lives Matter movement (BLM). The subsequent police killings of Michael

Brown, Eric Garner, and other black men in cities across America has further fueled the movement, which has gained widespread attention and directed public debate to the issues surrounding race and equality. The Black Lives Matter movement is above all an effort to confront racist practices tied to control over black bodies in public and domestic spaces. The phrase "Black Lives Matter" turns attention to "all of the ways in which Black people are intentionally left powerless at the hands of the state" ("About the Black Lives Matter").

The organization's local chapters have utilized a variety of direct actions that challenge the neoliberal order seeking to maintain control over and discipline residents within city spaces. Black Lives Matter activists have blocked traffic on streets and major bridges from San Francisco to New York City. During the 2015 holiday shopping season, BLM activists shouted "no justice, no profits!" as they protested along Chicago's "Miracle Mile" where shoppers were patronizing high-end boutiques and eateries. And BLM activists halted holiday traffic heading to the Minneapolis-St. Paul National Airport ("Black Lives Matter Statement" 2015). Aware of the impact such an action held for the capitalist workings of the city, the group noted "black communities across the United States are taking brave actions to impede the flow of goods and commerce with peaceful protests to call for an immediate overhaul of the justice system both locally and nationally that will demand accountability for police, removal of grand juries in cases involving police shootings, an immediate halt to militarized police units and weapons, and extensive review of racialized police practices in black neighborhoods" ("Black Lives Matter Statement" 2015).

These actions not only disrupted traffic and business as usual, they symbolically upended the moral order of the city that both prohibits and sanctions specific behaviors and celebrates the city as the mark of cultural and corporate progress. Geographies have consequences (Soja 2010b) that impact the body directly. The Detroit area activist Martha Grevatt put the matter this way: "When we say black lives matter . . . it's not just about horrible killings of black men, women and children, it means black cities matter too" (personal interview, March 26, 2015). When Black Lives Matter activists take to the streets, they are, in part, asserting that black residents have a right to public space, to be black and in public without being suspect, without the burden of the racist hegemonic script of black masculinity, without fear of being confronted/shot by the police. Their efforts are, in part, a struggle over geography in the ways that Detroit residents have fought for the right to housing and Harlem residents have struggled for rights to clean air, and, more recently, the residents of Flint, Michigan (another black city), have fought for the right to clean drinking water.

Notably, the Black Lives Matter movement is "rooted in the experiences of Black people in [the U.S.] who actively resist" de-humanization in all its forms ("About the Black Lives Matter"). The previous chapters sought to understand the impact of urban growth rhetorics from the standpoint of those most impacted but often denied a voice in such discussions. Standpoint emphasizes that all knowledge is "saturated with history and social life" (Harding 1993, 57). Standpoint theory suggests that "all knowledge attempts are socially situated [but] that some of these objective social locations are better than others as starting points" for understanding our world (Harding 1993, 56). When considered in light of the processes of urban growth and renewal, Harding's statement suggests something that Detroiters and West Harlem residents have been saying all along; namely, that they should have a say in the policies that affect their lives, that they have knowledge and experiences that give them an insight into issues of housing and health that planners and developers do not have.

Theoretically, the analyses in the previous chapters wove together insights from critical geography, urban studies, and communication. Drawing specifically on the concept of space, I suggested the importance of a historical materialist view that understands the ways capitalism has been and continues to be implicated in the formation and experience of urban spaces. Contemporary scholarship, particularly beginning with the poststructuralist/postmodern "linguistic" turn and continuing through the "spatial turn" and the "affective turn," has eschewed the materialist underpinnings of Marxist thought as overly deterministic. Influenced by the writings of Foucault, Rorty, and Lyotard, scholars in fields including philosophy, English, sociology, and communication studies have promoted a discourse centered view of society and self that has replaced critique of material structures and systems (e.g., workplace exploitation, institutionalized racism) and study of collective agency with analysis of discursive formations and strategic strikes through which individuals can assert a localized agency.[3]

On my view, the continued relevance of the writings of Marx and Engels is remarkable even given the vast social and political differences between the time of their writings and the present day. The study of urban growth and struggle over the past century in many respects illustrates capitalist movement through space, the ways economic imperatives shape the growth of cities, and the salience of the sensuous laboring body as Marx detailed these issues in his writings. As academics and pundits are debating the relevance of Marxist thought, it seems that ordinary people—folks directly impacted by workplace exploitation and marginalization and crises in housing, education, and health—remain undeterred in their belief of the importance of collective action, solidarity on the part of the marginalized, and the impact of material institutions and structures on their bodies.

The task is to join what appear to be disparate resistance movements to a larger globalized movement for social justice and human rights. Black Lives Matter seeks justice in the face of all forms of anti-black racism, or what has been referred to as the "new Jim Crow" (Petersen-Smith 2015).[4] Local chapters of Black Lives Matter have worked in solidarity with struggles for Palestinian rights, a minimum living wage, and pro-democracy movements worldwide (Petersen-Smith 2015). Likewise, residents active in resisting Detroit's forced austerity and sweeping privatization of public services framed their endeavors as part of a larger resistance to the global trajectory of neoliberal policies imposed on poorer countries in Europe and in Central and South America. For scholars committed to turning theory into praxis, we may continue to explore and exercise rhetorical strategies effective at challenging institutions and systems (e.g., capitalism, two-party politics) that disguise as impartial and universally good. We might, as Detroit activist Martha Grevatt suggests, see Detroit—and I would add West Harlem—as templates for the rest of the country prompting people everywhere to be in solidarity with the efforts of black communities galvanizing for their homes, their health, and their lives. Keeping an eye on the optimistic moments of resistance that have resulted in victories such as marriage equality and the traction of Black Lives Matter, we may continue to believe, as environmental justice activist Vernice Miller (1993) asserted, "Struggle works!" (722).

NOTES

1. See also Murray, Burke, Marcius, and Parascandola (2014), Bloom and Imam (2014), Koeske (2014). The Murray et al. account had Garner weighing 400 pounds.

2. In the report, *War Comes Home*, the American Civil Liberties Union found state and local law enforcement agencies have been using federal funds to pay for the "weapons and tactics of war" (2). Notably, the militarization of the police has racialized implications as a majority of the hyperaggressive tactics and equipment have been deployed in the name of the War on Drugs, which has disproportionately targeted communities of color. During unrest in Ferguson, Missouri, in the wake of the shooting death of Michael Brown, local police wore Kevlar vests, helmets, and camouflage and were armed with automatic rifles and tear gas (Bouie 2014).

3. These contrasting views have been articulated by Cloud (1994; 2006), Gunn & Cloud (2010), and Triece (2001, 2013). For arguments supporting the discursification of materiality see Greene (1998, 2004).

4. Michelle Alexander's widely acclaimed book, *The New Jim Crow: Mass Incarceration in the Age of Colorblindness* describes the rampant imprisonment of hundreds of thousands of black men as a contemporary form of de facto racism.

Bibliography

A call for an international people's assembly against the banks and against austerity. (2013). Detroiters Resisting Emergency Management. Retrieved from http://www.d-rem.org/oct-5-6-international-peoples-assembly-against-the-banks-and-against-austerity/.

A hurricane without water: Fannie Mae, Freddie Mac, and the foreclosure crisis in metro Detroit. Flyer of Detroit Eviction Defense. Retrieved from http://detroitevictiondefense.org/.

Abbey-Lambertz, K. (2013, March 15). Michigan emergency management law in effect in 6 cities after Detroit appointment. *Huffington Post*. Retrieved from http://www.huffingtonpost.com/2013/03/15/michigan-emergency-manager-law-cities_n_2876777.html?

About the Black Lives Matter network. (n.d.). Black Lives Matter website. http://blacklivesmatter.com/about/.

Adler, W. M. (1995). *Land of opportunity*. Atlantic Monthly Press.

Aguilar, L. (2014a, October 24). 3 sites holding out in Red Wings arena district. *Detroit News*. Retrieved from http://www.detroitnews.com/story/business/real-estate/2014/10/24/ilitches-cass-corridor-arena/17811049/.

Aguilar, L. (2014b, March 6). Different strategies for Gilbert, Ilitches as they reshape Detroit. *Detroit News*. Page no longer available online.

Aguilar, L. (2014c, September 25). Ilitches set to launch new Wings arena and $650M dream. *Detroit News*. Retrieved from http://www.detroitnews.com/story/business/2014/09/25/detroit-red-wings-ilitch-cass-corridor-downtown-detroit/16192173/.

Aguilar, L. (2014d, October 1). Key policy roles for businesses, foundations in Detroit. *Detroit News*. Retrieved from http://www.detroitnews.com/story/business/2014/10/01/detroit-bankruptcy-kresge-foundation-dan-gilbert-rip-rapson-meeting-minds/16566475/.

Alcoff, L. (2006). *Visible identities: Race, gender, and the self*. Oxford: Oxford University Press.

Alexander, A., & Aouragh, M. (2014). Egypt's unfinished revolution: The role of the media revisited. *International Journal of Communication, 8*, 890–915.

Allagui, I. (2014). Waiting for spring: Arab resistance and change. *International Journal of Communication, 8*, 983–1007.

Allam, N. (2014). Blesses and curses: Virtual dissidence as a contentious performance in the Arab Spring's repertoire of contention. *International Journal of Communication, 8*, 853–870.

Allegretti, M. (2014, March 24). Introduction. Detroit: The next American city of opportunity. Manhattan Institute for Policy Research. Retrieved from http://www.manhattan-institute.org/multimedia/events/032414CSLL/.

Althusser, L. (1984). Ideology and ideological state apparatuses. In B. Brewster (Trans.), *Essays on ideology* (pp. 127–186). London: Verso.

American Civil Liberties Union. (2014). *War comes home: The excessive militarization of American policing*. ACLU Foundation. https://www.aclu.org/sites/default/files/field_document/jus14-warcomeshome-text-rel1.pdf.

Anderson, L. (2012). There is no alternative: The critical potential of alternative media for challenging neoliberal discourse. *tripleC, 10(2)*, 752–764.

Are you safe from environmental chemicals? (2010, March). *Harlem Community Voices*, 2.

Aristotle. (350 B. C. E.). *Politics*. Retrieved from http://classics.mit.edu/Aristotle/politics.7.seven.html.
Aristotle. (1954). *The rhetoric and the poetics of Aristotle*. Trans. W. Rhys Roberts. New York: The Modern Library.
Armstrong, H., Shumack, K. (2011). Ecologies of place: Emergent mapping practices, research perspectives and scenarios. *Global Media Journal-Australian Edition*. Retrieved from http://www.hca.uws.edu.au/gmjau/archive/v5_2011_2.
Arrieta, M., White, H. L., & Crook, E. D. (2008). Using zip code-level mortality data as a local health status indicator in Mobile, Alabama. *American Journal of Medical Science, 335*, 271–274.
Aune, J. A. (2001). *Selling the free market: The rhetoric of economic correctness*. New York: The Guilford Press.
Austen, B. (2014, July 13). Detroit, through rose-colored glasses. *New York Times Magazine*, 22–29, 37–38.
Babington, C. (2005). Some GOP legislators hit jarring notes in addressing Katrina. *Washington Post*. Retrieved from http://www.washingtonpost.com/wp-dyn/content/article/2005/09/09/AR2005090901930.html.
Babson, S. (2014, November 7). Reduce principal debt, fight home foreclosures. *Detroit News*. Retrieved from http://www.detroitnews.com/story/opinion/2014/11/06/fight-foreclosures-reduce-principal/18615959/.
Babson, S., Alpern, R., Elsila, D., and Revitte, J. (1986). *Detroit perspectives: The making of a union town*. Detroit: Wayne State University.
Back, L. (2005). "Home from home": Youth, belonging and place. In C. Alexander & C. Knowles (Eds.), *Making race matter: Bodies, space and identity* (pp. 19–41). New York: Palgrave Macmillan.
Bacon, J. (2003). Reading the reparations debate. *Quarterly Journal of Speech, 89*(3), 171–195.
Bailey, G. (2013, July). Accumulation by dispossession. *International Socialist Review*. Retrieved from http://isreview.org/issue/95/accumulation-dispossession.
Bailey, R. W. (1984). *The crisis regime: The MAC, the EFBC, and the political impact of the New York City financial crisis*. Albany: State University of New York Press.
Bambrough, R. (1963). Introduction to Politics. In R. Bambrough (introduction and commentary), *The philosophy of Aristotle* (pp. 379–381). New York: The New American Library.
Barney, T. (2009). Power lines: The rhetoric of maps as social change in the post-Cold War landscape. *Quarterly Journal of Speech, 95*(4), 412–434.
Barney, T. (2013). "'Gulag'-slavery, Inc.": The power of place and the rhetorical life of a Cold War map. *Rhetoric & Public Affairs, 16*(2), 317–354.
Bauer, K. (2009). On the politics and the possibilities of participatory mapping and GIS: Using spatial technologies to study common property and land use change among pastoralists in Central Tibet. *Cultural Geographies, 16*, 229–252.
Bauman, J. F. (1987). *Public housing, race, and renewal: Urban planning in Philadelphia, 1920–1974*. Philadelphia: Temple University Press.
Bay, M. (1998). "The world was thinking wrong about race": *The Philadelphia Negro* and nineteenth-century science. In M. B. Katz and T. J. Sugrue (Eds.), *W. E. B. DuBois, race, and the city: The Philadelphia Negro and its legacy* (pp. 41–60). Philadelphia: The University of Pennsylvania Press.
Beauregard, R. A. (2003). *Voices of decline: The postwar fate of U.S. cities*, 2nd Ed. New York: Routledge.
Benford, R. D. and Snow, D. A. (2000). Framing processes and social movements: An overview and assessment. *Annual Review of Sociology, 26*, 611–639.
Bennett, W. L. (2004). Communicating global activism: Strengths and vulnerabilities of networked politics. In W. van de Donk, B. D. Loader, P. G. Nixon, D. Rucht (Eds.), *Cyberprotest: New media, citizens and social movements* (pp. 123–147). London: Routledge.

Benson, L. (2009). Income, ZIP code, education are good indicators of health. MPRNews, October 9. Retrieved from http://www.mprnews.org/story/2009/10/05/social-determinants-of-health.

Berlant, L. (1997). *The queen of America goes to Washington city: Essays on sex and citizenship*. Durham, NC: Duke University Press.

Berman, L. (2014, October 2). Dan Gilbert's take on the blight stuff. *Detroit News*. Retrieved from http://www.detroitnews.com/story/opinion/columnists/laura-berman/2014/10/02/gilbert-blight-fight-detroit-berman/16570359/.

Beveridge, A. A., and Weber, S. (2008). Race and class in the developing New York and Los Angeles metropolises. In Ed. David Halle, *New York & Los Angeles: Politics, society and culture* (pp. 49–78). Chicago: The University of Chicago Press.

Birdsall, W. F. (2007). Web 2.0 as a social movement. *Webology, 4*. Retrieved from http://www.webology.org/2007/v4n2/a40.html.

Birdsell, D. S. (1987). Ronald Reagan on Lebanon and Grenada: Flexibility and interpretation in the application of Kenneth Burke's pentad. *Quarterly Journal of Speech, 73*, 267–279.

Bitzer, L. (1968). The rhetorical situation. *Philosophy and Rhetoric, 1*, 1–14.

Black. E. (1970). The second persona. *Quarterly Journal of Speech, 56*, 109–119.

Black, J. (1997). *Maps and politics*. Chicago: University of Chicago Press.

Black Lives Matter statement. (2015, Dec.). Black Lives Matter website. http://blacklivesmatter.com/black-lives-matter-statement-no-business-as-usual-black-xmas-is-here/.

Blackwell, B. (2014, Nov. 26). Tamir Rice's father has history of domestic violence. http://www.cleveland.com/metro/index.ssf/2014/11/tamir_rices_father_has_history.html.

Blair, C., Dickinson, G., & Ott, B. L. (2010). Introduction: Rhetoric/Memory/Place. In G. Dickinson, C. Blair, & B. L. Ott (Eds.), *Places of public memory: The rhetoric of museums and memorials* (pp. 1–54).Tuscaloosa: The University of Alabama Press.

Bloom, D. E., and Imm, J. (2014, Dec. 8). New York man dies after chokehold by police. CNN. http://www.cnn.com/2014/07/20/justice/ny-chokehold-death/

Bobo, L., Kluegel, J. R., and Smith, R. A. (1997). Laissez-faire racism: The crystallization of a kinder, gentler, antiblack ideology. In S. A. Tuch and J. K. Martin (Eds.), *Racial attitudes in the 1990s: Continuity and change* (pp. 15–42). Westport, CN: Praeger.

Bodnar, J. (1992). *Remaking America: Public memory, commemoration, and patriotism in the twentieth century*. Princeton, NJ: Princeton University Press.

Body-Gendrot, S. (2000). *The social control of cities? A comparative perspective*. Oxford: Blackwell Publishers.

Bouie, J. (2014, March 12). What Paul Ryan gets wrong about "inner-city" poverty. *The Daily Beast*. Retrieved from http://www.thedailybeast.com/articles/2014/03/12/what-paul-ryan-gets-wrong-about-inner-city-poverty.html.

Bouie, J. (2014, August 13). The militarization of the police. *Slate*. http://www.slate.com/articles/news_and_politics/politics/2014/08/police_in_ferguson_military_weapons_threaten_protesters.html.

Boyer, P. (1978). *Urban masses and moral order in America, 1820–1920*. Cambridge, MA: Harvard University Press.

Brecher, C, Horton, R. D., with Cropf, R. A., and Mead, D. M. (1993). *Power failure: New York City politics and policy since 1960*. New York: Oxford University Press.

Brodock, K. (2010). Economic and social factor: The digital (activism) divide. In M. Joyce (Ed.), *Digital activism decoded: The new mechanics of change* (pp. 71–84). New York: IDEBATE Press.

Brookfield, S. (2003). Putting the critical back into critical pedagogy: A commentary on the path of dissent. *Journal of Transformative Education, 1*(2), 141–149.

Brouwer, D. (1998). The precarious visibility politics of self-stigmatization: The case of HIV/AIDS tattoos. *Text and Performance Quarterly, 18*, 114–136.

Brown, P. (1992). Popular epidemiology and toxic waste contamination: Lay and professional ways of knowing. *Journal of Health and Social Behavior, 33*, 267–281.

Brown, P. (1993). When the public knows better: Popular epidemiology challenges the system. *Environment: Science and Policy for Sustainable Development, 35*(8), 16–41.

Bryant, J. (2014). Moving people out of Detroit. *Voice of Detroit.* Retrieved from http://voiceofdetroit.net/2014/02/04/moving-people-out-of-detroit/.

Bukowski, D. (2010, September 29). Bing's Detroit—the next New Orleans? *Voice of Detroit.* Retrieved from http://voiceofdetroit.net/2010/09/29/bings-detroit-the-next-new-orleans/.

Bukowski, D. (2011, November 26). Bing, council declare war on retirees, try to take 13th check; public hearing Tues. No. 29, 9:30 AM. *Voice of Detroit.* Retrieved from http://voiceofdetroit.net/2011/11/26/bing-council-declare-war-on-retirees-try-to-take-13th-check/.

Bukowski, D. (2013a, December 15). City council, state, feds, non-profits in bed with developers destroying black Detroit. *Voice of Detroit.* Retrieved from http://voiceofdetroit.net/2013/12/15/city-council-state-feds-non-profits-in-bed-with-developers-destroying-black-detroit/.

Bukowski, D. (2013b, April 8). Only Wall Street wins in Detroit crisis reaping $474 million fee. *Voice of Detroit.* Retrieved from http://voiceofdetroit.net/2013/04/08/only-wall-street-wins-in-detroit-crisis-reaping-474-million-fee/.

Bukowski, D. (2013c, January 27). Tax abatement 'deal with devil' in downtown Griswold tenants' eviction has gone to hell. *Voice of Detroit.* Retrieved from http://voiceofdetroit.net/2014/01/27/tax-abatement-deal-with-devil-in-downtown-griswold-tenants-eviction-has-gone-to-hell/.

Bukowski, D. (2014, February 18). Downtown Detroit's Griswold Apartments: "I see white people"; Council hearing Thurs. Feb. 20. *Voice of Detroit.* Retrieved from http://voiceofdetroit.net/2014/02/18/downtown-detroits-griswold-apartments-i-see-white-people-council-hearing-thurs-feb-20/.

Bukowski, D. (2015, June 21). Turn Detroit's lights on! *Voice of Detroit.* Retrieved from http://voiceofdetroit.net/2015/06/21/turn-detroits-lights-on/.

Bullard, R. D. (Ed.). (1994). *Unequal protection: Environmental justice and communities of color.* San Francisco: Sierra Club Books.

Bullard, R. D. (Ed.). (1994). Environmental justice for all. In R. D. Bullard (Ed.), *Unequal protection: Environmental justice and communities of color* (pp. 3–22). San Francisco: Sierra Club Books.

Bullard, R. D. (2000). *Dumping in Dixie: Race, class and environmental quality*, 3rd Ed. Boulder, CO: Westview Press.

Bullard, R. D. (2001). Environmental justice in the 21st century: Race still matters. *Phylon, 49*, 151–171.

Bullard, R. D., Mohai, P., Saha, R., & Wright, B. (2007). *Toxic wastes and race at twenty, 1987–2007.* Cleveland, OH: United Church of Christ.

Bullard, R. D., & Wright, B. (Eds.). (2009). *Race, Place, and environmental justice after Hurricane Katrina: Struggles to reclaim, rebuild, and revitalize New Orleans and the Gulf Coast.* Boulder, CO: Westview Press.

Burch, E. A., & Harry, J. C. (2004). Counter-hegemony and environmental justice in California newspapers: Source use patterns in stories about pesticides and farm workers. *J & MC Quarterly, 81*, 559–577.

Burgess, E. W. (1925). The growth of the city: An introduction to a research project. In . In R. E. Park, E. W. Burgess, R. D. McKenzie (Eds.), *The city* (pp. 47–62). Chicago: University of Chicago Press.

Burke, K. (1966). *Language as symbolic action.* Berkeley: University of California Press.

Burke, K. (1969a). *A grammar of motives.* Berkeley: University of California Press.

Burke, K. (1969b). *A rhetoric of motives.* Berkeley: University of California Press.

Butterworth, M. L. (2007). Race in "The Race": Mark McGwire, Sammy Sosa, and heroic constructions of whiteness. *Critical Studies in Media Communication, 24*(3), 228–244.

Caldeira, T. P. R. (1999). Fortified enclave: The new urban segregation. In S. M. Low (Ed.). *Theorizing the city: The new urban anthropology reader* (pp. 83–107). New Brunswick, NJ: Rutgers University Press.
Call to Action. (2014, May). flyer. Detroiters Resisting Emergency Management. Retrieved from http://www.d-rem.org/call-to-action-may-day-solidarity-against-emergency-management-in-michigan/.
Campbell, K. K. (1973). The rhetoric of women's liberation: An oxymoron. *Quarterly Journal of Speech, 59*, 74–86.
Campbell, K. K., & Jamieson, K. H. (1978). Form and genre in rhetorical criticism: An introduction. In K. K. Campbell, K. H. Jamieson (Eds.), *Form and genre: Shaping rhetorical action* (pp. 9–32). Falls Church, VA: Speech Communication Association.
Campbell, M. (2014, June 2). City of Detroit trash pickup services begin new era of privatization. CBS Detroit. Retrieved from http://detroit.cbslocal.com/2014/06/02/city-of-detroit-trash-pickup-services-begin-new-era-of-privatization/.
Caro, R. (1974). *The power broker: Robert Moses and the fall of New York*. New York: Alfred A. Knopf.
Carpenter, R. H. (1977). Frederick Jackson Turner and the rhetorical impact of the frontier thesis. *Quarterly Journal of Speech, 63*, 117–129.
CBS's Mideast "cycle of violence." (2006). Fairness & Accuracy in Reporting. Retrieved from http://fair.org/take-action/action-alerts/cbss-mideast-cycle-of-violence/.
Charland, M. (1987). Constitutive rhetoric: The case of the Peuple Québécois. *Quarterly Journal of Speech, 73*, 133–150.
Chinyelu, M. (1999). *Harlem ain't nothin' but a third world country: The global economy, empowerment zones and the colonial status of Africans in America*. New York: Mustard Seed Press.
Clines, F. X. (1993). Candidates attack the squeegee men. *New York Times*, September 26, p. 39.
Cloud, D. L. (1994). The materiality of discourse as oxymoron: A challenge to critical rhetoric. *Western Journal of Communication, 58*, 141–163.
Cloud, D. L. (2003). Therapy, silence, and war: Consolation and the end of deliberation in the "affected" public. *Poroi, 2*(1), 125–142. Available at: http://dx.doi.org/10.13008/2151-2957.1060.
Cloud, D. L. (2006). *The Matrix* and critical theory's desertion of the real. *Communication and Critical/Cultural Studies 3*, 329–354.
Cole, L. W., & Foster, S. R. (2001). *From the ground up: Environmental racism and the rise of the environmental justice movement*. New York: New York University Press.
Collin, R. W., & Harris, W. (1993). Race and waste in two Virginia communities. In R. D. Bullard (Ed.), *Confronting environmental racism: Voices from the grassroots* (pp. 93–106). Boston, MA: South End Press.
Collins, P. H. (1986). Learning from the outsider within: The sociological significance of black feminist thought. *Social Problems, 33*, S14–S32
Collins, P. H. (1991). *Black feminist thought: Knowledge, consciousness, and the politics of empowerment*. New York: Routledge.
Collins, P. H. (1994). Shifting the center: Race, class, and feminist theorizing about motherhood. In E. N. Glenn, G. Chang, & L. R. Forcey (Eds.), *Mothering: Ideology, experience, and agency* (pp. 45–65). New York: Routledge.
Colombia will end coca crop-dusting, citing health concerns. (2015, May 18). National Public Radio. Retrieved from http://www.npr.org/templates/transcript/transcript.php?storyId=406988063.
Community outreach education core. WE ACT website. Page no longer available.
Community stressors and susceptibility to air pollution in urban asthma. WE ACT website. Retrieved from http://www.weact.org/Projects/CleanAirQuality/CommunityStressors/tabid/610/Default.aspx.
Conley, D. (2010). Grid and swerve. *Critical Studies in Media Communication, 27*, 24–38.
Conley, D., and Dickinson, G. (2010). Textural democracy. *Critical Studies in Media Communication, 27*, 1–7.

Cooper, M. (1999). Spatial discourses and social boundaries: Re-imagining the Toronto waterfront. In S. M. Low (Ed.). *Theorizing the city: The new urban anthropology reader* (pp. 377–399). New Brunswick, NJ: Rutgers University Press.

Corburn, J. (2005). *Street science: Community knowledge and environmental health justice.* Cambridge, MA: The MIT Press.

Corrigan, Z. (2013a, June 20). As developers gentrify Detroit, evictions increase. World Socialist website. Retrieved from http://www.wsws.org/en/articles/2013/06/20/detr-j20.html?view=print.

Corrigan, Z. (2013b, August 1). Detroit's downtown 'development' plan: A blueprint written by and for the corporate elite. World Socialist website. Retrieved from https://www.wsws.org/en/articles/2013/08/01/gent-j01.html.

Cosgrove, D. (1999). Introduction: Mapping meaning. In D. Cosgrove (Ed.), *Mappings* (pp. 1–23). London: Reaktion Books Ltd.

Cox, R. J. (1990). Memory, critical theory, and the argument from history. *Argumentation & Advocacy, 27*(1), 1–13.

Crenshaw, C. (1997). Resisting whiteness' rhetorical silence. *Western Journal of Communication, 61*(3), 253–278.

Cross, M., & Keith, M. (Eds.). (1993). *Racism, the city and the state.* London: Routledge.

Davey, M. (2014a, May 27). Detroit urged to tear down 40,000 buildings. *New York Times.* Retrieved from http://www.nytimes.com/2014/05/28/us/detroit-task-force-says-blight-cleanup-will-cost-850-million.html?_r=0.

Davey, Monica. (2014b, July 22). Detroit's retirees vote to lower pensions, in support of bankruptcy plan. *New York Times.* Retrieved from http://www.nytimes.com/2014/07/22/us/detroits-retirees-vote-to-lower-pensions-in-support-of-bankruptcy-plan.html?_r=0.

Davidson, K. (2012). Detroit has tons of vacant land. But forty square miles? http://michiganradio.org/post/detroit-has-tons-vacant-land-forty-square-miles#stream/0.

Davis, P. (2013). Memoryscapes in transition: Black history museums, new south narratives, and urban regeneration. *Southern Communication Journal, 78*(2), 107–127.

Davisson, A. (2011). Beyond the borders of red and blue states: Google Maps as a site of rhetorical invention in the 2008 presidential election. *Rhetoric & Public Affairs, 14*(1), 101-124.

Defend Detroit city pensions & services—make the banks pay. (2014). Moratorium NOW! Retrieved from http://moratorium-mi.org/emergency-town-hall-meeting-sunday-march-2-3-pm/

Detroit bankruptcy exit plan: Pension cuts, millions for blight. (2014, February 21). *Detroit News.* Page no longer available online.

Detroit emergency manager Kevyn Orr pleased with Judge Rhodes's confirmation of city of Detroit's Plan of Adjustment. (2014, November 7). Retrieved from http://www.prnewswire.com/news-releases/detroit-emergency-manager-kevyn-orr-pleased-with-judge-rhodess-confirmation-of-city-of-detroits-plan-of-adjustment-281946161.html.

Detroit eviction defense: Who we are. Retrieved from http://detroitevictiondefense.org/coalition.php.

Detroit future city: Detroit strategic framework plan. (2012, December). Retrieved from http://detroitfuturecity.com/framework/.

Detroit state of emergency. (2013, November 27). *Michigan Citizen.* Page no longer available online.

Detroit streetlight repairs ahead of schedule. (2014, Dec. 4). *Detroit Free Press.* Retrieved from http://www.freep.com/story/news/local/michigan/detroit/2014/12/04/new-streetlights-detroit-progress/19866749/.

Detroit: The next American city of opportunity. (2014, March 24). Manhattan Institute. Link to the video has been made private since the author viewed it in March 2014.

Di Chiro, G. (1992). Defining environmental justice. *Socialist Review, 22*, 93–130.

Dickinson, G. (2006). The Pleasantville effect: Nostalgia and the visual framing of (white) suburbia. *Western Journal of Communication, 70*, 212–233.

Dickinson, G., & Ott, B. L. (2014). Two memory scholars reflect on the politics of remembering. *Spectra*, March/May, 18–21.

Dill, K. (2015, May 5). Quicken's Dan Gilbert: Detroit is ready to compete for talent with Silicon Valley. *Forbes*. Retrieved from http://www.forbes.com/sites/kathryndill/2015/05/05/quickens-dan-gilbert-detroit-is-ready-to-compete-for-talent-with-silicon-valley/.

Ding, H. (2013). Transcultural risk communication and viral discourses: Grassroots movements to manage global risks of H1N1 flu pandemic. *Technical Communication Quarterly*, 22, 126–49.

Dotson Newman, O. (2014). Personal interview with the author. May 28.

Downey, J., and N. Fenton. (2003). New media, counter publicity and the public sphere. *New Media & Society*, 5, 185–202.

Downing, J. (2008). Social movement theories and alternative media: An evaluation and critique. Communication, Culture & Critique, 1, 40–50.

Downing, J. D. H., T. Villarreal Ford, G. Gil, and L. Stein. (2001). *Radical media: Rebellious communication and social movements*. Thousand Oaks, CA: Sage Publications.

Dreier, P., Mollenkopf, J., & Swanstrom, T. (2001). *Place matters: Metropolitics for the twenty-first century*. Lawrence, Kansas: University Press of Kansas.

D-REM objection to debtor's motion to approve settlement. (2014, March 17). Detroiters Resisting Emergency Management. Retrieved from http://www.d-rem.org/bankruptcyobjection/.

D-REM statement on "The Albert." (2014, March 21). Retrieved from http://www.d-rem.org/d-rem-statement-on-the-albert/.

DuBois, W. E. B. (1899/1996). *The Philadelphia Negro: A social study*. Philadelphia: The University of Pennsylvania Press.

DuBois, W. E. B. (1903). *The souls of black folk*. New York: Penguin Group.

Duffy, M. J. (2010). Code Orange: How the internet, cell phones and new technologies helped shape the Ukrainian Revolution of 2004. *Atlanta Review of Journalism History*, 11, 69–84.

Dunlap, D. W. (1989, May 17). Atop a Harlem waste plant, a park grows. *New York Times*, B1.

Dutta, M. J. (2011). *Communicating social change: Structure, culture, and agency*. New York: Routledge.

Dutta, M. J., & Pal, M. (2007). The internet as a site of resistance: The case of the Narmada Bachao Andolan. In S. Duhe (Ed.), *New media and public relations* (pp. 203–215). New York: Peter Lang.

Dyer, R. (1998). White. *Screen*, 29(4), 44–65.

Eagleton, T. (1991). *Ideology: An introduction*. London: Verso.

Eisenbrey, R. (2013). CNN opinion: What bled Detroit dry? It's not pensions. *Voice of Detroit*. Retrieved from http://voiceofdetroit.net/2013/12/21/cnn-opinion-what-bled-detroit-dry-its-not-pensions/.

Ellis, T. (2013, November 18). Developers, HUD, non-profits collude to move Detroit seniors, disabled out of downtown Griswold Apts. *Voice of Detroit*. Retrieved from http://voiceofdetroit.net/2013/11/18/developers-hud-non-profits-collude-to-move-detroit-seniors-disabled-out-of-downtown-griswold-apts/.

Emergency management is racism. (2013, August 21). *Michigan Citizen*. Page no longer available online.

Engels, F. (1845/2005). The great towns. excerpted from The condition of the working class in England in 1844. In R. T. LeGates & F. Stout (Eds.), *The city reader*, 3rd Ed., (pp. 58–66). London: Routledge.

Engels, F. (1890/1978). Letters on historical materialism. In R. C. Tucker (Ed.), *The Marx-Engels reader*, 2nd Ed. (pp. 760–768). New York: W. W. Norton & Company.

Entman, R. M., & Rojecki, A. (2000). *The black image in the white mind: Media and race in America*. Chicago: The University of Chicago Press.

Environmental justice advocacy & government accountability. WE ACT website. Retrieved from http://www.weact.org/SandBox/Test1/tabid/202/Default.aspx.

Environmental justice in the United States: Threats to quality of life. (2002). Atlanta, GA: Environmental Justice Resource Center.
Escobar, A. (1995). *Encountering development: The making and unmaking of the third world*. Princeton, NJ: Princeton University Press.
Ewalt, J. P. (2011). Mapping injustice: The *World is Witness*, place-framing, and the politics of viewing on Google Earth. *Communication, Culture & Critique, 4*, 333–354.
Faith leaders for EJ sketch plan for achieving food justice. (2010, September). *Harlem Community Voices*, 4.
Falola, B. I35 borderland. Retrieved from http://www.racheltanurmemorialprize.org/i35-borderland/.
Fannie Mae head greeted with protest. (n.d.). Detroit Eviction Defense. Retrieved from http://detroitevictiondefense.org/news.php#tax2015.
Ferretti, C. (2014a, February 21). Detroit plans $1.5B in capital improvement, looks at leasing airport and parking. *Detroit News*. Page no longer available online.
Ferretti, C. (2014b, March 13). Orr touts successes, maps out more Detroit improvements. *Detroit News*. Page no longer available online.
Ferris, D. (1994). A call for justice and equal environmental protection. In R. D. Bullard (Ed.), *Unequal protection: Environmental justice and communities of color* (pp. 298–319). San Francisco: Sierra Club Books.
Finley, A. (2013, August 5). Journal interview with Kevyn Orr: How Detroit can rise again. *Wall Street Journal*, 16.
Finn, R. (2014, August 3). Busy. Noisy. Homey. *New York Times*, 8.
Fischer, F. (1990). *Technocracy and the politics of expertise*. Newbury Park, Calif: Sage Publications.
Fischer, F. (2000). *Citizens, experts, and the environment: The politics of local knowledge*. Durham, NC: Duke University Press.
Fisher, W. R. (1980). Rationality and the logic of good reasons. *Philosophy and Rhetoric, 13*(2), 121–130.
Fisher, W. R. (1982). Romantic democracy, Ronald Reagan, and presidential heroes. *Western Journal of Speech Communication, 46*, 299–310.
Fisher. W. R. (1984). Narration as a human communication paradigm: The case of public moral argument. *Communication Monographs, 51*, 1–22.
Ford, G. (2013, March 26). Vampire capitalism comes to Detroit, MI and Dekalb County, GA. *Voice of Detroit*. Retrieved from http://voiceofdetroit.net/2013/03/26/vampire-capitalism-comes-to-detroit-mi-and-dekalb-county-ga/.
Ford, G. (2014). Detroit's agony shows why black America needs a people's plan for the cities. *Black Agenda Report*. Retrieved from http://www.blackagendareport.com/content/detroit%E2%80%99s-agony-shows-why-black-america-needs-people%E2%80%99s-plan-cities.
Ford, T. V. and G. Gil. (2001). Radical internet use. In J. D. H. Downing, with T. V. Ford, G. Gil, and L. Stein, *Radical media: Rebellious communication and social movements* (pp. 201–234). Thousand Oaks, CA: Sage Publications, Inc.
Foroohar, R. (2014, August 28). Detroit: America's emerging market. *Time*. Retrieved from http://time.com/3204249/detroit-americas-emerging-market/.
Foster, J. B. (2010). The financialization of accumulation. *Monthly Review*. Retrieved from http://monthlyreview.org/2010/10/01/the-financialization-of-accumulation/.
Foucault, M. (1980). *Power/Knowledge: Selected interviews and other writings, 1972–1977*. New York: Pantheon Books.
Frangonikolopoulos, C. A., & Chapsos, I. (2012). Explaining the role and the impact of the social media in the Arab Spring. *GMJ: Mediterranean Edition, 8*, 10–20.
Fraser, N. (1990). Rethinking the public sphere: A contribution to the critique of an actually existing democracy. *Social Text, 25/26*, 56–80.
Freeman, L. (2006). *There goes the 'hood: Views of gentrification from the ground up*. Philadelphia: Temple University Press.
Freund, D. M. (2007). *Colored property: State policy and white racial politics in suburban America*. Chicago: University of Chicago Press.

Fried, J. P. (1976). City's housing administrator proposes "planned shrinkage" of some slums. *New York Times*, February 3.

Friedenberg, D. M. (1992). *Life, liberty, and the pursuit of land*. Buffalo, NY: Prometheus Books.

Fuchs, C. (2012). Some reflections on Manuel Castells' book *Networks of Outrage and Hope. Social Movements in the Internet Age*. tripleC, 10, 775–797.

Furay, S. (2013, December 5). People's forum uses hip hop and Detroit culture to oppose EM. *Michigan Citizen*. Page no longer available online.

Gaist, T. (2013, December 17). Bankruptcy judge moves to privatize Detroit public lighting system. World Socialist website. Retrieved from http://www.wsws.org/en/articles/2013/12/17/dplr-d17.html.

Gallagher, J. (2012, April 1). With so much space, so few options—Detroit's vast vacant lots are a burden. *Detroit Free Press*. Retrieved from http://archive.freep.com/article/20120401/NEWS01/204010467/With-so-much-space-so-few-options-Detroit-s-vast-vacant-lots-are-a-burden.

Gallagher, J. (2013, May 2). Griswold apartments low-income housing to be redeveloped. *Detroit Free Press*. Retrieved from http://archive.freep.com/article/20130502/BUSINESS06/305020093/Griswold-Building-Capitol-Park-downtown-Detroit.

Gallagher, J. (2014a, July 27). One downtown, two empires: Mike Ilitch and Dan Gilbert reshape Detroit. *Detroit Free Press*. Retrieved from http://archive.freep.com/article/20140727/NEWS01/307270087/Gilbert-Ilitch-Red-Wings-Tigers-Quicken-Detroit

Gallagher, J. (2014b, September 28). Detroit's on a development fast track. *Detroit Free Press*. Retrieved from http://www.freep.com/story/news/local/michigan/detroit/2014/09/28/downtown-m-rail-arena-bridge/16343825/.

Gallagher, J., & Walsh, T. (2014, December 10). Little Caesars HQ latest entry in downtown upswing. *Detroit Free Press*. Retrieved from http://www.freep.com/story/money/business/michigan/2014/12/10/ilitch-little-caesars-detroit/20192073/.

Galusky, W. (2003). Identifying with information: Citizen empowerment, the internet, and the environmental anti-toxins movement. In M. McCaughey and M. D. Ayers (Eds.), *Cyberactivism: Online activism in theory and practice* (pp. 185–205). New York: Routledge.

Gans, H. J. (1982). *The urban villagers: Group and class in the life of Italian-Americans*. New York: The Free Press.

Garbage, pests & pesticides campaign has deep roots in WE ACT's efforts to improve Harlem's environment. (2009, June). *Harlem Community Voices*, 5.

Garcia-Navarro, L. (2013). Once unsafe, Rio's shantytowns see rapid gentrification. National Public Radio. Retrieved from http://www.npr.org/blogs/parallels/2013/06/10/187325080/once-unsafe-rios-shanty-towns-see-rapid-gentrification

Garcia-Navarro, L. (2014, February 27). As Brazil gears up for Olympics, some poor families get moved out. National Public Radio. Retrieved from http://www.npr.org/sections/parallels/2014/02/27/276514012/as-brazil-gears-up-for-olympics-some-poor-families-get-moved-out.

Gaventa, J. (1993). The powerful, the powerless, and the experts: Knowledge in the information age. In M. Brydon-Miller, B. Hall, T. Jackson, & P. Park (Eds.), *Voices of change: Participatory research in the United States and Canada* (pp. 20–46). Toronto: OISE Press.

Geertz, C. (1983). *Local knowledge: Further essays in interpretive anthropology*. New York: Basic Books.

Gentrification is apartheid. (2014, January 6). *Michigan Citizen*. Page no longer available online.

Georgakas, D., and Surkin, M. (1975). *Detroit: I do mind dying. A study in urban revolution*. New York: St. Martin's Press.

Ghonim, W. (2012). *Revolution 2.0: The power of the people is greater than the people in power, a memoir*. Boston: Houghton Mifflin Harcourt.

Gibb, C. (2006). Deterritorialized people in hyperspace: Creating and debating Harari identity over the internet. In K. Landzelius (Ed.), *Native on the net: Indigenous and diasporic peoples in the virtual age* (pp. 169–185). London: Routledge.

Gideon, V. (2006). Canadian aboriginal peoples tackle e-health: Seeking ownership versus integration. In K. Landzelius (Ed.), *Native on the net: Indigenous and diasporic peoples in the virtual age* (pp. 61–79). London: Routledge.

Gilens, M. (1999). *Why Americans hate welfare: Race, media and the politics of antipoverty policy*. Chicago: University of Chicago Press.

Ginossar, T., & Nelson, S. (2010). Reducing the health and digital divides: A model for using community-based participatory research approach to e-health interventions in low-income Hispanic communities. *Journal of Computer-Mediated Communication, 15*(4), 530–551.

Giroux, H. A. (1997). *Pedagogy and the politics of hope: Theory, culture, and schooling*. Boulder, CO: Westview Press.

Giroux, H. A. (2003). Spectacles of race and pedagogies of denial: Anti-black racist pedagogy under the reign of neoliberalism. *Communication Education, 52*, 191–211.

Glink, I. (2012). U.S. housing market remains deeply segregated. Retrieved from http://www.cbsnews.com/news/us-housing-market-remains-deeply-segregated/

Goings, K. W., & Mohl, R. A. (1996). Toward a new African American urban history. In K. W. Goings & R. A. Mohl (Eds.), *The new African American urban history* (pp. 1–16). Thousand Oaks: Sage.

Gold, A. R. (1991a, August 14). Flaws may cost millions at Harlem sewage plant. *New York Times*, A1.

Gold, A. R. (1991b, August 16). Turning sewage plants into friendly neighbors. *New York Times*, B3.

Goldberg, D. T. (1993). "Polluting the body politic": Racist discourse and urban location. In M. Cross & M. Keith (Eds.), *Racism, the city and the state* (pp. 45–60). London: Routledge.

Goldberg, D. T. (2009). *The threat of race: Reflections on racial neoliberalism*. NJ: Wiley-Blackwell.

Goldsmith, W. W. (2000). From the metropolis to globalization: The dialectics of race and urban form. In P. Marcuse & R. van Kempen (Eds.), *Globalizing cities: A new spatial order?* (pp. 37–55). Oxford: Blackwell.

Gonzalez, M. (n.d.). Don't mourn, organize: Power and passion for environmental justice and democracy. Bioneers Media: Videos, voices and words inspiring global citizens. Retrieved from http://media.bioneers.org/listing/dont-mourn-organize-power-and-passion-for-environmental-justice-and-democracy-mary-gonzalez/.

Goodman, J. D., and J. Goldstein. (2014, Aug. 19). Grand jury to take up death linked to police chokehold in Staten Island. *New York Times*. http://www.nytimes.com/2014/08/20/nyregion/eric-garner-staten-island-police-chokehold-case-to-go-to-grand-jury.html?_r=0.

Goodnough, A. (2016, Jan. 29). Flint weighs scope of harm to children caused by lead in water. *New York Times*. http://www.nytimes.com/2016/01/30/us/flint-weighs-scope-of-harm-to-children-caused-by-lead-in-water.html?_r=0.

Gray, H. (1989). Television, black Americans, and the American dream. *Critical Studies in Mass Communication, 6*, 376–386.

Greaves, C. (2004, March/April). Bad air linked to low birth weight, small head size. *Uptown Eye*, p. 5.

Greene, R. W. (1998). Another materialist rhetoric. *Critical Studies in Media Communication, 15*(1), 21–40.

Greene, R. W. (2004). "Rhetoric and capitalism: Rhetorical agency as communicative labor." *Philosophy and Rhetoric, 37*,188-206.

Greene, R. W. (2010). Spatial materialism: Labor, location, and transnational literacy. *Critical Studies in Media Communication, 27*, 105-110.

Gregory, S. (1998). *Black Corona: Race and the politics of place in an urban community*. Princeton, NJ: Princeton University Press.

Grevatt, M. (2015). Personal interview with the author. March 26.
Griffin, W. H. Jr. (2014). Personal interview with the author. March 23.
Griffin, W. H. Jr. (2014). Letter to Dan Gilbert. Photocopy given to the author by Griffin.
Griswold tenants speak out on threatened eviction. (2013). *World Socialist website*, July 1. http://www.wsws.org/en/articles/2013/07/01/intr-j01.html.
Gross, A. (1990). *The rhetoric of science*. Cambridge: Harvard University Press.
Gross, L. (2003). The gay global village in cyberspace. In Eds. N. Couldry and J. Curran, *Contesting media power: Alternative media in a networked world*. Lanham, Md.: Rowman & Littlefield. 259–273.
Grossberg, L. (1993). Cultural studies and/in new worlds. *Critical Studies in Mass Communication, 10*, 1–22.
Grossman, K. (1994). The People of Color Environmental Summit. In R. D. Bullard (Ed.), *Unequal protection: Environmental justice and communities of color* (pp. 272–297). San Francisco: Sierra Club Books.
Grosz, E. A. (1994). *Volatile bodies: Toward a corporeal feminism*. Indiana University Press.
Gunaratne, S. A. (2006). Public sphere and communicative rationality: Interrogating Habermas's eurocentrism. *Journalism & Communication Monographs, 8*(2), 93–156.
Gunn, J. & Cloud, D. L. (2010). Agentic orientation as magical voluntarism. *Communication Theory, 20*, 50–78.
Gutiérrez, G. (1994). Mothers of East Los Angeles strike back. In R. D. Bullard (Ed.), *Unequal protection: Environmental justice and communities of color* (pp. 220–233). San Francisco: Sierra Club Books.
Habermas, J. (1984). *The theory of communicative action: Reason and the rationalization of society*. Boston: Beacon Press.
Hackworth, J. (2006). *The neoliberal city: Governance, ideology, and development in American urbanism*. Ithaca: Cornell University Press.
Haglund, L. (2010). *Limiting resources: Market-led reform and the transformation of public goods*. University Park, PA: The Pennsylvania State University.
Hallstein, D. L. O. (2000). Where standpoint stands now: An introduction and commentary. *Women's Studies in Communication, 23*, 1–15.
Hammerback, J. C. (1994). José Antonio's rhetoric of fascism. *Southern Communication Journal, 59*, 181–195.
Harding, S. (1993). Rethinking standpoint epistemology: "What is strong objectivity?" In L. Alcoff & E. Potter (Eds.), *Feminist Epistemologies* (49–82). New York: Routledge.
Harley, J. B. (2001). *The new nature of maps*. Baltimore: John Hopkins University Press.
Harley, J. B. (2011). Deconstructing the map. In M. Dodge, R. Kitchin, & C. Perkins (Eds.), *The map reader: Theories of mapping practice and cartographic representation* (pp. 56–64). Hoboken, NJ: Wiley-Blackwell.
HARP isn't enough! (n.d.). Detroit Eviction Defense flyer. Retrieved from http://detroitevictiondefense.org/flyers/2014/MelWatt-HARP_isnt_enough_10-3-14.pdf
Harris, R. (2004). Encouraging emergent moments: The personal, critical, and rhetorical in the writing classroom. *Pedagogy: Critical Approaches to Teaching Literature, Language, Composition, and Culture, 4*(3), 401–418.
Harris, R. A., Ed. (1997). *Landmark essays on rhetoric of science: Case studies*. Mahwah, N.J.: Hermagoras Press.
Hartsock, N. (1983a). *Money, sex, and power: Toward a feminist historical materialism*. New York: Longman.
Hartsock, N. (1983b). The feminist standpoint: Developing the ground for a specifically feminist historical materialism. In S. Harding & M. B. Hintikka (Eds.), *Discovering reality: Feminist perspectives on epistemology, metaphysics, methodology, and philosophy of science* (pp. 283–310). Boston, MA: D. Reidel Publishing Company.
Harvey, D. (1975). The geography of capitalist accumulation: A reconstruction of the Marxian theory. *Antipode, 7*(2), 9–21.

Harvey, D. (1983). Geography. In T. Bottomore, L. Harris, V. G. Kieman, & R. Miliband (Eds.). *A dictionary of Marxist thought* (pp. 189–192). Cambridge, MA: Harvard University Press.
Harvey, D. (1984). On the history and present condition of geography: An historical materialist manifesto. *The Professional Geographer, 36*, 1–11.
Harvey, D. (1989). *The condition of postmodernity: An enquiry into the origins of cultural change*. Oxford: Basil Blackwell.
Harvey, D. (1998). The body as an accumulation strategy. *Environment & Planning D: Society & Space, 16*, 401–421.
Harvey, D. (2000). *Spaces of hope*. Berkeley: University of California Press.
Harvey, D. (2003). *The new imperialism*. Oxford: Oxford University Press.
Harvey, D. (2005). *A brief history of neoliberalism*. Oxford: Oxford University Press.
Harvey, D. (2006a). Neo-Liberalism as creative destruction. *Geografiska Annaler Series B: Human Geography, 88*(2), 145–158.
Harvey, D. (2006b). *The limits to capital*. London: Verso.
Harvey, D. (2009). *Social justice and the city*. Athens: The University of Georgia Press.
Harvey, D. (2013). On why struggles over urban space matter: An interview with David Harvey. Conducted by Hiba Bou Akar and Nada Moumtaz. Jadaliyya. Retrieved from http://www.jadaliyya.com/pages/index/15156/on-why-struggles-over-urban-space-matter_an-interv.
Hasian, M. Jr., & Frank, R. E. (1999). Rhetoric, history, and collective memory: Decoding the Goldhagen Debates. *Western Journal of Communication, 63(1)*, 95–114.
Hekman, S. (1997). Truth and method: Feminist standpoint theory revisited. *Signs: Journal of Women in Culture and Society, 22*, 341–365.
Helms, M., Gray, K., Egan, P., & Spangler, T. (2014, February 22). Orr's Detroit bankruptcy plan puts pressure on pensioners, state, to ante up. *Detroit Free Press*. Retrieved from http://archive.freep.com/article/20140221/NEWS06/302220011/govern-or-rick-snyder-detroit-bankruptcy-plan-of-adjustment.
Herrada, E. (2013, July 25). Statement of the Honorable Elena Herrada, elected school board in exile. *Michigan Citizen*. Page no longer online.
Hicks, M. (2014, November 21). Neighbors get glimpse of Red Wings arena proposal. *Detroit News*. Retrieved from http://www.detroitnews.com/story/news/local/wayne-county/2014/11/21/red-wings-arena-neighbors-proposal/19375373/.
Higgins, R. R. (1994). Race, pollution, and the mastery of nature. *Environmental Ethics, 16*, 251–264.
Himelboim, I., & Han, J. Y. (2014). Cancer talk on twitter: Community structure and information sources in breast and prostate cancer social networks. *Journal of Health Communication: International Perspectives, 19*(2), 210–225.
Hine, D. C. (1996). Black migration to the urban Midwest: The gender dimension, 1915–1945. In K. W. Goings & R. A. Mohl (Eds.), *The new African American urban history* (pp. 240–265). Thousand Oaks: Sage.
Hirsch, A. R. (1983). *Making the second ghetto: Race & housing in Chicago 1940-1960*. Cambridge: Cambridge University Press.
History of WE ACT. WE ACT website. Retrieved from http://www.weact.org/Home/WEACTHistory/tabid/180/Default.aspx
Hoerl, K. (2012). Selective amnesia and racial transcendence in news coverage of President Obama's inauguration. *Quarterly Journal of Speech, 98(2)*, 178–202.
Holloway, L. (1992, September 1). 28 acres of roof and a place to play in West Harlem. *New York Times*, B1.
Hooghe, M., Vissers, S., Stolle, D., & Mahéo, V. (2010). The potential of internet mobilization: An experimental study on the effect of internet and face-to-face mobilization efforts. *Political Communication, 27*, 406–431.
hooks, b. (1984). *Feminist theory from margin to center*. Boston: South End Press.
hooks, b. (1992). *Black looks: Race and representation*. Boston: South End Press.
Horner, A., & Keane, A. (2000). *Body matters: Feminism, textuality, corporeality*. Manchester University Press.

Howell, S. (2014, March 6). Week 48 of the occupation. *Michigan Citizen*. Page no longer available online.

Humphreys, S. (2008). Grassroots creativity and community in new media environments: Yarn Harlot and the 4000 knitting Olympians. *Continuum: Journal of Media & Cultural Studies, 22*(3), 419–433.

Hyra, D. S. (2008). *The new urban renewal: The economic transformation of Harlem and Bronzeville*. Chicago: University of Chicago Press.

In U.S. media, Palestinians attack, Israel retaliates. (2002). Fairness & Accuracy in Reporting. Retrieved from http://fair.org/take-action/action-alerts/in-u-s-media-palestinians-attack-israel-retaliates/.

Internet usages statistics. (2014). Retrieved from http://www.internetworldstats.com/stats.htm.

Jackson, K. T. (1980). Race, ethnicity, and real estate appraisal: The Home Owners' Loan Corporation and the Federal Housing Administration. *Journal of Urban History, 6*, 419–452.

Jackson, K. T. (1985). *Crabgrass frontier: The suburbanization of the United States*. New York: Oxford Press.

Jackson II, R. L. (2006). *Scripting the black masculine body: Identity, discourse, and racial politics in popular media*. Albany: State University of New York.

Jargowsky, P. (2014). Architecture of segregation: Civil unrest, the concentration of poverty, and public policy. Century Foundation report. http://jargowsky.camden.rutgers.edu/2015/08/14/architecture-of-segregation/.

Jeffries, Z. (2013, May 2). Urban renewal displaces residents. *Michigan Citizen*. Page no longer available online.

Jenson, R. J., & Hammerback, J. C. (1998). "Your tools are really the people": The rhetoric of Robert Parris Moses. *Communication Monographs, 65*, 126–140.

Johnstone, H. W. (1973). Rationality and rhetoric in philosophy. *Quarterly Journal of Speech, 59*, 381-389.

Jones, B., & Mukherjee, R. (2010). From California to Michigan: Race, rationality, and neoliberal governmentality. *Communication and Critical/Cultural Studies, 7*(4), 401–422.

Jones, J. (1998). "Lifework" and its limits: The problem of labor in *The Philadelphia Negro*. In M. B. Katz and T. J. Sugrue (Eds.), *W. E. B. DuBois, race and the city: The Philadelphia negro and its legacy* (pp. 103–126). Philadelphia: University of Pennsylvania Press.

Jordan, J. (2013, June 14). Detroit emergency manager: A historical look vs. standard version. *Voice of Detroit*. Retrieved from http://voiceofdetroit.net/2013/06/18/detroit-emergency-manager-a-historical-look-vs-standard-version/.

Joyce, M. (Ed.). (2010). *Digital activism decoded: The new mechanics of change*. New York: IDebate Press.

Judge backs Snyder, Orr in bankruptcy. (2013, December 3). *Michigan Citizen*. Page no longer available online.

Juris, J. S. (2008). *Networking futures: The movements against corporate globalization*. Durham, NC: Duke University Press.

Kahn, R., and D. Kellner. (2004). New media and internet activism: From the "Battle of Seattle" to blogging. *New Media & Society, 6*, 87–95.

Kaplan, D. N. (2008). Dispatches from the street. *Journal of International and Intercultural Communication, 1*(4), 269–289.

Katz, M. B., & Sugrue, T. J. (1998). *W. E. B. DuBois, race, and the city: The Philadelphia negro and its legacy*. Philadelphia: University of Pennsylvania Press.

Keil, R. (2002). "Common-Sense" neoliberalism: Progressive conservative urbanism in Toronto, Canada. *Antipode, 34*(3), 578–601.

Keith, M., & Cross, M. (1993). Racism and the postmodern city. In M. Cross & M. Keith (Eds.), *Racism, the city and the state* (pp. 1–30). London: Routledge.

Keith, M. & Pile, S. (1993a). Introduction Part I: The politics of place. In M. Keith & S. Pile (Eds.), *Place and the politics of identity* (pp. 1–21). London: Routledge.

Keith, M. & Pile, S. (1993b). Introduction Part 2: The place of politics. In M. Keith & S. Pile (Eds.), *Place and the politics of identity* (pp. 22–40). London: Routledge.

Kelling, G., and Wilson, J. Q. (1982, March). Broken windows. *The Atlantic*. http://www.theatlantic.com/magazine/archive/1982/03/broken-windows/304465/.

Kitchin, R., & Dodge, M. (2011). Rethinking maps. In M. Dodge, R. Kitchin, & C. Perkins (Eds.), *The map reader: Theories of mapping practice and cartographic representation* (pp. 108–114). Hoboken, NJ: Wiley-Blackwell.

Klein, N. (2000). *No logo: Taking aim at the brand bullies*. London: Flamingo.

Kleniewski, N. (1984). From industrial to corporate city: The role of urban renewal. In W. K. Tabb, & L. Sawers (Eds.), *Marxism and the metropolis: New perspectives in urban political economy* (pp. 205–222). New York: Oxford University Press.

Koeske, Z. (2014, August 1). Eric Garner's death caused by chokehold, ruled a homicide, medical examiner says. Retrieved from http://www.silive.com/news/index.ssf/2014/08/chokehold_caused_eric_garners.html.

Krauss, C. (1989). Community struggles and the shaping of democratic consciousness. *Sociological Forum, 4*(2), 227–239.

Krauss, C. (1993). Women and toxic waste protests: Race, class and gender as resources of resistance. *Qualitative Sociology, 16*, 247–262.

Krauss, C. (1994). Women of color on the front line. In *Unequal protection: Environmental justice and communities of color* (pp. 256–271). San Francisco: Sierra Club Books.

Kruikemeier, S., van Noort, G., Vliegenthart, R., & de Vreese, C. H. (2014). Unraveling the effects of active and passive forms of political internet use: Does it affect citizens' political involvement? *New Media & Society, 16*(6), 903–920.

Kurth, J., Wilkinson, M., & Aguilar, L. (2013, October 4). Six decades in Detroit: How abandonment, racial tensions and financial missteps bankrupted the city. *Detroit News*. Retrieved from http://www.detroitnews.com/article/20131004/METRO01/310040001.

Kusmer, K. (1996). African Americans in the city since World War II: From the industrial to the postindustrial era. In K. W. Goings & R. A. Mohl (Eds.), *The new African American urban history* (pp. 320–368). Thousand Oaks: Sage.

Laclau, E., and Mouffe, C. (1985). *Hegemony and socialist strategy: Towards a radical democratic politics*. London: Verso.

Lagos, T. G., Coopman, T. M., & Tomhave, J. (2014). "Parallel poleis": Towards a theoretical framework of the modern public sphere, civic engagement and the structural advantages of the internet to foster and maintain parallel socio-political institutions. *New Media & Society, 16*(3), 398–414.

Lambert, L. (2012, March 26). More Americans move to cities in past decade. Retrieved from http://www.reuters.com/article/2012/03/26/usa-cities-population-idUSL2E8EQ5AJ20120326.

Landzelius, K. (2006). Introduction. *Native on the net: Indigenous and diasporic peoples in the virtual age*. London: Routledge.

Lead poisoning remains a problem in low-income, communities of color in New York City. (2009, September). *Harlem Community Voices*, 3.

Leadership is key to Detroit's revival. (2013, August 12). *Detroit News*. Retrieved from http://www.detroitnews.com/article/20130812/OPINION01/308120002/1008/OPINION01/Editorial-Leadership-key-Detroit-s-revival.

Lefebvre, H. (1976). Reflections on the politics of space. *Antipode, 8*, 30–37.

Lefebvre, H. (1991). *The production of space*. trans. D. Nicholson-Smith. Oxford: Blackwell.

Lefebvre, H. (2009). *State, space, world: Selected essays*. Minneapolis: University of Minnesota Press.

Lessenberry, J. (2014). Detroit bondholders will be paid 74 cents on the dollar; working women can relate. Retrieved from http://michiganradio.org/post/detroit-bondholders-will-be-paid-74-cents-dollar-working-women-can-relate#stream/0.

Levy, C. (1993, April 18). Sanitation cutbacks hit poorer districts hardest. *New York Times*, 37.

Lewis, E. (1996). Connecting memory, self, and the power of place in African American urban history. In K. W. Goings & R. A. Mohl (Eds.), *The new African American urban history* (pp.116–141). Thousand Oaks, CA: Sage Publications.
Light, B., Griffiths, M., & Lincoln, S. (2012). 'Connect and create': Young people, YouTube and Graffiti communities. *Continuum, 26*(3), 343–355.
Lim, M. (2012). Clicks, cabs, and coffee houses: Social media and oppositional movements in Egypt, 2004–2011. *Journal of Communication, 62*, 231–248.
Lipsitz, G. (1990). *Time passages: Collective memory and American popular culture*. Minneapolis: University of Minnesota Press.
Lipsitz, G. (2002). The possessive investment in whiteness. In P. S. Rothenberg (Ed.), *White privilege: Essential readings on the other side of racism* (pp. 61–84). New York: Worth Publishers.
Live it up in the D. Retrieved from http://opportunitydetroit.com/live/.
Loane, S. S., & D'Alessandro, S. (2013). Communication that changes lives: Social support within an online health community for ALS. *Communication Quarterly, 61*(2), 236–251.
Lukács, G. (1968). *History and class consciousness: Studies in Marxist dialectics*. Cambridge, MA: The M.I.T. Press.
Lyotard, J. F. (1984). *The postmodern condition*. Minneapolis: University of Minneapolis Press.
MacDonald, C. (2014, October 2). U. S. housing officials draw protest in Detroit. *Detroit News*. Retrieved from http://www.detroitnews.com/story/news/local/metro-detroit/2014/10/02/harp-officials-detroit/16596683/
Macek, S. (2006). *Urban nightmares: The media, the right, and the moral panic over the city*. Minneapolis: University of Minnesota Press.
Makagon, D. (2010). Bring on the shock troops: Artists and gentrification in the popular press. *Communication and Critical/Cultural Studies, 7*, 26–52.
Malanga, S. (2013, July 27). Cross country: The real reason the once great city of Detroit came to ruin. *Wall Street Journal*, A13.
Margai, F. (2010). *Environmental health hazards and social justice: Geographical perspectives on race and class disparities*. London: earthscan.
Markowitz, G., and Rosner, D. (2014). *Lead wars: The politics of science and the fate of America's children*. Berkeley: University of California Press.
Martin, D. (2003). "'Place-framing' as place-making: Constituting a neighborhood for organizing and activism. *Annals of the Association of American Geographers, 93*, 730-750.
Marx, K. (1844/1978). Economic and philosophic manuscripts of 1844. In R. C. Tucker (Ed.), *The Marx-Engels reader*, 2nd Ed. (pp. 66–125). New York: W. W. Norton & Company.
Marx, K. (1857-8/1973). *Grundrisse: Foundations of the critique of political economy*. trans. M. Nicolaus. New York: Random House.
Marx, K. (1867/1906). *Capital*. vol. 1. New York: The Modern Library.
Marx, K., & Engels, F. (1845/1970). *The German ideology*. New York: International Publishers.
Marx, K., & Engels, F. (1848/1965). *The communist manifesto*. New York: Washington Square Press, Inc.
Massey, D. B. (1994). *Space, place, and gender*. Minneapolis: University of Minnesota Press.
Massey, D. S., & Denton, N. A. (1993). *American apartheid: Segregation and the making of the underclass*. Cambridge, MA: Harvard University Press.
McCaughey, M., and Ayers, M. D. (Eds.). (2003). *Cyberactivism: Online activism in theory and practice*. New York: Routledge.
McChesney, R. (1999). *Rich media, poor democracy: Communication politics in dubious times*. Urbana: University of Illinois Press.
McCloskey, D. N. (1985). *The rhetoric of economics*. Madison: The University of Wisconsin Press.

McGee, M. C. (1975). In search of "The People": A rhetorical alternative. *Quarterly Journal of Speech, 61*, 235–249.

McGinty, T. J. (2015). Statement from County Prosecutor Timothy J. McGinty on the decision of the grand jury in the Tamir Rice case. Retrieved from http://prosecutor.cuyahogacounty.us/pdf_prosecutor/en-US/2015-1-28%20Statement%20on%20Grand%20Jury%20decision%20in%20the%20Tamir%20Rice%20case%20(00000002).pdf.

McGraw, B. (2013). Meet the downtown residents who say they are being pushed aside for the "new Detroit." Retrieved from http://www.deadlinedetroit.com/articles/4721/meet_the_downtown_residents_who_say_they_are_being _pushed_aside_for_the_new_detroit#.VXcUIqbj9Jn

McKerrow, R. (1989). Critical rhetoric: Theory and praxis. *Communication Monographs, 56*(2), 91–111.

McIntosh, P. (2011). White privilege: Unpacking the invisible knapsack. In *Gender through the prism of difference*, eds. Maxine Baca Zinn, Pierrette Hondagneu-Sotelo, Michael A. Messner. 235–38. New York: Oxford University Press.

Meisenbach, R. J., Remke, R. V., Buzzanell, P. M., & Liu. (2008). "They allowed": Pentadic mapping of women's maternity leave discourse as organizational rhetoric. *Communication Monographs, 75*, 1–24.

Miller, J. (2006). *Native America, discovered and conquered: Thomas Jefferson, Lewis & Clark, and manifest destiny*. Westport, CT: Praeger.

Miller, V., Hallstein, M., & Quass, S. (1996). Feminist politics and environmental justice: Women's community activism in West Harlem New York. In D. Rocheleau, B. Thomas-Slayter, & E. Waangari (Eds.), *Feminist political ecology: Global issues and local experiences* (pp. 62–85). London: Routledge.

Miller, V. D. (1993). Planning, power and politics: A case study of the land use and siting history of the North River water pollution control plant. *Fordham Urban Law Journal, 21*(3), 706–722.

Miller-Travis, V. (2013). Interview with Jessica Knoblauch. Ecology without equality. Retrieved from http://earthjustice.org/features/ourwork/down-to-earth-ecology-without-equality.

Mission & history. Retrieved from http://righttothecity.org/about/mission-history/.

Mitchell, D. (2003). *The right to the city: Social justice and the fight for public space*. New York: The Guildford Press.

Mock, B. (2009, March 22). Fighting for green justice. *American Prospect*. Retrieved from http://prospect.org/article/fighting-green-justice.

Mohl, R. A. (1993). Race and space in the modern city: Interstate-95 and the black community in Miami. In A. R. Hirsch and R. A. Mohl (Eds.), *Urban policy in the twentieth century* (pp. 100–158). New Brunswick, NJ: Rutgers University Press.

Mollenkopf, J. (1981). Neighbourhood political development and the politics of urban growth: Boston and San Francisco 1958–78. *International Journal of Urban and Regional Research, 5*(1), 15–39.

Moody, K. (2007). *From welfare state to real estate: Regime change in New York City, 1974 to the present*. New York: The New Press.

Morse, J. (1999). A report to the Secretary of War of the United States, on Indian Affairs. In S. T. Joshi, (Ed.), *Documents of American prejudice: An anthology of writings on race from Thomas Jefferson to David Duke* (pp. 231–37). New York, N. Y.: Basic Books. [1822].

Moses, M. (1993). Farmworkers and pesticides. In R. D. Bullard, Ed., *Confronting environmental racism: Voices from the grassroots* (pp. 161–78). Cambridge, MA: South End Press.

Mother Clara Hale bus depot re-construction task force meeting (2008, March 18). Meeting minutes. Page no longer available online.

Moynihan, D. P. (1965). The Negro family: The case for national action. In L. Rainwater & W. L. Yancy (Eds.), *The Moynihan report and the politics of controversy* (pp. 45–94). Cambridge: M.I.T. Press.

Mujica, J. (1992). Coloring the hazards: Risk maps, research, and education to fight health hazards. *American Journal of Industrial Medicine, 22,* 767–770.
Murray, K., Burke, K., Marcius, C. R., and Parascandola R. (2014, Dec. 3). "Staten Island man dies after NYPD cop puts him chokehold." *Daily News.* http://www.nydailynews.com/new-york/staten-island-man-dies-puts-choke-hold-article-1.1871486
Nagourney, A. (2001). Quality of life is high priority for Bloomberg. *New York Times,* December 27. http://www.nytimes.com/2001/12/27/nyregion/quality-of-life-is-high-priority-for-bloofmberg.html.
Naison, M. (1986). From eviction resistance to rent control: Tenant activism in the Great Depression. In R. Lawson with assistance of M. Naison (Eds.), *The tenant movement in New York City, 1904-1984* (pp. 94–133). New Brunswick: Rutgers University Press.
Nakayama, T. K., & Krizek, R. L. (1995). Whiteness: A strategic rhetoric. *Quarterly Journal of Speech, 81,* 291–309.
Neavling, S., and M. Helms. (2011, Nov. 16). Mayor Bing expected to unveil plan to privatize Detroit bus, lighting systems. *Detroit Free Press.* Retrieved from http://archive.freep.com/article/20111116/NEWS01/111160429/Mayor-Bing-expected-unveil-plan-privatize-Detroit-bus-lighting-systems.
Newport, F. (2014). Gallup review: Black and white attitudes toward police. Retrieved from http://www.gallup.com/poll/175088/gallup-review-black-white-attitudes-toward-police.aspx.
New uptown diesel leadership council to check MTA. (2004, March/April). *The Uptown Eye,* 7.
New York State Transportation Equity Alliance (NYSTEA). WE ACT website. Page no longer available online.
Newfield, J., and Barrett, W. (1989). *City for sale: Ed Koch and the betrayal of New York.* New York: Harper & Row, Publishers.
Newport, F. (2014, Aug. 20). Gallup review: Black and white attitudes towards police. http://www.gallup.com/poll/175088/gallup-review-black-white-attitudes-toward-police.aspx
Newsome, G. (2013, March 8). Challenging assumptions about progress in the face of emergency management. *Michigan Citizen.* Page no longer available online.
Norris, H. (1991). Dislocation without relocation. In W. W. Henrickson (Ed.), *Detroit perspectives: Crossroads and turning points* (pp. 474–476). Detroit: Wayne State University Press.
Northern Manhattan garbage, pests & pesticides campaign. WE ACT website. Page no longer available online.
Oct 5 & 6: International people's assembly against the banks and against austerity. (2013, September 5). Detroiters Resisting Emergency Management. Retrieved from http://www.d-rem.org/oct-5-6-international-peoples-assembly-against-the-banks-and-against-austerity/.
"Opportunity in Detroit ad debuts during series." (2012, October). *Crain's Detroit Business.* Retrieved from http://www.crainsdetroit.com/article/20121029/FREE/121029872/opportunity-in-detroit-ad-debuts-during-series.
O'Reilly, T. (2007). What is Web 2.0? Design patterns and business models for the next generation of software. *Communications and Strategies, 65,* 17–37.
Ott, B. L., & Burgchardt, C. R. (2013). On critical-rhetorical pedagogy: Dialoging with Schindler's List. *Western Journal of Communication, 77*(1), 14–33.
Pal, M., & Dutta, M. J. (2012). Organizing resistance on the internet: The case of the international campaign for justice in Bhopal. *Communication, Culture & Critique, 5,* 230–251.
Pal, M., & Dutta, M. J. (2013). "Land is our mother": Alternative meanings of development in subaltern organizing. *Journal of International and Intercultural Communication, 6*(3), 203–220.

Papacharissi, Z. (2002). The virtual sphere: The internet as a public sphere. *New Media & Society, 4*, 9–27.
Park, R. (1925). The city: Suggestions for the investigation of human behavior in the urban environment. In R. E. Park, E. W. Burgess, R. D. McKenzie (Eds.), *The city* (pp. 1–46). Chicago: University of Chicago Press.
Peeples, J. A., & DeLuca, K. M. (2006). The truth of the matter: Motherhood, community and environmental justice. *Women's Studies in Communication, 29*(1), 59–87.
People's forum II: Next generation state of emergency! (November 2013). http://www.d-rem.org/peoples-forum-ii-next-generation-state-of-emergency/.
People's plan for restructuring toward a sustainable Detroit. (2014, February 24). Detroiters Resisting Emergency Management. Retrieved from http://www.d-rem.org/peoples-plan/.
#People'sPlan press release: Community groups release plan for Detroit based on resident's needs. Detroiters Resisting Emergency Management. Retrieved from http://www.d-rem.org/peoplesplan-press-release-community-groups-release-plan-for-detroit-based-on-residents-needs/.
Perelman, C., and L. Olbrechts-Tyteca. (1969). *The new rhetoric: A treatise on argumentation*. trans. J. Wilkinson and P. Weaver. Notre Dame, IN: University of Notre Dame Press.
Pérez-Peña. (1994, January 5). Settlement in Harlem suit over odors. *New York Times*, B1.
Persky, S., Sanderson, S. C., & Koehly, L. M. (2013). Online communication about genetics and body weight: Implications for health behavior and internet-based education. *Journal of Health Communication, 18*(2), 241–249.
Peters, J. (2014, Dec. 5). Loose cigarettes today, civil unrest tomorrow: The racist, classist origins of broken windows policing. *Slate*. http://www.slate.com/articles/news_and_politics/crime/2014/12/edward_banfield_the_racist_classist_origins_of_broken_windows_policing.html.
Petersen-Smith, K. (2015). "Black Lives Matter: A new movement takes shape." *International Socialist Review*. Spring. http://isreview.org/issue/96/black-lives-matter.
Petray, T. L. (2011). Protest 2.0: Online interactions and Aboriginal activists. *Media Culture & Society, 33*, 923–940.
Pezzullo, P. C. (2001). Performing critical interruptions: Stories, rhetorical invention, and the environmental justice movement. *Western Journal of Communication, 65*(1), 1-25.
Plyushteva, A. (2009). The right to the city and the struggles over public citizenship: Exploring the links. *The Urban Reinventors Online Journal*, issue 3/09.
Powell, J. A. (2009). Reinterpreting metropolitan space as a strategy for social justice. In M. Paloma Pavel (Ed.), *Breakthrough communities: Sustainability and justice in the next American metropolis* (pp. 23–32). Cambridge: The MIT Press.
Prakesh, S. (2004, Fall). MTA agrees to meet directly with community residents. *Uptown Eye*, 5.
Prelli, L. (1993). *A rhetoric of science*. Carbondale: Southern Illinois University Press.
Preventing lead poisoning in immigrant homes. (2011, August). *Harlem Community Voices*, 5.
Prevost, L. (2014, July 20). The data-driven search: Websites are giving buyers hyper-specific community data. *New York Times*, 8.
Principles of environmental justice. (1991). http://www.ejnet.org/ej/principles.html
Pulido, L. (1996). Development of the "people of color" identity in the environmental justice movement of the Southwestern United States. *Socialist Review, 26*, 145–180.
Pulido, L. (2000). Rethinking environmental racism: White privilege and urban development in Southern California. *Annals of the Association of American Geographers, 90*(1), 12–40.
Quality of life program for New York City. (n.d.). Pamphlet presented by New York City Economic Development Corporation. http://www.nycedc.com/system/files/files/program/QualityLifeBrochure_0.pdf

Raab, B. 2013. "Almost death by zip code": Study suggests link between health and wealth. NBC News. Retrieved from http://www.nbcnews.com/feature/in-plain-sight/almost-death-zip-code-study-suggests-link-between-health-wealth-v19397882.

Rahimi, B. (2011). The agonistic social media: Cyberspace in the formation of dissent and consolidation of state power in postelection Iran. *Communication Review, 14*, 158–78.

Ramirez, C. E. (2014, February 20). Revitalized neighborhoods pushed in Future City's 2014–15 priorities. *Detroit News*. Page no longer available online.

Rankine, C. (2014). *Citizen: An American lyric*. Minneapolis: Graywolf Press.

Reimagine [r]evolution. (2012, July 1). *Michigan Citizen*. Page no longer available online.

Residents worry worsening operations at North River will endanger health—again. (2010, March). *Harlem Community Voices*, 1.

Rothstein, M. (1993, April 4). Creating parks in a crowded metropolis. *New York Times*, R1.

Rothstein, R. (2014). The making of Ferguson: Public policies at the root of its troubles. Economic Policy Institute report, October, 15. http://www.epi.org/publication/making-ferguson/.

Rothstein, R. (2015). Historian says don't sanitize how our government create ghettos. Fresh Air. radio transcript. http://www.wbur.org/npr/406699264/historian-says-dont-sanitize-how-our-government-created-the-ghettos.

Routledge, P. (2000). "Our resistance will be as transnational as capital": Convergence space and strategy in globalizing resistance. *Geo Journal, 52*, 25–33.

Rugh, J. S., & Massey, D. S. (2010). Racial segregation and the American foreclosure crisis. *American Sociological Review, 75*(5), 629–651.

Rushing, J. H. (1983). The rhetoric of the American western myth. *Communication Monographs, 50*, 14–32.

Rybas, N., & Gajjala, R. (2007). Developing cyberethnographic research methods for understanding digitally mediated identities. *Forum: Qualitative Social Research, 8*. Retrieved from http://www.qualitative-research.net/index.php/fqs/article/viewArticle/282.

Saco, D. (2002). *Cybering democracy: Public space and the internet*. Minneapolis: University of Minnesota Press.

Said. E. W. (1993). *Culture and imperialism*. New York: Alfred A. Knopf.

Salter, L. (2003). Democracy, new social movements, and the internet: A Habermasian analysis. In M. McCaughey and M. D. Ayers (Eds.), *Cyberactivism: Online activism in theory and practice* (pp. 117–144). New York: Routledge.

Sampson, R. J., & Raudenbush, S. W. (2005). Neighborhood stigma and the perception of disorder. *Focus, 24*(1), 7–11.

Sands, D. (2013). Fannie Mae, Freddie Mac cancel appearance at Metro Detroit foreclosure hearing. *Huffpost Detroit*. Retrieved from http://www.huffingtonpost.com/2013/05/18/detroit-foreclosure-hearing-fannie-mae-freddie-mac_n_3293854.html.

Sassen, S. (1996). Analytic borderlands: Race, gender and representation in the new city. In A. D. King (Ed.), *Re-Presenting the city: Ethnicity, capital and culture in the 21st-century metropolis* (pp. 183–202). Washington Square, New York: New York University Press.

Sastry, S., & Dutta, M. J. (2013). Global health interventions and the 'common sense' of neoliberalism: A dialectical analysis of PEPFAR. *Journal of International and Intercultural Communication, 6*(1), 21–39.

Schneider, K. (2011, November 29). Cleveland turns uptown into new downtown. *New York Times*. Retrieved from http://www.nytimes.com/2011/11/30/realestate/commercial/cleveland-ignites-job-growth-with-rebuilding-project.html.

Schwartz, J. (1986). Tenant power in the Liberal City, 1943–1971. In R. Lawson with assistance of M. Naison (Eds.), *The tenant movement in New York City, 1904–1984* (pp. 134–208). New Brunswick: Rutgers University Press.

Schwartz, J. (1993). *The New York approach: Robert Moses, urban liberals, and redevelopment of the inner city.* Columbus: Ohio State University Press.

Segal, D. (2013, April 14). Motor City missionary. *New York Times*, Sunday Business 1, 4.

Severo, R. (1989, November 30). Odors from plant anger many in Harlem. *New York Times*, B1.

Shaffer, C. (2014, November 24). Tamir Rice's neighborhood has history of gangs, violence. Retrieved from http://www.cleveland.com/metro/index.ssf/2014/11/cleveland_neighborhood_where_t.html.

Shakow, A. & A. Irwin. (2000). Terms reconsidered: Decoding development discourse. In J. Y. Kim, J. V. Millen, A. Irwin, & J. Gershman (Eds.), *Dying for Growth: Global inequality and the health of the poor* (pp. 44–61). Monroe, Maine: Common Courage Press.

Shepard. P. (1993). Issues of community empowerment. *Fordham Urban Law Journal,* 21, 739–755.

Shepard, P. (2005/2006). Breathe at your own risk: Transit justice in West Harlem. *Race, Poverty & the Environment,* 12(1), 51–53.

Shepard, P. (2008). 2008 Jane Jacobs Medal recipient for lifetime achievement. video. Retrieved from http://www.weact.org/Home/Contact/PeggyMShepard/PeggyShepardVideo/tabid/489/Default.aspx.

Shepard, P. (n.d.). video. WE ACT website. Page no longer available.

Shepard, P., Corbin-Mark, C., & Foster, S. (2006, October 18). Testimony to the Council of the City of New York, Committee on Transportation.

Shor, I. (1992). *Empowering education: Critical teaching for social change.* Chicago: University of Chicago Press.

Shrader-Frechette, K. (2005). *Environmental justice: Creating equality, reclaiming democracy.* Oxford: Oxford University Press.

Sibley, D. (1995). *Geographies of exclusion: Society and difference in the West.* London: Routledge.

Siegal, N. (1999, July). Will a Harlem plant become a son of Fresh Kills. *New York Times.*

Simons, H. (1972). Persuasion in social conflicts: A critique of prevailing conceptions and a framework for future research. *Speech Monographs,* 39, 227–47.

Sites, W. (2003). *Remaking New York: Primitive globalization and the politics of urban community.* Minneapolis: University of Minnesota Press.

Slotkin, R. (1973). *Regeneration through violence: The mythology of the American frontier, 1600–1860.* Middletown, Conn.: Wesleyan University Press.

Smith, C. (2006). *The plan of Chicago: Daniel Burnham and remaking of the American city.* Chicago: University of Chicago Press.

Smith, N. (1982). Gentrification and uneven development. *Economic Geography,* 58(2), 139–155.

Smith, N. (1990). *Uneven development: Nature, capital and the production of space.* Oxford: Basil Blackwell.

Smith, N. (1996). *The new urban frontier: Gentrification and the revanchist city.* London: Routledge.

Smith, N. (2002). New globalism, new urbanism: Gentrification as global urban strategy. *Antipode,* 34(3), 427–450.

Smith, S. J. (1993). Residential segregation and the politics of racialization. In M. Cross & M. Keith (Eds.), *Racism, the city and the state* (pp. 128–143). London: Routledge.

Snavely, B. (2014, March 25). Detroit seeking offers for private management of water and sewerage department. *Detroit Free Press.* Retrieved from http://archive.freep.com/article/20140325/NEWS01/303250100/Detroit-Water-Department-Keyvn-Orr-bids.

Snell, R., & Livengood, C. (2014, March 31). Orr proposes steeper cuts if retirees don't support debt-cutting deal. *Detroit News.* Page no longer available online.

Snyder, R. (2014, March 24). Detroit: The next American city of opportunity. Manhattan Institute for Policy Research. Retrieved from http://www.manhattan-institute.org/multimedia/events/032414CSLL/.

Snyder, Orr strike upbeat note about Detroit at NYC policy forum. (2014, March 24). *Detroit News*. Page no longer available online.

Soja, E. (2010a). *Postmodern geographies: The reassertion of space in critical social theory*. London: Verso.

Soja, E. (2010b). *Seeking spatial justice*. Minneapolis: University of Minnesota Press.

Solomonow, S. (2001, Fall). WE ACT files discrimination complaint against the MTA. *Uptown Eye*, 1.

Sparke, M. (1998). A map that roared and an original atlas: Canada, cartography, and the narration of a nation. *Annals of the Association of American Geographers, 88*(3), 463–495.

Specter, M. (1992c, June 22). Harlem groups file suit to fight sewage odors. *New York Times*, B3.

Specter, M. (1992b, April 17). Stench at sewage plant is traced; millions pledged for repair work. *New York Times*, A1.

Spencer, J. A. (1986). New York City tenant organizations and the post-World War I housing crisis. In R. Lawson with assistance of M. Naison (Eds.), *The tenant movement in New York City, 1904–1984* (pp. 51–93). New Brunswick: Rutgers University Press.

Statement from Orr's office. (2014, February 21). Retrieved from http://www.mlive.com/news/detroit/index.ssf/2014/02/detroit_emergency_manager_kevy_3.html

Stephens, T. (2014, March 19). Detroit lives! *Counter Punch*. Retrieved from http://www.counterpunch.org/2014/03/19/detroit-lives/.

Stormer, N. (2010). Mediating biopower and the case of prenatal space. *Critical Studies in Media Communication, 27*, 8–23.

Strachan, M. (2014, August 8). White people create app to avoid, um, 'sketchy' areas. *Huffington Post*. Retrieved from http://www.huffingtonpost.com/2014/08/08/sketchfactor-app-white-creators_n_5660205.html?page_version=legacy&view=print&comm_ref=false.

Starr, R. (1976). Making New York smaller. *New York Times*, November 14.

Streeter, T. (2013). Policy, politics, and discourse. *Communication, Culture & Critique, 6*, 488-501.

Stewart, T. L. (2007). *The mysterious benedict society*. New York: Little , Brown and Company.

Stuckey, M. E. (2011). The Donner Party and the rhetoric of westward expansion. *Rhetoric & Public Affairs, 14*, 229–260.

Stuckler, D., & Basu, S. (2013). *The body economic: Why austerity kills*. New York, NY: Basic Books.

Sturken, M. (1997). *Tangled memories: The Vietnam War, and AIDS epidemic, and the politics of remembering*. Berkeley: University of California Press.

Sugrue, T. J. (1996). *The origins of the urban crisis: Race and inequality in postwar Detroit*. Princeton, NJ: Princeton University Press.

Susser, I., & J. Schneider. (2003). Wounded cities: Destruction and reconstruction in a globalized world. In J. Schneider & I. Susser (Eds.), *Wounded cities: Destruction and reconstruction in a globalized world* (pp. 1–23). Oxford: Berg.

Sutton, J. S. (2012). Space in tropes, an opaque but visible relationship. *Review of Communication, 12*(1), 30–43.

Sze, J. (2007). *Noxious New York: The racial politics of urban health and environmental justice*. Cambridge, MA: The MIT Press.

Szulc, Ł., & Dhoest, A. (2013). The internet and sexual identity formation: Comparing internet use before and after coming out. *Communications-The European Journal of Communication Research, 38*(4), 347–365.

Taylor, M. M. (2003). *Harlem: Between heaven and hell*. Minneapolis: University of Minnesota Press.

Telford, J. (2013, December 22). Fascism & classism in Detroit and Lansing. Detroiters Resisting Emergency Management. Retrieved from http://www.d-rem.org/fascism-classism-in-detroit-and-lansing/.

The greenest, cleanest depot possible: Rebuilding Mother Clara Hale Depot. (2010). New York, NY: WE ACT for Environmental Justice.

The MTA accountability campaign. WE ACT website. Page no longer available online.

The Northern Manhattan climate action plan. WE ACT website. http://www.weact.org/climate.

Thelen, D. (1989). Memory and American history. *Journal of American History*, 75(4), 1117–1129.

Thomas, J. M. (1997). *Redevelopment and race: Planning a finer city in postwar Detroit*. Baltimore: The Johns Hopkins University Press.

Thomas, R. W. (1992). *Life for us is what we make it: Building black community in Detroit, 1915–1945*. Bloomington: Indiana University Press.

Thompson, H. A. (2001). *Whose Detroit? Politics, labor, and race in a modern American city*. Ithaca: Cornell University Press.

Tonn, M. B. (1996). Militant motherhood: Labor's Mary Harris "Mother Jones." *Quarterly Journal of Speech*, 82, 1–21.

Toxic Substance Control Act (TSCA) reform in the works. (2011, August). *Harlem Community Voices*, 1.

Travis, T. (2013). The real cause of Detroit's fiscal crisis and its solution. *Voice of Detroit*. Retrieved from http://voiceofdetroit.net/2013/03/17/the-real-cause-of-detroits-fiscal-crisis-and-its-solution/.

Triece, M. E. (2001). *Protest and popular culture: Women in the U.S. labor movement, 1894-1917*. Boulder, CO: Westview Press.

Triece, M. E. (2003). Appealing to the "intelligent worker": Rhetorical reconstitution and the influence of firsthand experience in the rhetoric of Leonora O'Reilly. *Rhetoric Society Quarterly*, 33(2), 5–24.

Triece, M. E. (2007). *On the picket line: Strategies of working class women during the Depression*. Urbana: University of Illinois Press.

Triece, M. E. (2013). *"Tell it like it is": Women in the National Welfare Rights Movement*. Columbia, S.C.: University of South Carolina Press.

Tuchman, G. (1978). *Making news: A study in the construction of reality*. New York: The Free Press.

Tulton, L. (2004). "The R-A-P on MTS." *Uptown Eye*, March/April 2004.

Turbeville, W. C. (2013). The Detroit Bankruptcy. Dēmos. Retrieved from http://www.demos.org/publication/detroit-bankruptcy.

U.S. General Accounting Office. (1983). Siting of hazardous waste landfills and their correlation with racial and economic status of surrounding communities.

Van de Donk, W., B. D. Loader, P. G. Nixon, and D. Rucht (Eds.). (2004). *Cyberprotest: New media, citizens and social movements*. New York: Routledge.

Vitale, A. S. (2008). *City of disorder: How the quality of life campaign transformed New York politics*. New York: New York University Press.

Wailoo, K. (2001). *Dying in the city of the blues: Sickle cell anemia and the politics of race and health*. Chapel Hill: University of North Carolina Press.

Walker, G. (2012). *Environmental justice: Concepts, evidence and politics*. London: Routledge.

Warf, B., & Arias, S. (2009). Introduction: The reinsertion of space in the humanities and social sciences. In B. Warf & S. Arias (Eds.), *The spatial turn: Interdisciplinary perspectives* (pp. 1–10). London: Routledge.

WE ACT and Columbia University Children's Center launch "Healthy Home, Healthy Child campaign." (2001, Fall). *Uptown Eye*, 6.

WE ACT—Dedicated to empowering communities to fight for environmental justice. (2009, June 23). *Harlem Community Voices*, 1.

"We object!" Rally highlights mass opposition to Snyder-Orr "plan of adjustment." (2014, March 31). Detroiters Resisting Emergency Management. Retrieved from http://www.d-rem.org/we-object-rally-highlights-mass-opposition-to-snyder-orr-plan-of-adjustment/

Weaver, R. (1989). Language is sermonic. In J. L. Golden, G. F. Berquist, & W. E. Coleman (Eds.), *The rhetoric of western thought* (pp. 304–317). Dubuque, Iowa: Kendall/Hunt Publishing Company.

Welcome to The Albert. Retrieved from https://vimeo.com/88779497.

Westra, L, & Wenz, P. S. (Eds.). (1995). *Faces of environmental racism: Confronting issues of global justice*. Lanham, MD: Rowman & Littlefield Publishers, Inc.

Why are the Feds destroying our 'hoods? (2013). Detroit Eviction Defense. Retrieved from http://detroitevictiondefense.org/past-events.php#fanniemae2.

Whyte, L. E. (2014). THINK: In Detroit, foundations ride to the rescue. *Detroit News*. Page is no longer available online.

Wiley, S. B. C. (2005). Spatial materialism: Grossberg's Deleuzean cultural studies. *Cultural Studies, 19*, 63–99.

Willard, C. A. (1989). The creation of publics: Notes on Goodnight's historical relativity. *Argumentation and Advocacy, 26*, 45–59.

Williams, P. 1991. *The alchemy of race and rights*. Cambridge: Harvard University Press.

Williams, P. (2014). Drop dead, Detroit! *New Yorker*, January 27.

Winerip, M. (1993, May 23). Up on the roof, Harlem gains acres of beauty. *New York Times*, 29.

Wischusen, P. (2013, August 21). "Emergency management is racism." *Michigan Citizen*. Page no longer available online.

Wood, D., & Fels, J. (2011). Design on signs/ Myth and meaning in maps. In M. Dodge, R. Kitchin, & C. Perkins (Eds.), *The map reader: Theories of mapping practice and cartographic representation* (pp. 48–55). Hoboken, NJ: Wiley-Blackwell.

Woodward Avenue: Michigan's main street. (2007, March 12). *Detroit News*. Retrieved from http://www.detroitnews.com/article/20070312/METRO/703120330.

Wright, B. (2008). New Orleans black diaspora: Will the residents come back? Retrieved from http://reimaginerpe.org/node/1810.

Wright, J. (2014). Address given to Michigan Roundtable for Diversity and Inclusion. https://www.youtube.com/watch?v=pqA5na2CTSw.

Wylie-Kellerman, B. (2013). Detroit: Coming to a city near you. Detroiters Resisting Emergency Management. Retrieved from http://www.d-rem.org/detroit-coming-to-a-city-near-you/.

Youmans, W. L., & York, J. C. (2012). Social media and the activist toolkit: User agreements, corporate interests, and the information infrastructure of modern social movements. *Journal of Communication, 62*, 315–329.

Zukin, S. (1982). *Loft living: Culture and capital in urban change*. Baltimore: The Johns Hopkins University Press.

Zukin, S. (1991). *Landscapes of power: From Detroit to Disney World*. Berkeley: University of California Press.

Zukin, S. (1998). Politics and aesthetics of public space: The "American" model. Retrieved from http://www.publicspace.org/en/text-library/eng/a013-politics-and-aesthetics-of-public-space-the-american-model.

Zukin, S. (2007). Reading *The Urban Villagers* as a cultural document: Ethnicity, modernity, and capital. *City & Community, 6*(1), 39–48.

Zukin, S. (2008). Consuming authenticity: From outposts of difference to means of exclusion. *Cultural Studies, 22*, 724–748.

Zukin, S. (2009). Changing landscapes of power: Opulence and the urge for authenticity. *International Journal of Urban and Regional Research, 33*, 543–553.

Index

1214 Griswold: residents of, vii, 31, 35, 36, 78; real estate company, 31, 74, 75–76

accumulation by dispossession, 8, 32, 64, 65, 150
agency, xxii, 22, 32, 33, 49, 50–60
architecture of segregation, 143, 161
Aristotle, 20, 27n9, 124, 150
automobile industry: activism in, 36; racism in, 36; workers in, 36–37. *See also* Dodge Revolutionary Union Movement

bankruptcy, xiii, 9, 32, 38, 45, 48–49, 52, 57, 61n5, 61n9, 65, 67–68, 70, 77, 80, 92
Black Lives Matter, xi, xxii, 145–146
blight, 35, 45, 52, 58, 60, 61n1, 66, 77, 91, 96, 97
broken windows theory, 118–120, 143
Brown, Michael, xxiiin1, 143–144, 145, 148n2
Burke, Kenneth, 20, 123
Burnham, Daniel, 1, 4
bus depots, 107, 109, 112, 114–115, 127–128, 130–131, 132–134

capitalism, xii, xiv–xviii, 2–5, 8, 9–10, 17, 21, 22–23, 64–67, 69, 77, 139, 147. *See also* historical materialism
cartography. *See* mapping
Chicago School, 3, 4, 5. *See also* Park, Robert
citizen science. *See* street science
City Beautiful Movement, 4, 5
Cleveland, Ohio, xiv, xxiiin1, 1, 2, 18, 19, 27n2, 27n6, 39, 144
community-based participatory research, xviii, 111–137, 117–118, 121, 129, 134–135. *See also* street science; participatory action research
conscious remembering, 47–49. *See also* memory
constitutive rhetoric, 54, 56
Corbin-Mark, Cecil, 114–115, 129, 130, 131–132, 134
counterhegemonic narrative, x, xi, xviii, xix, xxi, 50, 54, 56–60, 73, 76, 77, 82
countermapping. *See* mapping
Crawford, John, xxiiin1, 143–144, 145
creative destruction, xiv–xv, 3, 64, 65
cyberprotest, xi, 27n12, 142. *See also* Internet

DED. *See* Detroit Eviction Defense
D-REM. *See* Detroiters Resisting Emergency Management
demystification, xi, 72–74, 82, 142
deindustrialization, xiv, xviii, xxi, 11, 15, 32, 37, 38, 39, 42, 48, 70, 88, 140, 141
Detroit Eviction Defense, 54, 59–60, 74
Detroit Future City, 46, 59, 68–70, 71, 79
Detroiters Resisting Emergency Management, xxi, 48–49, 54, 56, 57, 59, 74, 76, 77, 80, 82, 142
devalorization. *See* valorization
displacement, ix, xii–xiii, xv, xxi, 6, 7, 8, 10, 31, 32, 48, 58, 69–70, 71, 72, 82, 87, 102, 103, 140, 141
Dodge Revolutionary Union Movement, 36
DuBois, W. E. B., 11, 27n7, 73
Dump Dirty Diesel Campaign, 114–115, 131, 133

empowerment zones, 95
Engels, Friedrich, xiv, xv, xvi, 1, 3–5, 11, 21, 22, 64, 65, 103–104, 147
environmental justice, xxii, 89, 97, 98, 104, 105, 106–107, 108, 109, 110, 111, 112, 115, 117, 126, 127–129, 132, 135, 147; history of, 98–100; women's efforts in, 100–102
epistemic advantage, xvii, 55, 59, 73, 132

Federal Housing Act, 6, 7, 91, 96, 97
Federal Housing Administration, 5, 7, 11, 34, 35, 59
financialization, xxiii, 8, 16, 32, 65, 88
fiscal crisis, 48, 92–93
foreclosure, 16, 32, 37, 46, 54, 58, 59, 80
free market. *See* market logic

Garner, Eric, xxiiin1, 143–144, 145, 148n1
gentrification, xi, xv, 9, 10, 11, 21, 22, 26, 27n5, 32, 59, 75, 93, 94, 105, 137
geographies of injustice, x, xiii, xv, 11
Gilbert, Dan, xiii, 39, 51, 52–53, 57, 58, 61n11, 65, 71, 72, 74, 78, 141
Giuliani, Rudy, 9, 94, 118, 119, 131
Goldberg, David Theo, x, xi, 17, 53
Gray, Freddie, 143
Great Migration, 32, 89
Great Recession, 8, 32, 35, 37, 67

Harlem, history of, 89
highway construction, xxi, 5, 12, 27n8, 37, 48, 91, 97, 140
historical materialism, xii, xvi, 21–23, 104, 147. *See also* capitalism
home owners associations, 12, 33, 90, 94
Home Owners' Loan Corporation, 5, 11–12, 13, 14, 34, 105
housing covenants, ix, 12, 33, 140
Harvey, David, x, xii, xiii, xiv, xvii, xix, 3, 4, 5, 7–8, 17, 22, 27n10, 63, 64, 65, 83n2, 104, 124, 126
Hurricane Katrina, 9, 37, 87, 102

Ilitch, Mike, 39, 51–52, 52–53, 53, 61n11, 77, 141

individualism, x, xx, 10, 50, 54, 56, 58, 105, 141, 142, 145
Internet, 23, 23–26, 27n11, 27n13, 54, 111, 142. *See also* cyberprotest

laissez faire racism, 94–95
Lefebvre, Henri, xiv, xv, 17, 22, 56, 94

MNOW!. *See* Moratorium NOW!
mapping, xi, xviii, 3, 11, 70, 104, 105, 106, 121; counterhegemonic uses of, xxii, 105, 107, 108, 109, 110, 111, 111–112, 114, 115, 117, 142; hegemonic uses of, 105; verbal, 105, 107, 112, 114
market logic, x, xi, xiii, xxi, 5, 56, 59, 63, 68, 69, 78, 121, 142
memory, xiii, 32, 40–42, 42, 44, 45, 46–47, 49, 50, 51, 140–141, 143. *See also* conscious remembering
Martin, Trayvon, ix, 15, 145
Marx, Karl, xiv–xv, xvi–xvii, xix, xxiiin3, 3, 21, 22, 27n10, 55, 58, 64, 65, 72–73, 82n1, 103–104, 122, 128, 147
Miller, Vernice, 91, 92, 98, 100, 102, 117, 124, 129, 131, 147
Moratorium NOW!, 54, 56, 57, 59, 74, 80, 81, 142
Moses, Robert, 6, 91, 92, 96, 116n5

naturalization, xix, xx, xxi, xxii, 5, 10, 140
neoliberalism, x–xi, xix–xxii, 7–9, 10, 16, 40, 48, 50, 59, 65, 66, 67, 68, 69, 70, 71–72, 74, 81, 92–93, 94, 105, 112, 117, 120, 121, 139, 140, 145–146, 147; hallmarks of, 140–143
North River Sewage Treatment Plant, 91, 97, 98, 100, 112, 117, 118, 124–127, 129, 132, 136

opportunity, x, xiii, xx, xxi, 34, 35, 47, 50, 67, 68, 70–72, 74, 75–77, 79, 81, 82, 112, 113, 142
Opportunity Detroit, 39, 51, 61n8, 71–72, 78
Orr, Kevyn, 38, 43, 47, 48, 50, 51, 52, 53, 56–57, 65, 67–68, 72, 79

Paradise Valley, 12, 31, 34, 43
Park, Robert, 1, 2, 4–5
participatory action research, 121
participatory mapping. *See* mapping
People's Plan For Restructuring, 56–57, 58–59, 79
Plan of Adjustment, 56, 57, 67–68, 70, 79, 80
police, 33, 37, 38, 68, 119, 145, 148n2; Black residents' view of, 139; killings at the hands of, xi, xxiiin1, 139–140, 143–144, 145–146
privatization, xix, 8–9, 9, 27n6, 38, 56, 65–67, 68, 70, 72, 77, 81

quality of life, xvi, 69, 94, 98, 102, 115, 118, 119–120, 129–131, 137, 143

rationality, x, 42, 63, 66–68, 72, 74, 80, 90, 105, 108, 120, 121, 142–143
redlining, xviii, xx, 2, 6, 11, 12, 34, 48, 89, 105
regeneration, x, xi, xii, xv, xvi, xviii, xix, xxi, xxiii, 10, 34, 121
rent strikes, 96–97
rhetoric of collectivity, 32, 56, 58
rhetoric of technology, xxiii, 88, 97, 118, 122–128. *See also* technocratic ideology
rhetorical punctuation, 45–46
rhetorical situation, xii, xvi, xix, 32, 89
Rice, Tamir, xxiiin1, 143–145
rust belt, xiv, xxi, 1, 7, 61n4

segregation, 2, 5, 6, 11, 11–16, 34, 36, 43, 44, 59, 64, 87, 91, 95, 96, 120, 140, 142, 143
selective amnesia, xviii, xx, 32, 42, 45, 140. *See also* strategic forgetting
Shepard, Peggy, 97, 98, 111, 114–115, 127, 129, 130, 131, 132, 134, 136
sketch factor, 2, 26n1, 91
slum clearance, 6, 15, 35, 91, 96. *See also* urban renewal
spatial fix, 5, 7, 65
spatial turn, 20, 103, 147
Smith, Neil, xiii, xiv, 4, 5, 9–10, 27n5, 39, 65, 66

Soja, Edward, xiii, xiv–xv, xvi, xxii, 5, 18, 22, 39, 56, 64, 65, 95, 114, 146
standpoint, xvii–xviii, 27n12, 55, 73, 101–102, 104, 122, 123, 128, 132, 146
strategic forgetting, xviii, xx, 32, 42, 45, 47, 140, 141. *See also* selective amnesia
street science, xi, xviii, xxii, 88, 90, 117–118, 121, 122, 132, 136, 142
suburbanization. *See* suburbs
suburbs, xii, 1, 3, 5, 6, 7, 9, 10, 12, 37, 48, 75, 80, 93, 140
Sugrue, Thomas J., ix, xiii, xix, 1, 7, 11–16, 27n7, 31, 32, 33, 34, 35, 37, 43, 44, 46, 61n3, 61n4, 90, 105
Sweet, Ossian, 33, 34

technocratic ideology, 121, 122–124, 128, 142
toxic dumping, xi, xv, xxi, 2, 26, 87, 88, 93, 98–101, 102, 104, 106, 110–111, 126, 127–128, 133, 135, 142
Toxic Waste and Race in the United States, 99, 117, 122

uneven development, 5, 7, 9–10, 22, 32, 65–66, 78, 92
urban reformers, 4, 90
urban renewal. *See* gentrification

valorization, xxiii, 1, 3, 6, 10, 22, 39, 66, 93

WE ACT For Environmental Justice, xviii, xxii, 98, 100, 102, 105–106, 107–115, 117, 125, 126, 128–133, 134, 135–137, 137n4, 142
white flight, xiii, 1, 6, 7, 37, 42, 48, 70, 89, 93
white privilege, xx, 34–35, 42, 44, 45, 47, 51, 53, 55, 99, 122, 142–143
white violence, 12, 15, 32–33, 36, 89, 94, 143
whiteness, xix, xx, xxi, xxiii, 12, 32, 42, 45, 47, 50, 53, 55, 67, 73, 76, 142

zip code, xviii, 22, 104, 107, 108, 116n6
zoning, 90, 91, 117, 140

About the Author

Mary E. Triece is a professor in the School of Communication and interim director of women's studies at the University of Akron where she has taught for 18 years. Triece's books include *Protest and Popular Culture: Women in the U.S. Labor Movement, 1894–1917*; *On the Picket Line: Strategies of Working-Class Women during the Depression*, which won the 2008 Bonnie Ritter Book Award; *Tell It Like It Is: Women in the National Welfare Rights Movement*; and *Race and Hegemonic Struggle in the United States*, co-edited with Michael G. Lacy. Triece has also published articles in *Critical Studies in Mass Communication*, *Women's Studies in Communication*, *Rhetoric Society Quarterly*, and *Western Journal of Communication*. Triece resides in Cleveland, Ohio, with her husband, two children, and three cats.